HENRIK IBSEN:
The Last Plays

Henrik IBSEN: The Last Plays

Introduced and translated by WILLIAM ARCHER

A MERMAID
DRAMABOOK

 HILL AND WANG · NEW YORK

Library of Congress catalog card number: 59-8154

FIRST DRAMABOOK PRINTING FEBRUARY 1959
SECOND PRINTING FEBRUARY 1960
THIRD PRINTING JUNE 1964
FOURTH PRINTING MAY 1967

Manufactured in the United States of America
by The Colonial Press Inc., Clinton, Mass.

CONTENTS

HENRIK IBSEN:
The Last Plays

LITTLE EYOLF

Play in Three Acts

(1894)

INTRODUCTION

Little Eyolf was written in Christiania during 1894, and published in Copenhagen on December 11 in that year. By this time Ibsen's correspondence has become so scanty as to afford us no clue to what may be called the biographical antecedents of the play. Even of anecdotic history very little attaches to it. For only one of the characters has a definite model been suggested. Ibsen himself told his French translator, Count Prozor, that the original of the Rat-Wife was "a little old woman who came to kill rats at the school where he was educated. She carried a little dog in a bag, and it was said that children had been drowned through following her." This means that Ibsen did not himself adapt to his uses the legend so familiar to us in Browning's *Pied Piper of Hamelin*, but found it ready adapted by the popular imagination of his native place, Skien. "This idea," Ibsen continued to Count Prozor, "was just what I wanted for bringing about the disappearance of Little Eyolf, in whom the infatuation[1] and the feebleness of his father are reproduced, but concentrated, exaggerated, as one often sees them in the son of such a father." Dr. Elias tells us that a well-known lady artist, who in middle life suggested to Ibsen the figure of Lona Hessel, was in later years the model for the Rat-Wife. There is no inconsistency between these two accounts of the matter. The idea was doubtless suggested by his recollection of the ratcatcher of Skien, while traits of manner and physiognomy might be borrowed from the lady in question.

The *Literary Remains* contain a first draft of *Little Eyolf*, with several gaps in it, and yet fairly complete. It shows once more how after having invented a play, the poet set about reinventing it, and how the reinvention was apt to determine its poetic value. In this case he had

---

[1] The French word used by Count Prozor is "infatuation." I can think of no other rendering for it; but I do not quite know what it means as applied to Allmers and Eyolf.

3

extraordinary difficulty with the characters' names, which
he changed about incessantly. His first list of characters
ran thus:

> Harald Borgheim.
> Johanna, his wife.
> Rita, his sister.
> Alfred, his son, eleven years old.
> Eivind Almer, road engineer.
> Miss Varg, Johanna's aunt.

Miss Varg is the character who ultimately became the
grimly fascinating Rat-Wife. After he ceased to be "Borgheim" Allmers became "Skioldheim." Eyolf, after beginning as "Alfred" was for some time "Eivind." Rita was
"Andrea" all through the second act. Not till the third
act was reached had the names been finally allotted. It
seems that the poet's first idea was simply to study a
rather commonplace wife's jealousy of a rather commonplace child. The lameness of Eyolf was an afterthought;
there is no trace of it in the draft. And as Eyolf is not
lame, the terrible cry of "the crutch is floating" must
also have been an afterthought, as well as the almost
intolerable scene of recrimination between Allmers and
Rita as to the accident which caused his lameness. In
fact, nearly everything that gives the play its depth, its
horror, and its elevation came as an afterthought. There
is a slight—a very slight—hint of the "evil eye" motive,
but the idea is in no way developed. Instead of the exquisite beauty of Rita's resolve to try to "make her peace
with the great open eyes," and to fill the blank within
her with "something that is a little like love," we have
a page of almost common sentimentalizing over Eyolf's
continued existence in their hearts. And instead of Alfred's wonderful tale of his meeting with Death in the
mountains, we find a poem which he reads to Rita!—
the verses Ibsen had written as a first hint for *The
Master Builder*. In no case, perhaps, did Ibsen's revision
work such a transfiguration as in this play.

The verse quoted on p. 33 is the last line of a very
well-known poem by Johann Sebastian Welhaven, en-
titled *Republikanerne*, written in 1839. An unknown guest
in a Paris restaurant has been challenged by a noisy party
of young Frenchmen to join them in drinking a health to
Poland. He refuses; they denounce him as a craven and
a slave; he bares his breast and shows the scars of wounds

received in fighting for the country whose lost cause has become a subject for conventional enthusiasm and windy rhetoric.

> De saae paa hverandre. Han vandred sin vei.
> De havde champagne, men rörte den ei.

"They looked at each other. He went on his way. There stood their champagne, but they did not touch it." The champagne incident leads me to wonder whether the relation between Rita and Allmers may not have been partly suggested to Ibsen by the relation between Charlotte Stieglitz and her weakling of a husband. Their story must have been known to him through George Brandes' *Young Germany*, if not more directly. "From time to time," says Dr. Brandes, "there came over her what she calls her champagne-mood; she grieves that this is no longer the case with him." [2] Did the germ of the incident lie in these words?

The first performance of the play in Norway took place at the Christiania Theatre on January 15, 1895, Fru Wettergren playing Rita and Fru Dybwad, Asta. In Copenhagen (March 13, 1895) Fru Oda Nielsen and Fru Hennings played Rita and Asta respectively, while Emil Poulsen played Allmers. The first German Rita (Deutsches Theater, Berlin, January 12, 1895) was Frau Agnes Sorma, with Reicher as Allmers. Six weeks later Frl. Sandrock played Rita at the Burgtheater, Vienna. In May, 1895, the play was acted by M. Lugné-Poë's company in Paris. The first performance in English took place at the Avenue Theatre, London, on the afternoon of November 23, 1896, with Miss Janet Achurch as Rita, Miss Elizabeth Robins as Asta, and Mrs. Patrick Campbell as the Rat-Wife. Miss Achurch's Rita made a profound impression. Mrs. Patrick Campbell afterwards played the part in a short series of evening performances. In the spring of 1895 the play was acted in Chicago by a company of Scandinavian amateurs, presumably in Norwegian, but it was not acted in English in America until Madame Nazimova added it to her repertory in the season of 1907-1908.

As the external history of *Little Eyolf* is so short, I

---

[2] *Main Currents of Nineteenth Century Literature,* Vol. VI, p. 299.

am tempted to depart from my usual practice, and say a few words as to its matter and meaning.

George Brandes, writing of this play, has rightly observed that "a kind of dualism has always been perceptible in Ibsen; he pleads the cause of Nature, and he castigates Nature with mystic morality; only sometimes Nature is allowed the first voice, sometimes morality. In *The Master Builder* and in *Ghosts* the lover of Nature in Ibsen was predominant; here, as in *Brand* and *The Wild Duck*, the castigator is in the ascendant." So clearly is this the case in *Little Eyolf* that Ibsen seems almost to fall into line with Mr. Thomas Hardy. To say nothing of analogies of detail between *Little Eyolf* and *Jude the Obscure*, there is this radical analogy, that they are both utterances of a profound pessimism, both indictments of Nature.

But while Mr. Hardy's pessimism is plaintive and passive, Ibsen's is stoical and almost bracing. It is true that in this play he is no longer the mere "indignation-pessimist" whom Dr. Brandes quite justly recognized in his earlier works. His analysis has gone deeper into the heart of things, and he has put off the satirist and the iconoclast. But there is in his thought an incompressible energy of revolt. A pessimist in contemplation, he remains a meliorist in action. He is not, like Mr. Hardy, content to let the flag droop half-mast high; his protagonist still runs it up to the masthead, and looks forward steadily to the "heavy day of work" before him. But although the note of the conclusion is resolute, almost serene, the play remains nonetheless an indictment of Nature, or at least of that egoism of passion which is one of her most potent subtleties. In this view, Allmers becomes a type of what we may roughly call the "free moral agent"; Eyolf, a type of humanity conceived as passive and suffering, thrust will-less into existence, with boundless aspirations and cruelly limited powers; Rita, a type of the egoistic instinct which is "a consuming fire"; and Asta, a type of the beneficent love which is possible only so long as it is exempt from "the law of change." Allmers, then, is self-conscious egoism, egoism which can now and then break its chains, look in its own visage, realize and shrink from itself; while Rita, until she has passed through the awful crisis which forms the matter of the play, is unconscious, reckless, and ruthless egoism, exigent and jealous, "holding to its rights," and incapable even of rising into the secondary stage of maternal love. The off-spring and the victim of these egoisms is Eyolf, "little wounded warrior," who longs to scale the heights and dive into the depths, but must remain forever chained to the crutch of human infirmity. For years Allmers has been a restless and half-reluctant slave to Rita's imperious temperament. He has dreamed and theorized about "responsibility," and has kept Eyolf poring over his books, in the hope that, despite his misfortune, he may one day minister to parental vanity. Finally he breaks away from Rita, for the first time "in all these ten years," goes up "into the infinite solitudes," looks Death in the face, and returns shrinking from passion, yearning toward selfless love, and filled with a profound and remorseful pity for the lot of poor maimed humanity. He will "help Eyolf to bring his desires into harmony with what lies attainable before him." He will "create a conscious happiness in his mind." And here the drama opens.

Before the Rat-Wife enters, let me pause for a moment to point out that here again Ibsen adopts that characteristic method which, in writing of *The Lady from the Sea* and *The Master Builder*, I have compared to the method of Hawthorne. The story he tells is not really, or rather not inevitably, supernatural. Everything is explicable within the limits of nature; but supernatural agency is also vaguely suggested, and the reader's imagination is stimulated, without any absolute violence to his sense of reality. On the plane of everyday life, then, the Rat-Wife is a crazy and uncanny old woman, fabled by the peasants to be a werewolf in her leisure moments, who goes about the country killing vermin. Coming across an impressionable child, she tells him a preposterous tale, adapted from the old "Pied Piper" legends, of her method of fascinating her victims. The child, whose imagination has long dwelt on this personage, is in fact hypnotized by her, follows her down to the sea, and, watching her row away, turns dizzy, falls in, and is drowned. There is nothing impossible, nothing even improbable, in this. At the same time, there cannot be the least doubt, I think, that in the poet's mind the Rat-Wife is the symbol of Death, of the "still, soft darkness" that is at once so fearful and so fascinating to humanity. This is clear not only in the text of her single scene, but in the fact that

Allmers, in the last act, treats her and his "fellow traveler" of that night among the mountains, not precisely as identical, but as interchangeable, ideas. To tell the truth, I have even my own suspicions as to who is meant by "her sweetheart," whom she "lured" long ago, and who is now "down where all the rats are." This theory I shall keep to myself; it may be purely fantastic, and is at best inessential. What is certain is that death carried off little Eyolf, and that, of all he was, only the crutch is left, mute witness to his hapless lot.

He is gone; there was so little to bind him to life that he made not even a moment's struggle against the allurement of the "long, sweet sleep." Then, for the first time, the depth of the egoism which had created and conditioned his little life bursts upon his parents' horror-stricken gaze. Like accomplices in crime, they turn upon and accuse each other—"sorrow makes them wicked and hateful." Allmers, as the one whose eyes were already half opened, is the first to carry the war into the enemy's country; but Rita is not slow to retort, and presently they both have to admit that their recriminations are only a vain attempt to drown the voice of self-reproach. In a sort of fierce frenzy they tear away veil after veil from their souls, until they realize that Eyolf never existed at all, so to speak, for his own sake, but only for the sake of their passions and vanities. "Isn't it curious," says Rita, summing up the matter, "that we should grieve like this over a little stranger boy?"

In blind self-absorption they have played with life and death, and now "the great open eyes" of the stranger boy will be forever upon them. Allmers would fain take refuge in a love untainted by the egoism, and unexposed to the revulsions, of passion. But not only is Asta's pity for Rita too strong to let her countenance this desertion: she has discovered that her relation to Allmers is *not* "exempt from the law of change," and she "takes flight from him—and from herself." Meanwhile it appears that the agony which Allmers and Rita have endured in probing their wounds has been, as Halvard Solness would say, "salutary self-torture." The consuming fire of passion is now quenched, but "it has left an empty place within them," and they feel a common need "to fill it up with something that is a little like love." They come to remember that there are other children in the world on whom reckless instinct has thrust the gift of life—neglected children, stunted and maimed in mind if not in body. And now that her egoism is seared to the quick, the mother instinct asserts itself in Rita. She will take these children to her—these children to whom her hand and her heart have hitherto been closed. They shall be outwardly in Eyolf's place, and perhaps in time they may fill the place in her heart that should have been Eyolf's. Thus she will try to "make her peace with the great open eyes." For now, at last, she has divined the secret of the unwritten book on "human responsibility," and has realized that motherhood means—atonement.

So I read this terrible and beautiful work of art. This, I think, is *a* meaning inherent in it—not perhaps *the* meaning, and still less all the meanings. Indeed, its peculiar fascination for me, among all Ibsen's works, lies in the fact that it seems to touch life at so many different points. But I must not be understood as implying that Ibsen constructed the play with any such definitely allegoric design as is here set forth. I do not believe that this creator of men and women ever started from an abstract conception. He did not first compose his philosophic tune and then set his puppets dancing to it. The germ in his mind was dramatic, not ethical; it was only as the drama developed that its meanings dawned upon him; and he left them implicit and fragmentary, like the symbolism of life itself, seldom formulated, never worked out with schematic precision. He simply took a cutting from the tree of life, and, planting it in the rich soil of his imagination, let it ramify and burgeon as it would.

Even if one did not know the date of *Little Eyolf,* one could confidently assign it to the latest period of Ibsen's career, on noting a certain difference of scale between its foundations and its superstructure. In his earlier plays, down to and including *Hedda Gabler,* we feel his invention at work to the very last moment, often with more intensity in the last act than in the first; in his later plays he seems to be in haste to pass as early as possible from invention to pure analysis. In this play, after the death of Eyolf (surely one of the most inspired "situations" in all drama) there is practically no external action whatsoever. Nothing happens save in the souls of the characters; there is no further invention, but rather what one may perhaps call inquisition. This does not prevent the second act from being quite the most poignant, or the third act from being one of the most moving, that Ibsen ever wrote. Far from wishing to depreciate the play, I rate it more highly, perhaps, than most critics—among the very greatest of Ibsen's achievements. I merely note as a characteristic of the poet's latest manner this disparity of scale between the work foreshadowed, so to speak, and the work completed. We shall find it still more evident in the case of *John Gabriel Borkman.*

CHARACTERS

ALFRED ALLMERS, *landed proprietor and man of letters, formerly a tutor*

MRS. RITA ALLMERS, *his wife*

EYOLF, *their child, nine years old*

MISS ASTA ALLMERS, *Alfred's younger half sister*

ENGINEER BORGHEIM

THE RAT-WIFE

The action takes place on ALLMERS'S *property, bordering on the fiord, twelve or fourteen miles from Christiania.*

LITTLE EYOLF

ACT FIRST

A pretty and richly decorated garden room, full of furniture, flowers, and plants. At the back, open glass doors, leading out to a veranda. An extensive view over the fiord. In the distance, wooded hillsides. A door in each of the side walls, the one on the right a folding door, placed far back. In front on the right, a sofa, with cushions and rugs. Beside the sofa, a small table, and chairs. In front, on the left, a larger table, with armchairs around it. On the table stands an open handbag. It is an early summer morning, with warm sunshine.

MRS. RITA ALLMERS stands beside the table, facing toward the left, engaged in unpacking the bag. She is a handsome, rather tall, well-developed blonde, about thirty years of age, dressed in a light-colored morning gown.

Shortly after, MISS ASTA ALLMERS enters by the door on the right, wearing a light brown summer dress, with hat, jacket, and parasol. Under her arm she carries a locked portfolio of considerable size. She is slim, of middle height, with dark hair, and deep, earnest eyes. Twenty-five years old.

ASTA [*as she enters*]. Good morning, my dear Rita.

Rita [*turns her head, and nods to her*]. What! is that you, Asta? Come all the way from town so early?

Asta [*takes off her things, and lays them on a chair beside the door*]. Yes, such a restless feeling came over me. I felt I must come out today, and see how little Eyolf was getting on—and you too. [*Lays the portfolio on the table*

13

beside the sofa.] So I took the steamer, and here I am.

Rita [*smiling to her*]. And I daresay you met one or other of your friends on board? Quite by chance, of course.

Asta [*quietly*]. No, I did not meet a soul I knew. [*Sees the bag.*] Why, Rita, what have you got there?

Rita [*Still unpacking*]. Alfred's traveling bag. Don't you recognize it?

Asta [*joyfully, approaching her*]. What! Has Alfred come home?

Rita. Yes, only think—he came quite unexpectedly by the late train last night.

Asta. Oh, then that was what my feeling meant! It was that that drew me out here! And he hadn't written a line to let you know? Not even a post card?

Rita. Not a single word.

Asta. Did he not even telegraph?

Rita. Yes, an hour before he arrived—quite curtly and coldly. [*Laughs.*] Don't you think that was like him, Asta?

Asta. Yes; he goes so quietly about everything.

Rita. But that made it all the more delightful to have him again.

Asta. Yes, I am sure it would.

Rita. A whole fortnight before I expected him!

Asta. And is he quite well? Not in low spirits?

Rita [*closes the bag with a snap, and smiles at her*]. He looked quite transfigured as he stood in the doorway.

Asta. And was he not the least bit tired either?

Rita. Oh, yes, he seemed to be tired enough—very tired, in fact. But, poor fellow, he had come on foot the greater part of the way.

Asta. And then perhaps the high mountain air may have been rather too keen for him.

Rita. Oh, no; I don't think so at all. I haven't heard him cough once.

Asta. Ah, there you see now! It was a good thing, after all, that the doctor talked him into taking this tour.

Rita. Yes, now that it is safely over.—But I can tell you it has been a terrible time for me, Asta. I have never cared to talk about it—and you so seldom came out to see me, too——

Asta. Yes, I daresay that wasn't very nice of me—but——

Rita. Well, well, well, of course you had your school to

attend to in town. [*Smiling.*] And then our road-maker friend—of course he was away too.

Asta. Oh, don't talk like that, Rita.

Rita. Very well, then; we will leave the road maker out of the question.—You can't think how I have been longing for Alfred! How empty the place seemed! How desolate! Ugh, it felt as if there had been a funeral in the house!

Asta. Why, dear me, only six or seven weeks——

Rita. Yes; but you must remember that Alfred has never been away from me before—never so much as twenty-four hours. Not once in all these ten years.

Asta. No; but that is just why I really think it was high time he should have a little outing this year. He ought to have gone for a tramp in the mountains every summer—he really ought.

Rita [*half smiling*]. Oh yes, it's all very well for you to talk. If I were as—as reasonable as you, I suppose I should have let him go before—perhaps. But I positively could not, Asta! It seemed to me I should never get him back again. Surely you can understand that?

Asta. No. But I daresay that is because I have no one to lose.

Rita [*with a teasing smile*]. Really? No one at all?

Asta. Not that I know of. [*Changing the subject.*] But tell me, Rita, where is Alfred? Is he still asleep?

Rita. Oh, not at all. He got up as early as ever today.

Asta. Then he can't have been so very tired after all.

Rita. Yes, he was last night—when he arrived. But now he has had little Eyolf with him in his room for a whole hour and more.

Asta. Poor little white-faced boy! Has he to be forever at his lessons again?

Rita [*with a slight shrug*]. Alfred will have it so, you know.

Asta. Yes; but I think you ought to put down your foot about it, Rita.

Rita [*somewhat impatiently*]. Oh, no; come now, I really cannot meddle with that. Alfred knows so much better about these things than I do. And what would you have Eyolf do? He can't run about and play, you see—like other children.

Asta [*with decision*]. I will talk to Alfred about this.

Rita. Yes, do; I wish you would.—Oh! here he is.

ALFRED ALLMERS, *dressed in light summer clothes, enters by the door on the left, leading* EYOLF *by the hand. He is a slim, lightly-built man of about thirty-six or thirty-seven, with gentle eyes, and thin brown hair and beard. His expression is serious and thoughtful.* EYOLF *wears a suit cut like a uniform, with gold braid and gilt military buttons. He is lame, and walks with a crutch under his left arm. His leg is shrunken. He is undersized, and looks delicate, but has beautiful intelligent eyes.*

Allmers [*drops* EYOLF's *hand, goes up to* ASTA *with an expression of marked pleasure, and holds out both his hands to her*]. Asta! My dearest Asta! To think of your coming! To think of my seeing you so soon!

Asta. I felt I must—— Welcome home again!

Allmers [*shaking her hands*]. Thank you for coming.

Rita. Doesn't he look well?

Asta [*gazes fixedly at him*]. Splendid! Quite splendid! His eyes are so much brighter! And I suppose you have done a great deal of writing on your travels? [*With an outburst of joy.*] I shouldn't wonder if you had finished the whole book, Alfred?

Allmers [*shrugging his shoulders*]. The book? Oh, the book——

Asta. Yes, I was sure you would find it go so easily when once you got away.

Allmers. So I thought too. But, do you know, I didn't find it so at all. The truth is, I have not written a line of the book.

Asta. Not a line?

Rita. Oho! I wondered when I found all the paper lying untouched in your bag.

Asta. But, my dear Alfred, what have you been doing all this time?

Allmers [*smiling*]. Only thinking and thinking and thinking.

Rita [*putting her arm round his neck*]. And thinking a little, too, of those you had left at home?

Allmers. Yes, you may be sure of that. I have thought a great deal of you—every single day.

Rita [*taking her arm away*]. Ah, that is all I care about.

Asta. But you haven't even touched the book! And yet you can look so happy and contented! That is not what you generally do—I mean when your work is going badly.

Allmers. You are right there. You see, I have been such a fool hitherto. All the best that is in you goes into thinking. What you put on paper is worth very little.

Asta [*exclaiming*]. Worth very little!

Rita [*laughing*]. What an absurd thing to say, Alfred.

Eyolf [*looks confidingly up at him*]. Oh, yes Papa, what you write is worth a great deal!

Allmers [*smiling and stroking his hair*]. Well, well, since you say so——— But I can tell you, someone is coming after me who will do it better.

Eyolf. Who can that be? Oh, tell me!

Allmers. Only wait—you may be sure he will come, and let us hear of him.

Eyolf. And what will you do then?

Allmers [*seriously*]. Then I will go to the mountains again——

Rita. Fie, Alfred! For shame!

Allmers. —up to the peaks and the great waste places.

Eyolf. Papa, don't you think I shall soon be well enough for you to take me with you?

Allmers [*with painful emotion*]. Oh, yes, perhaps, my little boy.

Eyolf. It would be so splendid, you know, if I could climb the mountains, like you.

Asta [*changing the subject*]. Why, how beautifully you are dressed today, Eyolf!

Eyolf. Yes, don't you think so, Auntie?

Asta. Yes, indeed. Is it in honor of Papa that you have got your new clothes on?

Eyolf. Yes, I asked Mama to let me. I want so to let Papa see me in them.

Allmers [*in a low voice, to* RITA]. You shouldn't have given him clothes like that.

Rita [*in a low voice*]. Oh, he has teased me so long about them—he had set his heart on them. He gave me no peace.

Eyolf. And I forgot to tell you, Papa—Borgheim has bought me a new bow. And he has taught me how to shoot with it too.

Allmers. Ah, there now—that's just the sort of thing for you, Eyolf.

Eyolf. And next time he comes, I shall ask him to teach me to swim, too.

Allmers. To swim! Oh, what makes you want to learn swimming?

Eyolf. Well, you know, all the boys down at the beach can swim. I am the only one that can't.

Allmers [*with emotion, taking him in his arms*]. You shall learn whatever you like—everything you really want to.

Eyolf. Then do you know what I want most of all, Papa?

Allmers. No; tell me.

Eyolf. I want most of all to be a soldier.

Allmers. Oh, little Eyolf, there are many, many other things that are better than that.

Eyolf. Ah, but when I grow big, then I shall have to be a soldier. You know that, don't you?

Allmers [*clenching his hands together*]. Well, well, well: we shall see——

Asta [*seating herself at the table on the left*]. Eyolf! Come here to me, and I will tell you something.

Eyolf [*goes up to her*]. What is it, Auntie?

Asta. What do you think, Eyolf—I have seen the Rat-Wife.

Eyolf. What! Seen the Rat-Wife! Oh, you're only making a fool of me!

Asta. No; it's quite true. I saw her yesterday.

Eyolf. Where did you see her?

Asta. I saw her on the road, outside the town.

Allmers. I saw her, too, somewhere up in the country.

Rita [*who is sitting on the sofa*]. Perhaps it will be our turn to see her next, Eyolf.

Eyolf. Auntie, isn't it strange that she should be called the Rat-Wife?

Asta. Oh, people just give her that name because she wanders round the country driving away all the rats.

Allmers. I have heard that her real name is Varg.

Eyolf. Varg! That means a wolf, doesn't it?

Allmers [*patting him on the head*]. So you know that, do you?

Eyolf [*cautiously*]. Then perhaps it may be true, after all, that she is a werewolf at night. Do you believe that, Papa?

Allmers. Oh, no; I don't believe it. Now you ought to go and play a little in the garden.

Eyolf. Should I not take some books with me?

Allmers. No, no books after this. You had better go down to the beach to the other boys.

Eyolf [*shyly*]. No, Papa, I won't go down to the boys today.

Allmers. Why not?

Eyolf. Oh, because I have these clothes on.

Allmers [*knitting his brows*]. Do you mean that they make fun of—of your pretty clothes?

Eyolf [*evasively*]. No, they daren't—for then I would thrash them.

Allmers. Aha!—then why——?

Eyolf. You see, they are so naughty, these boys. And then they say I can never be a soldier.

Allmers [*with suppressed indignation*]. Why do they say that, do you think?

Eyolf. I suppose they are jealous of me. For you know, Papa, they are so poor, they have to go about barefoot.

Allmers [*softly, with choking voice*]. Oh, Rita—how it wrings my heart!

Rita [*soothingly, rising*]. There, there, there!

Allmers [*threateningly*]. But these rascals shall soon find out who is the master down at the beach!

Asta [*listening*]. There is someone knocking.

Eyolf. Oh, I'm sure it's Borgheim!

Rita. Come in.

The RAT-WIFE *comes softly and noiselessly in by the door on the right. She is a thin little shrunken figure, old and gray-haired, with keen, piercing eyes, dressed in an old-fashioned flowered gown, with a black hood and cloak. She has in her hand a large red umbrella, and carries a black bag by a loop over her arm.*

Eyolf [*softly, taking hold of* ASTA'S *dress*]. Auntie! That must surely be her!

The Rat-Wife [*curtseying at the door*]. I humbly beg pardon—but are your worships troubled with any gnawing things in the house?

Allmers. Here? No, I don't think so.

The Rat-Wife. For it would be such a pleasure to me to rid your worship's house of them.

Rita. Yes, yes; we understand. But we have nothing of the sort here.

The Rat-Wife. That's very unlucky, that is; for I just happened to be on my rounds now, and goodness knows when I may be in these parts again.——Oh, how tired I am!

Allmers [*pointing to a chair*]. Yes, you look tired.

The Rat-Wife. I know one ought never to get tired of doing good to the poor little things that are hated and persecuted so cruelly. But it takes your strength out of you, it does.

Rita. Won't you sit down and rest a little?

The Rat-Wife. I thank your ladyship with all my heart. [*Seats herself on a chair between the door and the sofa.*] I have been out all night at my work.

Allmers. Have you indeed?

The Rat-Wife. Yes, over on the islands. [*With a chuckling laugh.*] The people sent for me, I can assure you. They didn't like it a bit; but there was nothing else to be done. They had to put a good face on it, and bite the sour apple. [*Looks at* EYOLF, *and nods.*] The sour apple, little master, the sour apple.

Eyolf [*involuntarily, a little timidly*]. Why did they have to——?

The Rat-Wife. What?

Eyolf. To bite it?

The Rat-Wife. Why, because they couldn't keep body and soul together on account of the rats and all the little rat-children, you see, young master.

Rita. Ugh! Poor people! Have they so many of them?

The Rat-Wife. Yes, it was all alive and swarming with them. [*Laughs with quiet glee.*] They came creepy-crawly up into the beds all night long. They plumped into the milk cans, and they went pittering and pattering all over the floor, backwards and forwards, and up and down.

Eyolf [*softly, to* ASTA]. I shall never go there, Auntie.

The Rat-Wife. But then I came—I, and another along with me. And we took them with us, every one—the sweet little creatures! We made an end of every one of them.

Eyolf [*with a shriek*]. Papa—look! look!

Rita. Good Heavens, Eyolf.

Allmers. What's the matter?

Eyolf [*pointing*]. There's something wriggling in the bag!

Rita [*at the extreme left, shrieks*]. Ugh! Send her away, Alfred.

The Rat-Wife [*laughing*]. Oh, dearest lady, you needn't be frightened of such a little manikin.

Allmers. But what is the thing?

The Rat-Wife. Why, it's only little Mopsëman. [*Loosening the string of the bag.*] Come up out of the dark, my own little darling friend.

A little dog with a broad black snout pokes its head out of the bag.

[*Nodding and beckoning to* EYOLF.] Come along, don't be afraid, my little wounded warrior! He won't bite. Come here! Come here!

Eyolf [*clinging to* ASTA]. No, I dare not.

The Rat-Wife. Don't you think he has a gentle, lovable countenance, my young master?

Eyolf [*astonished, pointing*]. That thing there?

The Rat-Wife. Yes, this thing here.

Eyolf [*almost under his breath, staring fixedly at the dog*]. I think he has the horriblest—countenance I ever saw.

The Rat-Wife [*closing the bag*]. Oh, it will come—it will come, right enough.

Eyolf [*involuntarily drawing nearer, at last goes right up to her, and strokes the bag*]. But he is lovely—lovely all the same.

The Rat-Wife [*in a tone of caution*]. But now he is so tired and weary, poor thing. He's utterly tired out, he is. [*Looks at* ALLMERS.] For it takes the strength out of you, that sort of game, I can tell you, sir.

Allmers. What sort of a game do you mean?

The Rat-Wife. The luring game.

Allmers. Do you mean that it is the dog that lures the rats?

The Rat-Wife [*nodding*]. Mopsëman and I—we two do it together. And it goes so smoothly—for all you can see, at any rate. I just slip a string through his collar, and then I lead him three times round the house, and play on my Pan's pipes. When they hear that, they have got to come up from the cellars, and down from the garrets, and out of their holes, all the blessed little creatures.

Eyolf. And does he bite them to death then?

The Rat-Wife. Oh, not at all! No, we go down to the boat, he and I do—and then they follow after us, both the big ones and the little ratikins.

Eyolf [*eagerly*]. And what then—tell me!

The Rat-Wife. Then we push out from the land, and I scull with one oar and play on my Pan's pipes. And

Mopsëman, he swims behind. [*With glittering eyes*]. And all the creepers and crawlers, they follow and follow us out into the deep, deep waters. Ay, for they have to.

Eyolf. Why do they have to?

The Rat-Wife. Just because they want not to—just because they are so deadly afraid of the water. That is why they have got to plunge into it.

Eyolf. Are they drowned, then?

The Rat-Wife. Every blessed one. [*More softly.*] And there it is all as still, and soft, and dark as their hearts can desire, the lovely little things. Down there they sleep a long, sweet sleep, with no one to hate them or persecute them any more. [*Rises.*] In the old days, I can tell you, I didn't need any Mopsëman. Then I did the luring myself —I alone.

Eyolf. And what did you lure then?

The Rat-Wife. Men. One most of all.

Eyolf [*with eagerness*]. Oh, who was that one? Tell me!

The Rat-Wife [*laughing*]. It was my own sweetheart, it was, little heartbreaker!

Eyolf. And where is he now, then?

The Rat-Wife [*harshly*]. Down where all the rats are. [*Resuming her milder tone.*] But now I must be off and get to business again. Always on the move. [*To* Rita.] So your ladyship has no sort of use for me today? I could finish it all off while I am about it.

Rita. No, thank you; I don't think we require anything.

The Rat-Wife. Well, well, your sweet ladyship, you can never tell. If your ladyship should find that there is anything here that keeps nibbling and gnawing, and creeping and crawling, then just see and get hold of me and Mopsëman. Good-by, good-by, a kind good-by to you all. [*She goes out by the door on the right.*]

Eyolf [*softly and triumphantly, to* Asta]. Only think, Auntie, now I have seen the Rat-Wife too!

Rita *goes out upon the veranda, and fans herself with her pocket handkerchief. Shortly afterwards,* Eyolf *slips cautiously and unnoticed out to the right.*

Allmers [*takes up the portfolio from the table by the sofa*]. Is this your portfolio, Asta?

Asta. Yes. I have some of the old letters in it.

Allmers. Ah, the family letters——

Asta. You know you asked me to arrange them for you while you were away.

Allmers [*pats her on the head*]. And you have actually found time to do that, dear?

Asta. Oh, yes. I have done it partly out here and partly at my own rooms in town.

Allmers. Thanks, dear. Did you find anything particular in them?

Asta [*lightly*]. Oh, you know you always find something or other in such old papers. [*Speaking lower and seriously.*] It is the letters to mother that are in this portfolio.

Allmers. Those, of course, you must keep yourself.

Asta [*with an effort*]. No; I am determined that you shall look through them, too, Alfred. Sometime—later on in life. I haven't the key of the portfolio with me just now.

Allmers. It doesn't matter, my dear Asta, for I shall never read your mother's letters in any case.

Asta [*fixing her eyes on him*]. Then sometime or other—some quiet evening—I will tell you a little of what is in them.

Allmers. Yes, that will be much better. But do you keep your mother's letters—you haven't so many mementos of her.

He hands ASTA *the portfolio. She takes it, and lays it on the chair under her outdoor things.* RITA *comes into the room again.*

Rita. Ugh! I feel as if that horrible old woman had brought a sort of graveyard smell with her.

Allmers. Yes, she was rather horrible.

Rita. I felt almost sick while she was in the room.

Allmers. However, I can very well understand the sort of spellbound fascination that she talked about. The loneliness of the mountain peaks and of the great waste places has something of the same magic about it.

Asta [*looks attentively at him*]. What is it that has happened to you, Alfred?

Allmers [*smiling*]. To me?

Asta. Yes, something has happened—something seems almost to have transformed you. Rita noticed it too.

Rita. Yes, I saw it the moment you came. A change for the better, I hope, Alfred?

Allmers. It ought to be for the better. And it must and shall come to good.

Rita [*with an outburst*]. You have had some adventure on your journey! Don't deny it! I can see it in your face!

Allmers [*shaking his head*]. No adventure in the world —outwardly at least. But——

Rita [*eagerly*]. But——

Allmers. It is true that within me there has been something of a revolution.

Rita. Oh, Heavens——!

Allmers [*soothingly, patting her hand*]. Only for the better, my dear Rita. You may be perfectly certain of that.

Rita [*seats herself on the sofa*]. You must tell us all about it, at once—tell us everything!

Allmers [*turning to* ASTA]. Yes, let us sit down, too, Asta. Then I will try to tell you as well as I can.

He seats himself on the sofa at RITA's *side.* ASTA *moves a chair forward, and places herself near him.*

Rita [*looking at him expectantly*]. Well——?

Allmers [*gazing straight before him*]. When I look back over my life—and my fortunes—for the last ten or eleven years, it seems to me almost like a fairy tale or a dream. Don't you think so too, Asta?

Asta. Yes, in many ways I think so.

Allmers [*continuing*]. When I remember what we two used to be, Asta—we two poor orphan children——

Rita [*impatiently*]. Oh, that is such an old, old story.

Allmers [*not listening to her*]. And now here I am in comfort and luxury. I have been able to follow my vocation. I have been able to work and study—just as I had always longed to. [*Holds out his hands.*] And all this great —this fabulous good fortune we owe to you, my dearest Rita.

Rita [*half playfully, half angrily, slaps his hand*]. Oh, I do wish you would stop talking like that.

Allmers. I speak of it only as a sort of introduction.

Rita. Then do skip the introduction!

Allmers. Rita,—you must not think it was the doctor's advice that drove me up to the mountains.

Asta. Was it not, Alfred?

Rita. What was it, then?

Allmers. It was this: I found there was no more peace for me, there in my study.

Rita. No peace! Why, who disturbed you?

Allmers [*shaking his head*]. No one from without. But I felt as though I were positively abusing—or, say rather, wasting—my best powers—frittering away the time.

Asta [*with wide eyes*]. When you were writing at your book?

Allmers [*nodding*]. For I cannot think that my powers are confined to that alone. I must surely have it in me to do one or two other things as well.

Rita. Was that what you sat there brooding over?

Allmers. Yes, mainly that.

Rita. And so that is what has made you so discontented with yourself of late; and with the rest of us as well. For you know you were discontented, Alfred.

Allmers [*gazing straight before him*]. There I sat bent over my table, day after day, and often half the night too —writing and writing at the great thick book on "Human Responsibility." H'm!

Asta [*laying her hand upon his arm*]. But, Alfred—that book is to be your lifework.

Rita. Yes, you have said so often enough.

Allmers. I thought so. Ever since I grew up, I have thought so. [*With an affectionate expression in his eyes.*] And it was you that enabled me to devote myself to it, my dear Rita——

Rita. Oh, nonsense!

Allmers [*smiling to her*]. —you, with your gold, and your green forests——

Rita [*half laughing, half vexed*]. If you begin all that rubbish again, I shall beat you.

Asta [*looking sorrowfully at him*]. But the book, Alfred?

Allmers. It began, as it were, to drift away from me. But I was more and more beset by the thought of the higher duties that laid their claims upon me.

Rita [*beaming, seizes his hand*]. Alfred!

Allmers. The thought of Eyolf, my dear Rita.

Rita [*disappointed, drops his hand*]. Ah—of Eyolf!

Allmers. Poor little Eyolf has taken deeper and deeper hold of me. After that unlucky fall from the table—and especially since we have been assured that the injury is incurable——

Rita [*insistently*]. But you take all the care you possibly can of him, Alfred!

Allmers. As a schoolmaster, yes; but not as a father. And it is a father that I want henceforth to be to Eyolf.

Rita [*looking at him and shaking her head*]. I don't think I quite understand you.

Allmers. I mean that I will try with all my might to make his misfortune as painless and easy to him as it can possibly be.

Rita. Oh, but, dear—thank Heaven, I don't think he feels it so deeply.

Asta [*with emotion*]. Yes, Rita, he does.

Allmers. Yes, you may be sure he feels it deeply.

Rita [*impatiently*]. But, Alfred, what more can you do for him?

Allmers. I will try to perfect all the rich possibilities that are dawning in his childish soul. I will foster all the germs of good in his nature—make them blossom and bear fruit. [*With more and more warmth, rising.*] And I will do more than that! I will help him to bring his desires into harmony with what lies attainable before him. That is just what at present they are not. All his longings are for things that must forever remain unattainable to him. But I will create a conscious happiness in his mind.

He goes once or twice up and down the room. ASTA *and* RITA *follow him with their eyes.*

Rita. You should take these things more quietly, Alfred!

Allmers [*stops beside the table on the left, and looks at them*]. Eyolf shall carry on my lifework—if he wants to. Or he shall choose one that is altogether his own. Perhaps that would be best. At all events, I shall let mine rest as it is.

Rita [*rising*]. But, Alfred dear, can you not work both for yourself and for Eyolf?

Allmers. No, I cannot. It is impossible! I cannot divide myself in this matter—and therefore I efface myself. Eyolf shall be the complete man of our race. And it shall be my new lifework to make him the complete man.

Asta [*has risen and now goes up to him*]. This must have cost you a terribly hard struggle, Alfred?

Allmers. Yes, it has. At home here, I should never have conquered myself, never brought myself to the point of renunciation. Never at home!

Rita. Then that was why you went away this summer?

Allmers [*with shining eyes*]. Yes! I went up into the infinite solitudes. I saw the sunrise gleaming on the mountain peaks. I felt myself nearer the stars—I seemed almost to be in sympathy and communion with them. And then I found the strength for it.

Asta [*looking sadly at him*]. But you will never write any more of your book on "Human Responsibility"?

Allmers. No, never, Asta. I tell you I cannot split up my life between two vocations. But I will act out my "human responsibility"—in my own life.

Rita [*with a smile*]. Do you think you can live up to such high resolves at home here?

Allmers [*taking her hand*]. With you to help me, I can. [*Holds out the other hand.*] And with you too, Asta.

Rita [*drawing her hand away*]. Ah—with both of us! So, after all, you can divide yourself.

Allmers. Why, my dearest Rita——!

RITA *moves away from him and stands in the garden doorway. A light and rapid knock is heard at the door on the right.* ENGINEER BORGHEIM *enters quickly. He is a young man of a little over thirty. His expression is bright and cheerful, and he holds himself erect.*

Borgheim. Good morning, Mrs. Allmers. [*Stops with an expression of pleasure on seeing* ALLMERS.] Why, what's this? Home again already, Mr. Allmers?

Allmers [*shaking hands with him*]. Yes, I arrived last night.

Rita [*gaily*]. His leave was up, Mr. Borgheim.

Allmers. No, you know it wasn't, Rita——

Rita [*approaching*]. Oh, yes, but it was, though. His furlough had run out.

Borgheim. I see you hold your husband well in hand, Mrs. Allmers.

Rita. I hold to my rights. And besides, everything must have an end.

Borgheim. Oh, not everything—I hope. Good morning, Miss Allmers!

Asta [*holding aloof from him*]. Good morning.

Rita [*looking at* BORGHEIM]. Not everything, you say?

Borgheim. Oh, I am firmly convinced that there are some things in the world that will never come to an end.

Rita. I suppose you are thinking of love—and that sort of thing.

Borgheim [*warmly*]. I am thinking of all that is lovely!

Rita. And that never comes to an end. Yes, let us think of that, hope for that, all of us.

Allmers [*coming up to them*]. I suppose you will soon have finished your roadwork out here?

Borgheim. I have finished it already—finished it yesterday. It has been a long business, but, thank Heaven, that has come to an end.

Rita. And you are beaming with joy over that?

Borgheim. Yes, I am indeed!

Rita. Well, I must say——

Borgheim. What, Mrs. Allmers?

Rita. I don't think it is particularly nice of you, Mr. Borgheim.

Borgheim. Indeed! Why not?

Rita. Well, I suppose we sha'n't often see you in these parts after this.

Borgheim. No, that is true. I hadn't thought of that.

Rita. Oh, well, I suppose you will be able to look in upon us now and then all the same.

Borgheim. No, unfortunately that will be out of my power for a very long time.

Allmers. Indeed! How so?

Borgheim. The fact is, I have got a big piece of new work that I must set about at once.

Allmers. Have you indeed?—[*Pressing his hand.*]—I am heartily glad to hear it.

Rita. I congratulate you, Mr. Borgheim.

Borgheim. Hush, hush—I really ought not to talk openly of it as yet! But I can't help coming out with it! It is a great piece of roadmaking—up in the north—with mountain ranges to cross, and the most tremendous difficulties to overcome!—[*With an outburst of gladness.*] Oh, what a glorious world this is—and what a joy it is to be a roadmaker in it!

Rita [*smiling, and looking teasingly at him*]. Is it roadmaking business that has brought you out here today in such wild spirits?

Borgheim. No, not that alone. I am thinking of all the bright and hopeful prospects that are opening out before me.

Rita. Aha, then perhaps you have something still more exquisite in reserve!

Borgheim [*glancing toward* ASTA]. Who knows! When once happiness comes to us, it is apt to come like a spring flood. [*Turns to* ASTA.] Miss Allmers, would you not like to take a little walk with me? As we used to?

Asta [*quickly*]. No—no, thank you. Not now. Not to-day.

Borgheim. Oh, do come! Only a little bit of a walk! I have so much I want to talk to you about before I go.

Rita. Something else, perhaps, that you must not talk openly about as yet?

Borgheim. H'm, that depends——

Rita. But there is nothing to prevent your whispering, you know. [*Half aside.*] Asta, you must really go with him.

Asta. But, my dear Rita——

Borgheim [*imploringly*]. Miss Asta—remember it is to be a farewell walk—the last for many a day.

Asta [*takes her hat and parasol*]. Very well, suppose we take a stroll in the garden, then.

Borgheim. Oh, thank you, thank you!

Allmers. And while you are there you can see what Eyolf is doing.

Borgheim. Ah, Eyolf, by-the-by! Where is Eyolf today? I've got something for him.

Allmers. He is out playing somewhere.

Borgheim. Is he really! Then he has begun to play now? He used always to be sitting indoors over his books.

Allmers. There is to be an end of that now. I am going to make a regular open-air boy of him.

Borgheim. Ah, now, that's right! Out into the open air with him, poor little fellow! Good Lord, what can we possibly do better than play in this blessed world? For my part, I think all life is one long playtime!—Come, Miss Asta!

BORGHEIM *and* ASTA *go out on the veranda and down through the garden.*

Allmers [*stands looking after them*]. Rita—do you think there is anything between those two?

Rita. I don't know what to say. I used to think there was. But Asta has grown so strange to me—so utterly incomprehensible of late.

Allmers. Indeed! Has she? While I have been away?

Rita. Yes, within the last week or two.

Allmers. And you think she doesn't care very much about him now?

Rita. Not seriously; not utterly and entirely; not unreservedly—I am sure she doesn't. [*Looks searchingly at him.*] Would it displease you if she did?

Allmers. It would not exactly displease me. But it would certainly be a disquieting thought——

Rita. Disquieting?

Allmers. Yes; you must remember that I am responsible for Asta—for her life's happiness.

Rita. Oh, come—responsible! Surely Asta has come to years of discretion? I should say she was capable of choosing for herself.

Allmers. Yes, we must hope so, Rita.

Rita. For my part, I don't think at all ill of Borgheim.

Allmers. No, dear—no more do I—quite the contrary. But all the same——

Rita [*continuing*]. And I should be very glad indeed if he and Asta were to make a match of it.

Allmers [*annoyed*]. Oh, why should you be?

Rita [*with increasing excitement*]. Why, for then she would have to go far, far away with him! And she could never come out here to us, as she does now.

Allmers [*stares at her in astonishment*]. What! Can you really wish Asta to go away?

Rita. Yes, yes, Alfred!

Allmers. Why in all the world——?

Rita [*throwing her arms passionately round his neck*]. For then, at last, I should have you to myself alone! And yet—not even then! Not wholly to myself! [*Bursts into convulsive weeping.*] Oh, Alfred, Alfred—I cannot give you up!

Allmers [*gently releasing himself*]. My dearest Rita, do be reasonable!

Rita. I don't care a bit about being reasonable! I care only for you! Only for you in all the world! [*Again throwing her arms round his neck.*] For you, for you, for you!

Allmers. Let me go, let me go—you are strangling me!

Rita [*letting him go*]. How I wish I could! [*Looking at him with flashing eyes.*] Oh, if you knew how I have hated you——!

Allmers. Hated me——!

Rita. Yes—when you shut yourself up in your room and brooded over your work—till long, long into the night. [*Plaintively.*] So long, so late, Alfred. Oh, how I hated your work!

Allmers. But now I have done with that.

Rita [*with a cutting laugh*]. Oh, yes! Now you have given yourself up to something worse.

Allmers [*shocked*]. Worse! Do you call our child something worse?

Rita [*vehemently*]. Yes, I do. As he comes between you and me, I call him so. For the book—the book was not a living being, as the child is. [*With increasing impetuosity.*] But I won't endure it, Alfred! I will not endure it—I tell you so plainly!

Allmers [*looks steadily at her, and says in a low voice*]. I am often almost afraid of you, Rita.

Rita [*gloomily*]. I am often afraid of myself. And for that very reason you must not awake the evil in me.

Allmers. Why, good Heavens, do I do that?

Rita. Yes, you do—when you tear to shreds the holiest bonds between us.

Allmers [*urgently*]. Think what you're saying, Rita. It is your own child—our only child, that you are speaking of.

Rita. The child is only half mine. [*With another outburst.*] But you shall be mine alone! You shall be wholly mine! That I have a right to demand of you!

Allmers [*shrugging his shoulders*]. Oh, my dear Rita, it is of no use demanding anything. Everything must be freely given.

Rita [*looks anxiously at him*]. And that you cannot do henceforth?

Allmers. No, I cannot. I must divide myself between Eyolf and you.

Rita. But if Eyolf had never been born? What then?

Allmers [*evasively*]. Oh, that would be another matter. Then I should have only you to care for.

Rita [*softly, her voice quivering*]. Then I wish he had never been born.

Allmers [*flashing out*]. Rita! You don't know what you are saying!

Rita [*trembling with emotion*]. It was in pain unspeakable that I brought him into the world. But I bore it all with joy and rapture for your sake.

Allmers [*warmly*]. Oh, yes, I know, I know.

Rita [*with decision*]. But there it must end. I will live my life—together with you—wholly with you. I cannot go on being only Eyolf's mother—only his mother and nothing more. I will not, I tell you! I cannot! I will be all in all to you! To you, Alfred!

Allmers. But that is just what you are, Rita. Through our child——

Rita. Oh—vapid, nauseous phrases—nothing else! No, Alfred, I am not to be put off like that. I was fitted to become the child's mother, but not to be a mother to him. You must take me as I am, Alfred.

Allmers. And yet you used to be so fond of Eyolf.

Rita. I was so sorry for him—because you troubled yourself so little about him. You kept him reading and grinding at books. You scarcely even saw him.

Allmers [*nodding slowly*]. No; I was blind. The time had not yet come for me——

Rita [*looking in his face*]. But now, I suppose, it has come?

Allmers. Yes, at last. Now I see that the highest task I can have in the world is to be a true father to Eyolf.

Rita. And to me?—what will you be to me?

Allmers [*gently*]. I will always go on caring for you—with calm, deep tenderness. [*He tries to take her hands.*]

Rita [*evading him*]. I don't care a bit for your calm, deep tenderness. I want you utterly and entirely—and alone! Just as I had you in the first rich, beautiful days. [*Vehemently and harshly.*] Never, never will I consent to be put off with scraps and leavings, Alfred!

Allmers [*in a conciliatory tone*]. I should have thought there was happiness in plenty for all three of us, Rita.

Rita [*scornfully*]. Then you are easy to please. [*Seats herself at the table on the left.*] Now listen to me.

Allmers [*approaching*]. Well, what is it?

Rita [*looking up at him with a veiled glow in her eyes*]. When I got your telegram yesterday evening——

Allmers. Yes? What then?

Rita. —then I dressed myself in white——

Allmers. Yes, I noticed you were in white when I arrived.

Rita. I had let down my hair——

Allmers. Your sweet masses of hair——

Rita. —so that it flowed down my neck and shoulders——

Allmers. I saw it, I saw it. Oh, how lovely you were, Rita!

Rita. There were rose-tinted shades over both the lamps. And we were alone, we two—the only waking beings in the whole house. And there was champagne on the table.

Allmers. I did not drink any of it.

Rita [*looking bitterly at him*]. No, that is true. [*Laughs harshly.*] "There stood the champagne, but you tasted it not"—as the poet says. [*She rises from the armchair, goes with an air of weariness over to the sofa, and seats herself, half reclining, upon it.*]

Allmers [*crosses the room and stands before her*]. I was so taken up with serious thoughts. I had made up my mind to talk to you of our future, Rita—and first and foremost of Eyolf.

Rita [*smiling*]. And so you did——

Allmers. No, I had not time to—for you began to undress.

Rita. Yes, and meanwhile you talked about Eyolf. Don't you remember? You wanted to know all about little Eyolf's digestion.

Allmers [*looking reproachfully at her*]. Rita!

Rita. And then you got into your bed, and slept the sleep of the just.

Allmers [*shaking his head*]. Rita—Rita!

Rita [*lying at full length and looking up at him*]. Alfred?

Allmers. Yes?

Rita. "There stood your champagne, but you tasted it not."

Allmers [*almost harshly*]. No. I did not taste it.

He goes away from her and stands in the garden doorway. RITA *lies for some time motionless, with closed eyes.*

Rita [*suddenly springing up*]. But let me tell you one thing, Alfred.

Allmers [*turning in the doorway*]. Well?

Rita. You ought not to feel quite so secure as you do!

Allmers. Not secure?

Rita. No, you ought not to be so indifferent! Not so certain of your property in me!

Allmers [*drawing nearer*]. What do you mean by that?

Rita [*with trembling lips*]. Never in a single thought have I been untrue to you, Alfred! Never for an instant.

Allmers. No, Rita, I know that—I, who know you so well.

Rita [*with sparkling eyes*]. But if you disdain me——!

Allmers. Disdain! I don't understand what you mean!

Rita. Oh, you don't know all that might rise up within me, if——

Allmers. If?

Rita. If I should ever see that you did not care for me —that you did not love me as you used to.

Allmers. But, my dearest Rita—years bring a certain change with them—and that must one day occur even in us—as in everyone else.

Rita. Never in me! And I will not hear of any change in you either—I could not bear it, Alfred. I want to keep you to myself alone.

Allmers [*looking at her with concern*]. You have a terribly jealous nature——

Rita. I can't make myself different from what I am. [*Threateningly.*] If you go and divide yourself between me and anyone else——

Allmers. What then——?

Rita. Then I will take my revenge on you, Alfred!

Allmers. How "take your revenge"?

Rita. I don't know how.—Oh, yes, I do know, well enough!

Allmers. Well?

Rita. I will go and throw myself away——

Allmers. Throw yourself away, do you say?

Rita. Yes, that I will. I'll throw myself straight into the arms of—of the first man that comes in my way!

Allmers [*looking tenderly at her and shaking his head*]. That you will never do—my loyal, proud, truehearted Rita!

Rita [*putting her arms round his neck*]. Oh, you don't know what I might come to be if you—if you did not love me any more.

Allmers. Did not love you, Rita? How can you say such a thing!

Rita [*half laughing, lets him go*]. Why should I not spread my nets for that—that road-maker man that hangs about here?

Allmers [*relieved*]. Oh, thank goodness—you are only joking.

Rita. Not at all. He would do as well as anyone else.

Allmers. Ah, but I suspect he is more or less taken up already.

Rita. So much the better! For then I should take him

away from someone else; and that is just what Eyolf has done to me.

Allmers. Can you say that our little Eyolf has done that?

Rita [*pointing with her forefinger*]. There, you see! You see! The moment you mention Eyolf's name, you grow tender and your voice quivers! [*Threateningly, clenching her hands.*] Oh, you almost tempt me to wish——

Allmers [*looking at her anxiously*]. What do I tempt you to wish, Rita?——

Rita [*vehemently, going away from him*]. No, no, no— I won't tell you that! Never!

Allmers [*drawing nearer to her*]. Rita! I implore you— for my sake and for your own—do not let yourself be tempted into evil.

BORGHEIM *and* ASTA *come up from the garden. They both show signs of restrained emotion. They look serious and dejected.* ASTA *remains out on the veranda.* BORGHEIM *comes into the room.*

Borgheim. So that is over—Miss Allmers and I have had our last walk together.

Rita [*looks at him with surprise*]. Ah! And there is no longer journey to follow the walk?

Borgheim. Yes, for me.

Rita. For you alone?

Borgheim. Yes, for me alone.

Rita [*glances darkly at* ALLMERS]. Do you hear that? [*Turns to* BORGHEIM.] I'll wager it is someone with the evil eye that has played you this trick.

Borgheim [*looks at her*]. The evil eye?

Rita [*nodding*]. Yes, the evil eye.

Borgheim. Do you believe in the evil eye, Mrs. Allmers?

Rita. Yes. I have begun to believe in the evil eye. Especially in a child's evil eye.

Allmers [*shocked, whispers*]. Rita—how can you——?

Rita [*speaking low*]. It is you that make me so wicked and hateful, Alfred.

Confused cries and shrieks are heard in the distance, from the direction of the fiord.

Borgheim [*going to the glass door*]. What noise is that?

Asta [*in the doorway*]. Look at all those people running down to the pier!

Allmers. What can it be? [*Looks out for a moment.*] No

doubt it's those street urchins at some mischief again.

Borgheim [*calls, leaning over the veranda railings*]. I say, you boys down there! What's the matter?

Several voices are heard answering indistinctly and confusedly.

Rita. What do they say?

Borgheim. They say it's a child that's drowned.

Allmers. A child drowned?

Asta [*uneasily*]. A little boy, they say.

Allmers. Oh, they can all swim, every one of them.

Rita [*shrieks in terror*]. Where is Eyolf?

Allmers. Keep quiet—quiet. Eyolf is down in the garden, playing.

Asta. No, he wasn't in the garden.

Rita [*with upstretched arms*]. Oh, if only it isn't he!

Borgheim [*listens, and calls down*]. Whose child is it, do you say?

Indistinct voices are heard. BORGHEIM *and* ASTA *utter a suppressed cry, and rush out through the garden.*

Allmers [*in an agony of dread*]. It isn't Eyolf! It isn't Eyolf, Rita!

Rita [*on the veranda, listening*]. Hush! Be quiet! Let me hear what they are saying! [RITA *rushes back with a piercing shriek, into the room.*]

Allmers [*following her*]. What did they say?

Rita [*sinking down beside the armchair on the left*]. They said: "The crutch is floating!"

Allmers [*almost paralyzed*]. No! No! No!

Rita [*hoarsely*]. Eyolf! Eyolf! Oh, but they must save him!

Allmers [*half distracted*]. They must, they must! So precious a life! [*He rushes down through the garden.*]

ACT SECOND

A little narrow glen by the side of the fiord, on ALLMERS'S *property. On the left, lofty old trees overarch the spot. Down the slope in the background a brook comes leaping, and loses itself among the stones on the margin of the wood. A path winds along by the brookside. To the right there are only a few single trees, between which the fiord is visible. In front is seen the corner of a boat shed with a boat drawn up. Under the old trees on the left stands a table with a bench and one or two chairs, all made of thin birch staves. It is a heavy, damp day, with driving mist wreaths.*

ALFRED ALLMERS, *dressed as before, sits on the bench, leaning his arms on the table. His hat lies before him. He gazes absently and immovably out over the water.*

Presently ASTA ALLMERS *comes down the wood path. She is carrying an open umbrella.*

ASTA [*goes quietly and cautiously up to him*]. You ought not to sit down here in this gloomy weather, Alfred.

Allmers [*nods slowly without answering*].

Asta [*closing her umbrella*]. I have been searching for you such a long time.

Allmers [*without expression*]. Thank you.

Asta [*moves a chair and seats herself close to him*]. Have you been sitting here long? All the time?

Allmers [*does not answer at first. Presently he says*]. No, I cannot grasp it. It seems so utterly impossible.

Asta [*laying her hand compassionately on his arm*]. Poor Alfred!

Allmers [*gazing at her*]. Is it really true then, Asta? Or have I gone mad? Or am I only dreaming? Oh, if it were only a dream! Just think, if I were to waken now!

Asta. Oh, if I could only waken you!

Allmers [*looking out over the water*]. How pitiless the fiord looks today, lying so heavy and drowsy—leaden gray —with splashes of yellow—and reflecting the rain clouds.

Asta [*imploringly*]. Oh, Alfred, don't sit staring out over the fiord!

Allmers [*not heeding her*]. Over the surface, yes. But in the depths—there sweeps the rushing undertow——

Asta [*in terror*]. Oh, for God's sake—don't think of the depths!

Allmers [*looking gently at her*]. I suppose you think he is lying close outside here? But he is not, Asta. You must not think that. You must remember how fiercely the current sweeps out here—straight to the open sea.

Asta [*throws herself forward against the table, and,*

sobbing, buries her face in her hands]. Oh, God! Oh, God!

Allmers [*heavily*]. So you see, little Eyolf has passed so far—far away from us now.

Asta [*looks imploringly up at him*]. Oh, Alfred, don't say such things!

Allmers. Why, you can reckon it out for yourself—you that are so clever. In eight-and-twenty hours—nine-and-twenty hours—— Let me see——! Let me see——!

Asta [*shrieking and stopping her ears*]. Alfred!

Allmers [*clenching his hand firmly upon the table*]. Can you conceive the meaning of a thing like this?

Asta [*looks at him*]. Of what?

Allmers. Of this that has been done to Rita and me.

Asta. The meaning of it?

Allmers [*impatiently*]. Yes, the meaning, I say. For, after all, there must be a meaning in it. Life, existence—destiny, cannot be so utterly meaningless.

Asta. Oh, who can say anything with certainty about these things, my dear Alfred?

Allmers [*laughs bitterly*]. No, no; I believe you are right there. Perhaps the whole thing goes simply by haphazard—taking its own course, like a drifting wreck without a rudder. I daresay that is how it is. At least, it seems very like it.

Asta [*thoughtfully*]. What if it only seems——?

Allmers [*vehemently*]. Ah? Perhaps you can unravel the mystery for me? I certainly cannot. [*More gently.*] Here is Eyolf, just entering upon conscious life: full of such infinite possibilities—splendid possibilities perhaps: he would have filled my life with pride and gladness. And then a crazy old woman has only to come this way—and show a cur in a bag——

Asta. But we don't in the least know how it really happened.

Allmers. Yes, we do. The boys saw her row out over the fiord. They saw Eyolf standing alone at the very end of the pier. They saw him gazing after her—and then he seemed to turn giddy. [*Quivering.*] And that was how he fell over—and disappeared.

Asta. Yes, yes. But all the same——

Allmers. She has drawn him down into the depths—that you may be sure of, dear.

Asta. But, Alfred, why should she?

Allmers. Yes, that is just the question! Why should she?

There is no retribution behind it all—no atonement, I mean. Eyolf never did her any harm. He never called names after her; he never threw stones at her dog. Why, he had never set eyes either on her or her dog till yesterday. So there is no retribution; the whole thing is utterly groundless and meaningless, Asta. And yet the order of the world requires it.

Asta. Have you spoken to Rita of these things?

Allmers [*shakes his head*]. I feel as if I can talk better to you about them. [*Drawing a deep breath.*] And about everything else as well.

ASTA *takes sewing materials and a little paper parcel out of her pocket.* ALLMERS *sits looking on absently.*

What have you got there, Asta?

Asta [*taking his hat*]. Some black crape.

Allmers. Oh, what is the use of that?

Asta. Rita asked me to put it on. May I?

Allmers. Oh, yes; as far as I'm concerned——

She sews the crape on his hat.

[*Sitting and looking at her.*] Where is Rita?

Asta. She is walking about the garden a little, I think. Borgheim is with her.

Allmers [*slightly surprised*]. Indeed! Is Borgheim out here today again?

Asta. Yes. He came out by the midday train.

Allmers. I didn't expect that.

Asta [*sewing*]. He was so fond of Eyolf.

Allmers. Borgheim is a faithful soul, Asta.

Asta [*with quiet warmth*]. Yes, faithful he is, indeed. That is certain.

Allmers [*fixing his eyes upon her*]. You are really fond of him?

Asta. Yes, I am.

Allmers. And yet you cannot make up your mind to——?

Asta [*interrupting*]. Oh, my dear Alfred, don't talk of that!

Allmers. Yes, yes; tell me why you cannot?

Asta. Oh, no! Please! You really must not ask me. You see, it's so painful for me.—There now! The hat is done.

Allmers. Thank you.

Asta. And now for the left arm.

Allmers. Am I to have crape on it too?

Asta. Yes, that is the custom.

Allmers. Well—as you please.

She moves close up to him and begins to sew.

Asta. Keep your arm still—then I won't prick you.

Allmers [*with a half smile*]. This is like the old days.

Asta. Yes, don't you think so?

Allmers. When you were a little girl you used to sit just like this, mending my clothes. The first thing you ever sewed for me—that was black crape, too.

Asta. Was it?

Allmers. Round my student's cap—at the time of father's death.

Asta. Could I sew then? Fancy, I have forgotten it.

Allmers. Oh, you were such a little thing then.

Asta. Yes, I was little then.

Allmers. And then, two years afterwards—when we lost your mother—then again you sewed a big crape band on my sleeve.

Asta. I thought it was the right thing to do.

Allmers [*patting her hand*]. Yes, yes, it was the right thing to do, Asta. And then when we were left alone in the world, we two—— Are you done already?

Asta. Yes. [*Putting together her sewing materials.*] It was really a beautiful time for us, Alfred. We two alone.

Allmers. Yes, it was—though we had to toil so hard.

Asta. You toiled.

Allmers [*with more life*]. Oh, you toiled too, in your way, I can assure you—[*smiling*]—my dear, faithful—Eyolf.

Asta. Oh—you mustn't remind me of that stupid nonsense about the name.

Allmers. Well, if you had been a boy, you would have been called Eyolf.

Asta. Yes, if! But when you began to go to college—— [*Smiling involuntarily.*] I wonder how you could be so childish.

Allmers. Was it I that was childish?

Asta. Yes, indeed, I think it was, as I look back upon it all. You were ashamed of having no brother—only a sister.

Allmers. No, no, it was you, dear—you were ashamed.

Asta. Oh, yes, I too, perhaps—a little. And somehow or other I was sorry for you——

Allmers. Yes, I believe you were. And then you hunted up some of my old boy's clothes——

Asta. Your fine Sunday clothes—yes. Do you remember the blue blouse and knickerbockers?

Allmers [*his eyes dwelling upon her*]. I remember so well how you looked when you used to wear them.

Asta. Only when we were at home, alone, though.

Allmers. And how serious we were, dear, and how mightily pleased with ourselves. I always called you Eyolf.

Asta. Oh, Alfred, I hope you have never told Rita this?

Allmers. Yes, I believe I did once tell her.

Asta. Oh, Alfred, how could you do that?

Allmers. Well, you see—one tells one's wife everything—very nearly.

Asta. Yes, I suppose one does.

Allmers [*as if awakening, clutches at his forehead and starts up*]. Oh, how can I sit here and——

Asta [*rising, looks sorrowfully at him*]. What is the matter?

Allmers. He had almost passed away from me. He had passed quite away.

Asta. Eyolf!

Allmers. Here I sat, living in these recollections—and he had no part in them.

Asta. Yes, Alfred—little Eyolf was behind it all.

Allmers. No, he was not. He slipped out of my memory —out of my thoughts. I did not see him for a moment as we sat here talking. I utterly forgot him all that time.

Asta. But surely you must take some rest in your sorrow.

Allmers. No, no, no; that is just what I will not do! I must not—I have no right—and no heart for it, either. [*Going in great excitement toward the right.*] All my thoughts must be out there, where he lies drifting in the depths!

Asta [*following him and holding him back*]. Alfred—Alfred! Don't go to the fiord.

Allmers. I must go out to him! Let me go, Asta! I will take the boat.

Asta [*in terror*]. Don't go to the fiord, I say!

Allmers [*yielding*]. No, no—I will not. Only let me alone.

Asta [*leading him back to the table*]. You must rest from your thoughts, Alfred. Come here and sit down.

Allmers [*making as if to seat himself on the bench*]. Well, well—as you please.

Asta. No, I won't let you sit there.

Allmers. Yes, let me.

Asta. No, don't. For then you will only sit looking out ——[*Forces him down upon a chair, with his back to the right.*] There now. Now that's right. [*Seats herself upon the bench.*] And now we can talk a little again.

Allmers [*drawing a deep breath audibly*]. It was good to deaden the sorrow and heartache for a moment.

Asta. You must do so, Alfred.

Allmers. But don't you think it is terribly weak and unfeeling of me—to be able to do so?

Asta. Oh, no—I am sure it is impossible to keep circling forever round one fixed thought.

Allmers. Yes, for me it is impossible. Before you came to me, here I sat, torturing myself unspeakably with this crushing, gnawing sorrow——

Asta. Yes?

Allmers. And would you believe it, Asta——? H'm——

Asta. Well?

Allmers. In the midst of all the agony, I found myself speculating what we should have for dinner today.

Asta [*soothingly*]. Well, well, if only it rests you to——

Allmers. Yes, just fancy, dear—it seemed as if it did give me rest. [*Holds out his hand to her across the table.*] How good it is, Asta, that I have you with me. I am so glad of that. Glad, glad—even in my sorrow.

Asta [*looking earnestly at him*]. You ought most of all to be glad that you have Rita.

Allmers. Yes, of course I should. But Rita is no kin to me—it isn't like having a sister.

Asta [*eagerly*]. Do you say that, Alfred?

Allmers. Yes, our family is a thing apart. [*Half jestingly.*] We have always had vowels for our initials. Don't you remember how often we used to speak of that? And all our relations—all equally poor. And we have all the same color of eyes.

Asta. Do you think I have——?

Allmers. No, you take entirely after your mother. You are not in the least like the rest of us—not even like father. But all the same——

Asta. All the same——?

Allmers. Well, I believe that living together has, as it were, stamped us in each other's image—mentally, I mean.

Asta [*with warm emotion*]. Oh, you must never say that, Alfred. It is only I that have taken my stamp from you; and it is to you that I owe everything—every good thing in the world.

Allmers [*shaking his head*]. You owe me nothing, Asta. On the contrary——

Asta. I owe you everything! You must never doubt that. No sacrifice has been too great for you——

Allmers [*interrupting*]. Oh, nonsense—sacrifice! Don't talk of such a thing. I have only loved you, Asta, ever since you were a little child. [*After a short pause.*] And then it always seemed to me that I had so much injustice to make up for you.

Asta [*astonished*]. Injustice? You?

Allmers. Not precisely on my own account. But——

Asta [*eagerly*]. But——?

Allmers. On father's.

Asta [*half rising from the bench*]. On—father's! [*Sitting down again.*] What do you mean by that, Alfred?

Allmers. Father was never really kind to you.

Asta [*vehemently*]. Oh, don't say that!

Allmers. Yes, it is true. He did not love you—not as he ought to have.

Asta [*evasively*]. No, perhaps not as he loved you. That was only natural.

Allmers [*continuing*]. And he was often hard to your mother, too—at least in the last years.

Asta [*softly*]. Mother was so much, much younger than he—remember that.

Allmers. Do you think they were not quite suited to each other?

Asta. Perhaps not.

Allmers. Yes, but still—— Father, who in other ways was so gentle and warmhearted—so kindly toward everyone——

Asta [*quietly*]. Mother, too, was not always as she ought to have been.

Allmers. Your mother was not!

Asta. Perhaps not always.

Allmers. Toward father, do you mean?

Asta. Yes.

Allmers. I never noticed that.

Asta [*struggling with her tears, rises*]. Oh, my dear Alfred—let them rest—those who are gone. [*She goes toward the right.*]

Allmers [*rising*]. Yes, let them rest. [*Wringing his hands.*] But those who are gone—it is they that won't let us rest, Asta. Neither day nor night.

Asta [*looks warmly at him*]. Time will make it all seem easier, Alfred.

Allmers [*looking helplessly at her*]. Yes, don't you think it will?—But how I am to get over these terrible first days [*Hoarsely.*]—that is what I cannot imagine.

Asta [*imploringly, laying her hands on his shoulders*]. Go up to Rita. Oh, please do——

Allmers [*vehemently, withdrawing from her*]. No, no, no—don't talk to me of that! I cannot, I tell you. [*More calmly.*] Let me remain here, with you.

Asta. Well, I will not leave you.

Allmers [*seizing her hand and holding it fast*]. Thank you for that! [*Looks out for a time over the fiord.*] Where is my little Eyolf now? [*Smiling sadly to her.*] Can you tell me that—my big, wise Eyolf? [*Shaking his head.*] No one in all the world can tell me that. I know only this one terrible thing—that he is gone from me.

Asta [*looking up to the left, and withdrawing her hand*]. Here they are coming.

Mrs. ALLMERS *and* ENGINEER BORGHEIM *come down by the wood path, she leading the way. She wears a dark dress and a black veil over her head. He has an umbrella under his arm.*

Allmers [*going to meet her*]. How is it with you, Rita?

Rita [*passing him*]. Oh, don't ask.

Allmers. Why do you come here?

Rita. Only to look for you. What are you doing?

Allmers. Nothing. Asta came down to me.

Rita. Yes, but before Asta came? You have been away from me all the morning.

Allmers. I have been sitting here looking out over the water.

Rita. Ugh,—how can you?

Allmers [*impatiently*]. I like best to be alone now.

Rita [*moving restlessly about*]. And then to sit still! To stay in one place!

Allmers. I have nothing in the world to move for.

Rita. I cannot bear to be anywhere long. Least of all here—with the fiord at my very feet.

Allmers. It is just the nearness of the fiord——

Rita [*to* BORGHEIM]. Don't you think he should come back with the rest of us?

Borgheim [*to* ALLMERS]. I believe it would be better for you.

Allmers. No, no; let me stay where I am.

Rita. Then I will stay with you, Alfred.

Allmers. Very well; do so, then. You remain too, Asta.

Asta [*whispers to* BORGHEIM]. Let us leave them alone!

Borgheim [*with a glance of comprehension*]. Miss Allmers, shall we go a little further—along the shore? For the very last time?

Asta [*taking her umbrella*]. Yes, come. Let us go a little further.

ASTA *and* BORGHEIM *go out together behind the boat shed.* ALLMERS *wanders about for a little. Then he seats himself on a stone under the trees on the left.*

Rita [*comes up and stands before him, her hands folded and hanging down*]. Can you think the thought, Alfred—that we have lost Eyolf?

Allmers [*looking sadly at the ground*]. We must accustom ourselves to think it.

Rita. I cannot. I cannot. And then that horrible sight that will haunt me all my life long.

Allmers [*looking up*]. What sight? What have you seen?

Rita. I have seen nothing myself. I have only heard it told. Oh——!

Allmers. You may as well tell me at once.

Rita. I got Borgheim to go down with me to the pier——

Allmers. What did you want there?

Rita. To question the boys as to how it happened.

Allmers. But we know that.

Rita. We got to know more.

Allmers. Well?

Rita. It is not true that he disappeared all at once.

Allmers. Do they say that now?

Rita. Yes. They say they saw him lying down on the bottom. Deep down in the clear water.

Allmers [*grinding his teeth*]. And they didn't save him!

Rita. I suppose they could not.

Allmers. They could swim—every one of them. Did they tell you how he was lying whilst they could see him?

Rita. Yes. They said he was lying on his back. And with great, open eyes.

Allmers. Open eyes. But quite still?

Rita. Yes, quite still. And then something came and swept him away. They called it the undertow.

Allmers [*nodding slowly*]. So that was the last they saw of him.

Rita [*suffocated with tears*]. Yes.

Allmers [*in a dull voice*]. And never—never will anyone see him again.

Rita [*wailing*]. I shall see him day and night, as he lay down there.

Allmers. With great, open eyes.

Rita [*shuddering*]. Yes, with great, open eyes. I see them! I see them now!

Allmers [*rises slowly and looks with quiet menace at her*]. Were they evil, those eyes, Rita?

Rita [*turning pale*]. Evil——!

Allmers [*going close up to her*]. Were they evil eyes that stared up? Up from the depths?

Rita [*shrinking from him*]. Alfred——!

Allmers [*following her*]. Answer me! Were they a child's evil eyes?

Rita [*shrieks*]. Alfred! Alfred!

Allmers. Now things have come about—just as you wished, Rita.

Rita. I! What did *I* wish?

Allmers. That Eyolf were not here.

Rita. Never for a moment have I wished that! That Eyolf should not stand between us—that was what I wished.

Allmers. Well, well—he does not stand between us any more.

Rita [*softly, gazing straight before her*]. Perhaps now more than ever. [*With a sudden shudder.*] Oh, that horrible sight!

Allmers [*nods*]. The child's evil eyes.

Rita [*in dread, recoiling from him*]. Let me be, Alfred! I am afraid of you. I have never seen you like this before.

Allmers [*looks harshly and coldly at her*]. Sorrow makes us wicked and hateful.

Rita [*terrified, and yet defiant*]. That is what I feel, too.

ALLMERS *goes toward the right and looks out over the fiord.* RITA *seats herself at the table. A short pause.*

Allmers [*turning his head toward her*]. You never really and truly loved him—never!

Rita [*with cold self-control*]. Eyolf would never let me take him really and truly to my heart.

Allmers. Because you did not want to.

Rita. Oh, yes, I did. I did want to. But someone stood in the way—even from the first.

Allmers [*turning right round*]. Do you mean that *I* stood in the way?

Rita. Oh, no—not at first.

Allmers [*coming nearer her*]. Who, then?

Rita. His aunt.

Allmers. Asta?

Rita. Yes. Asta stood and barred the way for me.

Allmers. Can you say that, Rita?

Rita. Yes. Asta—she took him to her heart—from the moment that happened—that miserable fall.

Allmers. If she did so, she did it in love.

Rita [*vehemently*]. That is just it! I cannot endure to share anything with anyone! Not in love.

Allmers. We two should have shared him between us in love.

Rita [*looking scornfully at him*]. We? Oh, the truth is you have never had any real love for him either.

Allmers [*looks at her in astonishment*]. *I* have not——!

Rita. No, you have not. At first you were so utterly taken up by that book of yours—about Responsibility.

Allmers [*forcibly*]. Yes, I was. But my very book—I sacrificed for Eyolf's sake.

Rita. Not out of love for him.

Allmers. Why then, do you suppose?

Rita. Because you were consumed with mistrust of yourself. Because you had begun to doubt whether you had any great vocation to live for in the world.

Allmers [*observing her closely*]. Could you see that in me?

Rita. Oh, yes—little by little. And then you needed something new to fill up your life.—It seems *I* was not enough for you any longer.

Allmers. That is the law of change, Rita.

Rita. And that was why you wanted to make a prodigy of poor little Eyolf.

Allmers. That was not what I wanted. I wanted to make a happy human being of him.—That, and nothing more.

Rita. But not out of love for him. Look into yourself! [*With a certain shyness of expression.*] Search out all that lies under—and behind your action.

Allmers [*avoiding her eyes*]. There is something you shrink from saying.

Rita. And you too.

Allmers [*looks thoughtfully at her*]. If it is as you say, then we two have never really possessed our own child.

Rita. No. Not in perfect love.

Allmers. And yet we are sorrowing so bitterly for him.

Rita [*with sarcasm*]. Yes, isn't it curious that we should grieve like this over a little stranger boy?

Allmers [*with an outburst*]. Oh, don't call him a stranger!

Rita [*sadly shaking her head*]. We never won the boy, Alfred. Not I—nor you either.

Allmers [*wringing his hands*]. And now it is too late! Too late!

Rita. And no consolation anywhere—in anything.

Allmers [*with sudden passion*]. You are the guilty one in this!

Rita [*rising*]. I!

Allmers. Yes, you! It was your fault that he became—what he was! It was your fault that he could not save himself when he fell into the water.

Rita [*with a gesture of repulsion*]. Alfred—you shall not throw the blame upon me!

Allmers [*more and more beside himself*]. Yes, yes, I do! It was you that left the helpless child unwatched upon the table.

Rita. He was lying so comfortably among the cushions, and sleeping so soundly. And you had promised to look after him.

Allmers. Yes, I had. [*Lowering his voice.*] But then you came—you, you, you—and lured me to you.

Rita [*looking defiantly at him*]. Oh, better own at once that you forgot the child and everything else.

Allmers [*in suppressed desperation*]. Yes, that is true. [*Lower.*] I forgot the child—in your arms!

Rita [*exasperated*]. Alfred! Alfred—this is intolerable of you!

Allmers [*in a low voice, clenching his fists before her face*]. In that hour you condemned little Eyolf to death.

Rita [*wildly*]. You, too! You, too—if it is as you say!

Allmers. Oh, yes—call me to account, too—if you will. We have sinned, both of us. And so, after all, there was retribution in Eyolf's death.

Rita. Retribution?

Allmers [*with more self-control*]. Yes. Judgment upon you and me. Now, as we stand here, we have our deserts. While he lived, we let ourselves shrink away from him in secret, abject remorse. We could not bear to see it—the thing he had to drag with him——

Rita [*whispers*]. The crutch.

Allmers. Yes, that. And now, what we now call sorrow and heartache—is really the gnawing of conscience, Rita. Nothing else.

Rita [*gazing helplessly at him*]. I feel as if all this must end in despair—in madness for both of us. For we can never—never make it good again.

Allmers [*passing into a calmer mood*]. I dreamed about Eyolf last night. I thought I saw him coming up from the pier. He could run like other boys. So nothing had happened to him—neither the one thing nor the other. And the torturing reality was nothing but a dream, I thought. Oh, how I thanked and blessed—— [*Checking himself.*] H'm!

Rita [*looking at him*]. Whom?

Allmers [*evasively*]. Whom——?

Rita. Yes; whom did you thank and bless?

Allmers [*putting aside the question*]. I was only dreaming, you know——

Rita. One whom you yourself do not believe in?

Allmers. That was how I felt, all the same. Of course, I was sleeping——

Rita [*reproachfully*]. You should not have taught me to doubt, Alfred.

Allmers. Would it have been right of me to let you go through life with your mind full of empty fictions?

Rita. It would have been better for me; for then I

should have had something to take refuge in. Now I am utterly at sea.

Allmers [*observing her closely*]. If you had the choice now—— If you could follow Eyolf to where he is——?

Rita. Yes? What then?

Allmers. If you were fully assured that you would find him again—know him—understand him——?

Rita. Yes, yes; what then?

Allmers. Would you, of your own free will, take the leap over to him? Of your own free will leave everything behind you? Renounce your whole earthly life? Would you, Rita?

Rita [*softly*]. Now, at once?

Allmers. Yes; today. This very hour. Answer me—would you?

Rita [*hesitating*]. Oh, I don't know, Alfred. No! I think I should have to stay here with you, a little while.

Allmers. For my sake?

Rita. Yes, only for your sake.

Allmers. But afterwards? Would you then——? Answer!

Rita. Oh, what can I answer? I could not go away from you. Never! Never!

Allmers. But suppose now *I* went to Eyolf? And you had the fullest assurance that you would meet both him and me there. Then would you come over to us?

Rita. I should want to—so much! so much! But——

Allmers. Well?

Rita [*moaning softly*]. I could not—I feel it. No, no, I never could! Not for all the glory of heaven!

Allmers. Nor I.

Rita. No, you feel it so, too, don't you, Alfred! You could not either, could you?

Allmers. No. For it is here, in the life of earth, that we living beings are at home.

Rita. Yes, here lies the kind of happiness that we can understand.

Allmers [*darkly*]. Oh, happiness—happiness——

Rita. You mean that happiness—that we can never find it again? [*Looks inquiringly at him.*] But if——? [*Vehemently.*] No, no; I dare not say it! Nor even think it!

Allmers. Yes, say it—say it, Rita.

Rita [*hesitatingly*]. Could we not try to——? Would it not be possible to forget him?

Allmers. Forget Eyolf?

Rita. Forget the anguish and remorse, I mean.

Allmers. Can you wish it?

Rita. Yes,—if it were possible. [*With an outburst.*] For this—I cannot bear this forever! Oh, can we not think of something that will bring us forgetfulness!

Allmers [*shakes his head*]. What could that be?

Rita. Could we not see what traveling would do—far away from here?

Allmers. From home? When you know you are never really well anywhere but here.

Rita. Well, then, let us have crowds of people about us! Keep open house! Plunge into something that can deaden and dull our thoughts.

Allmers. Such a life would be impossible for me.—No,—rather than that, I would try to take up my work again.

Rita [*bitingly*]. Your work—the work that has always stood like a dead wall between us!

Allmers [*slowly, looking fixedly at her*]. There must always be a dead wall between us two, from this time forth.

Rita. Why must there——?

Allmers. Who knows but that a child's great, open eyes are watching us day and night.

Rita [*softly, shuddering*]. Alfred—how terrible to think of!

Allmers. Our love has been like a consuming fire. Now it must be quenched——

Rita [*with a movement toward him*]. Quenched!

Allmers [*hardly*]. It is quenched—in one of us.

Rita [*as if petrified*]. And you dare say that to me!

Allmers [*more gently*]. It is dead, Rita. But in what I now feel for you—in our common guilt and need of atonement—I seem to foresee a sort of resurrection——

Rita [*vehemently*]. I don't care a bit about any resurrection!

Allmers. Rita!

Rita. I am a warm-blooded being! I don't go drowsing about—with fishes' blood in my veins. [*Wringing her hands.*] And now to be imprisoned for life—in anguish and remorse! Imprisoned with one who is no longer mine, mine, mine!

Allmers. It must have ended so, sometime, Rita.

Rita. Must have ended so! The love that in the beginning rushed forth so eagerly to meet with love!

Allmers. My love did not rush forth to you in the beginning.

Rita. What did you feel for me, first of all?

Allmers. Dread.

Rita. That I can understand. How was it, then, that I won you after all?

Allmers [*in a low voice*]. You were so entrancingly beautiful, Rita.

Rita [*looks searchingly at him*]. Then that was the only reason? Say it, Alfred! The only reason?

Allmers [*conquering himself*]. No, there was another as well.

Rita [*with an outburst*]. I can guess what that was! It was "my gold, and my green forests," as you call it. Was it not so, Alfred?

Allmers. Yes.

Rita [*looks at him with deep reproach*]. How could you —how could you!

Allmers. I had Asta to think of.

Rita [*angrily*]. Yes, Asta! [*Bitterly.*] Then it was really Asta that brought us two together?

Allmers. She knew nothing about it. She has no suspicion of it, even to this day.

Rita [*rejecting the plea*]. It was Asta, nevertheless! [*Smiling, with a sidelong glance of scorn.*] Or, no—it was little Eyolf. Little Eyolf, my dear!

Allmers. Eyolf——?

Rita. Yes, you used to call her Eyolf, did you not? I seem to remember your telling me so—once, in a moment of confidence. [*Coming up to him.*] Do you remember it —that entrancingly beautiful hour, Alfred?

Allmers [*recoiling, as if in horror*]. I remember nothing! I will not remember!

Rita [*following him*]. It was in that hour—when your other little Eyolf was crippled for life!

Allmers [*in a hollow voice, supporting himself against the table*]. Retribution!

Rita [*menacingly*]. Yes, retribution!

ASTA *and* BORGHEIM *return by way of the boat shed. She is carrying some water lilies in her hand.*

Rita [*with self-control*]. Well, Asta, have you and Mr. Borgheim talked things thoroughly over?

Asta. Oh, yes—pretty well. [*She puts down her umbrella and lays the flowers upon a chair.*]

Borgheim. Miss Allmers has been very silent during our walk.

Rita. Indeed, has she? Well, Alfred and I have talked things out thoroughly enough——

Asta [*looking eagerly at both of them*]. What is this——?

Rita. Enough to last all our lifetime, I say. [*Breaking off.*] Come now, let us go up to the house, all four of us. We must have company about us in future. It will never do for Alfred and me to be alone.

Allmers. Yes, do you go ahead, you two. [*Turning.*] I must speak a word to you before we go, Asta.

Rita [*looking at him*]. Indeed? Well then, you come with me, Mr. Borgheim.

RITA *and* BORGHEIM *go up the wood path.*

Asta [*anxiously*]. Alfred, what is the matter?

Allmers [*darkly*]. Only that I cannot endure to be here any more.

Asta. Here! With Rita, do you mean?

Allmers. Yes. Rita and I cannot go on living together.

Asta [*seizes his arm and shakes it*]. Oh, Alfred—don't say anything so terrible!

Allmers. It is the truth I am telling you. We are making each other wicked and hateful.

Asta [*with painful emotion*]. I had never—never dreamed of anything like this!

Allmers. I did not realize it either, till today.

Asta. And now you want to——! What is it you really want, Alfred?

Allmers. I want to get away from everything here—far, far away from it all.

Asta. And to stand quite alone in the world?

Allmers [*nods*]. As I used to, before, yes.

Asta. But you are not fitted for living alone!

Allmers. Oh, yes. I was so in the old days, at any rate.

Asta. In the old days, yes; for then you had me with you.

Allmers [*trying to take her hand*]. Yes. And it is to you, Asta, that I now want to come home again.

Asta [*eluding him*]. To me! No, no, Alfred! That is quite impossible.

Allmers [*looks sadly at her*]. Then Borgheim stands in the way after all?

Asta [*earnestly*]. No, no; he does not! That is quite a mistake!

Allmers. Good. Then I will come to you—my dear, dear sister. I must come to you again—home to you, to be purified and ennobled after my life with——

Asta [*shocked*]. Alfred,—you are doing Rita a great wrong!

Allmers. I have done her a great wrong. But not in this. Oh, think of it, Asta—think of our life together, yours and mine. Was it not like one long holy day from first to last?

Asta. Yes, it was, Alfred. But we can never live it over again.

Allmers [*bitterly*]. Do you mean that marriage has so irreparably ruined me?

Asta [*quietly*]. No, that is not what I mean.

Allmers. Well, then we two will live our old life over again.

Asta [*with decision*]. We cannot, Alfred.

Allmers. Yes, we can. For the love of a brother and sister——

Asta [*eagerly*]. What of it?

Allmers. That is the only relation in life that is not subject to the law of change.

Asta [*softly and tremblingly*]. But if that relation were not——

Allmers. Not——?

Asta. ——not our relation?

Allmers [*stares at her in astonishment*]. Not ours? Why, what can you mean by that?

Asta. It is best I should tell you at once, Alfred.

Allmers. Yes, yes; tell me!

Asta. The letters to mother—— Those in my portfolio——

Allmers. Well?

Asta. You must read them—when I am gone.

Allmers. Why must I?

Asta [*struggling with herself*]. For then you will see that——

Allmers. Well?

Asta. ——that I have no right to bear your father's name.

Allmers [*staggering backwards*]. Asta! What is this you say!

Asta. Read the letters. Then you will see—and understand. And perhaps have some forgiveness—for mother, too.

Allmers [*clutching at his forehead*]. I cannot grasp this —I cannot realize the thought. You, Asta—you are not——

Asta. You are not my brother, Alfred.

Allmers [*quickly, half defiantly, looking at her*]. Well, but what difference does that really make in our relation? Practically none at all.

Asta [*shaking her head*]. It makes all the difference, Alfred. Our relation is not that of brother and sister.

Allmers. No, no. But it is nonetheless sacred for that— it will always be equally sacred.

Asta. Do not forget—that it is subject to the law of change, as you said just now.

Allmers [*looks inquiringly at her*]. Do you mean that——

Asta [*quietly, but with warm emotion*]. Not a word more—my dear, dear Alfred. [*Takes up the flowers from the chair.*] Do you see these water lilies?

Allmers [*nodding slowly*]. They are the sort that shoot up—from the very depth.

Asta. I pulled them in the tarn—where it flows out into the fiord. [*Holds them out to him.*] Will you take them, Alfred?

Allmers [*taking them*]. Thanks.

Asta [*with tears in her eyes*]. They are a last greeting to you, from—from little Eyolf.

Allmers [*looking at her*]. From Eyolf out yonder? Or from you?

Asta [*softly*]. From both of us. [*Taking up her umbrella.*] Now come with me to Rita. [*She goes up the wood path.*]

Allmers [*takes up his hat from the table, and whispers sadly*]. Asta. Eyolf. Little Eyolf——! [*He follows her up the path.*]

ACT THIRD

An elevation, overgrown with shrubs, in ALLMERS's *garden. At the back a sheer cliff, with a railing along its edge, and*

*with steps on the left leading downwards. An extensive
view over the fiord, which lies deep below. A flagstaff
with lines, but no flag, stands by the railing. In front, on
the right, a summerhouse, covered with creepers and wild
vines. Outside it, a bench. It is a late summer evening,
with clear sky. Deepening twilight.*

ASTA *is sitting on the bench, with her hands in her lap.
She is wearing her outdoor dress and a hat, has her parasol
at her side, and a little traveling bag on a strap over her
shoulder.*

BORGHEIM *comes up from the back on the left. He, too,
has a traveling bag over his shoulder. He is carrying a
rolled-up flag.*

BORGHEIM [*catching sight of* ASTA]. Oh, so you are up
here!

Asta. Yes, I am taking my last look out over the fiord.

Borgheim. Then I am glad I happened to come up.

Asta. Have you been searching for me?

Borgheim. Yes, I have. I wanted to say good-by to you
—for the present. Not for good and all, I hope.

Asta [*with a faint smile*]. You are persevering.

Borgheim. A road-maker has got to be.

Asta. Have you seen anything of Alfred? Or of Rita?

Borgheim. Yes, I saw them both.

Asta. Together?

Borgheim. No—apart.

Asta. What are you going to do with that flag?

Borgheim. Mrs. Allmers asked me to come up and
hoist it.

Asta. Hoist a flag just now?

Borgheim. Half-mast high. She wants it to fly both
night and day, she says.

Asta [*sighing*]. Poor Rita! And poor Alfred!

Borgheim [*busied with the flag*]. Have you the heart to
leave them? I ask, because I see you are in traveling dress.

Asta [*in a low voice*]. I must go.

Borgheim. Well, if you must, then——

Asta. And you are going, too, tonight?

Borgheim. I must, too. I am going by the train. Are you
going that way?

Asta. No. I shall take the steamer.

Borgheim [*glancing at her*]. We each take our own way, then?

Asta. Yes.

She sits and looks on while he hoists the flag half-mast high. When he has done he goes up to her.

Borgheim. Miss Asta—you can't think how grieved I am about little Eyolf.

Asta [*looks up at him*]. Yes, I am sure you feel it deeply.

Borgheim. And the feeling tortures me. For the fact is, grief is not much in my way.

Asta [*raising her eyes to the flag*]. It will pass over in time—all of it. All our sorrow.

Borgheim. All? Do you believe that?

Asta. Like a squall at sea. When once you have got far away from here, then——

Borgheim. It will have to be very far away indeed.

Asta. And then you have this great new roadwork, too.

Borgheim. But no one to help me in it.

Asta. Oh, yes, surely you have.

Borgheim [*shaking his head*]. No one. No one to share the gladness with. For it is gladness that most needs sharing.

Asta. Not the labor and trouble?

Borgheim. Pooh—that sort of thing one can always get through alone.

Asta. But the gladness—that must be shared with someone, you think?

Borgheim. Yes; for if not, where would be the pleasure in being glad?

Asta. Ah, yes—perhaps there is something in that.

Borgheim. Oh, of course, for a certain time you can go on feeling glad in your own heart. But it won't do in the long run. No, it takes two to be glad.

Asta. Always two? Never more? Never many?

Borgheim. Well, you see—then it becomes a quite different matter. Miss Asta—are you sure you can never make up your mind to share gladness and success and—and labor and trouble, with one—with one alone in all the world?

Asta. I have tried it—once.

Borgheim. Have you?

Asta. Yes, all the time that my brother—that Alfred and I lived together.

Borgheim. Oh, with your brother, yes. But that is altogether different. That ought rather to be called peace than happiness, I should say.

Asta. It was delightful, all the same.

Borgheim. There now—you see even that seemed to you delightful. But just think now—if he had not been your brother!

Asta [*makes a movement to rise, but remains sitting*]. Then we should never have been together. For I was a child then—and he wasn't much more.

Borgheim [*after a pause*]. Was it so delightful—that time?

Asta. Oh, yes, indeed it was.

Borgheim. Was there much that was really bright and happy in your life then?

Asta. Oh, yes, so much. You cannot think how much.

Borgheim. Tell me a little about it, Miss Asta.

Asta. Oh, there are only trifles to tell.

Borgheim. Such as——? Well?

Asta. Such as the time when Alfred had passed his examination—and had distinguished himself. And then, from time to time, when he got a post in some school or other. Or when he would sit at home working at an article— and would read it aloud to me. And then when it would appear in some magazine.

Borgheim. Yes, I can quite see that it must have been a peaceful, delightful life—a brother and sister sharing all their joys. [*Shaking his head.*] What I cannot understand is that your brother could ever give you up, Asta.

Asta [*with suppressed emotion*]. Alfred married, you know.

Borgheim. Was not that very hard for you?

Asta. Yes, at first. It seemed as though I had utterly lost him all at once.

Borgheim. Well, luckily it was not so bad as that.

Asta. No.

Borgheim. But, all the same—how could he! Go and marry, I mean—when he could have kept you with him, alone!

Asta [*looking straight in front of her*]. He was subject to the law of change, I suppose.

Borgheim. The law of change?

Asta. So Alfred calls it.

Borgheim. Pooh—what a stupid law that must be! I don't believe a bit in that law.

Asta [*rising*]. You may come to believe in it, in time.

Borgheim. Never in all my life! [*Insistently.*] But listen now, Miss Asta! Do be reasonable—for once in a way—in this matter, I mean——

Asta [*interrupting him*]. Oh, no, no—don't let us begin upon that again!

Borgheim [*continuing as before*]. Yes, Asta—I can't possibly give you up so easily. Now your brother has everything as he wishes it. He can live his life quite contentedly without you. He doesn't require you at all. Then this—this—that at one blow has changed your whole position here——

Asta [*with a start*]. What do you mean by that?

Borgheim. The loss of the child. What else should I mean?

Asta [*recovering her self-control*]. Little Eyolf is gone, yes.

Borgheim. And what more does that leave you to do here? You have not the poor little boy to take care of now. You have no duties—no claims upon you of any sort.

Asta. Oh, please, Mr. Borgheim—don't make it so hard for me.

Borgheim. I must; I should be mad if I did not try my uttermost. I shall be leaving town before very long, and perhaps I shall have no opportunity of meeting you there. Perhaps I shall not see you again for a long, long time. And who knows what may happen in the meanwhile?

Asta [*with a grave smile*]. So you are afraid of the law of change, after all?

Borgheim. No, not in the least. [*Laughing bitterly.*] And there is nothing to be changed, either—not in you, I mean. For I can see you don't care much about me.

Asta. You know very well that I do.

Borgheim. Perhaps, but not nearly enough. Not as I want you to. [*More forcibly.*] By Heaven, Asta—Miss Asta—I cannot tell you how strongly I feel that you are wrong in this! A little onward, perhaps, from today and tomorrow, all life's happiness may be awaiting us. And we must needs pass it by! Do you think we will not come to repent of it, Asta?

Asta [*quietly*]. I don't know. I only know that they are not for us—all these bright possibilities.

Borgheim [*looks at her with self-control*]. Then I must make my roads alone?

Asta [*warmly*]. Oh, how I wish I could stand by you in it all! Help you in the labor—share the gladness with you——

Borgheim. Would you—if you could?

Asta. Yes, that I would.

Borgheim. But you cannot?

Asta [*looking down*]. Would you be content to have only half of me?

Borgheim. No. You must be utterly and entirely mine.

Asta [*looks at him, and says quietly*]. Then I cannot.

Borgheim. Good-by then, Miss Asta.

He is on the point of going. ALLMERS *comes up from the left at the back.* BORGHEIM *stops.*

Allmers [*the moment he has reached the top of the steps, points, and says in a low voice*]. Is Rita in there—in the summerhouse?

Borgheim. No; there is no one here but Miss Asta.

ALLMERS *comes forward.*

Asta [*going toward him*]. Shall I go down and look for her? Shall I get her to come up here?

Allmers [*with a negative gesture*]. No, no, no—let it alone. [*To* BORGHEIM.] Is it you that have hoisted the flag?

Borgheim. Yes. Mrs. Allmers asked me to. That was what brought me up here.

Allmers. And you are going to start tonight?

Borgheim. Yes. Tonight I go away in good earnest.

Allmers [*with a glance at* ASTA]. And you have made sure of pleasant company, I daresay.

Borgheim [*shaking his head*]. I am going alone.

Allmers [*with a surprise*]. Alone!

Borgheim. Utterly alone.

Allmers [*absently*]. Indeed?

Borgheim. And I shall have to remain alone, too.

Allmers. There is something horrible in being alone. The thought of it runs like ice through my blood——

Asta. Oh, but, Alfred, you are not alone.

Allmers. There may be something horrible in that too, Asta.

Asta [*oppressed*]. Oh, don't talk like that! Don't think like that!

Allmers [*not listening to her*]. But since you are not going with him——? Since there is nothing to bind you——? Why will you not remain out here with me—and with Rita?

Asta [*uneasily*]. No, no, I cannot. I must go back to town now.

Allmers. But only in to town, Asta. Do you hear!

Asta. Yes.

Allmers. And you must promise me that you will soon come out again.

Asta [*quickly*]. No, no, I dare not promise you that, for the present.

Allmers. Well—as you will. We shall soon meet in town, then.

Asta [*imploringly*]. But, Alfred, you must stay at home here with Rita now.

Allmers [*without answering, turns to* Borgheim]. You may find it a good thing, after all, that you have to take your journey alone.

Borgheim [*annoyed*]. Oh, how can you say such a thing?

Allmers. You see, you can never tell whom you might happen to meet afterwards—on the way.

Asta [*involuntarily*]. Alfred!

Allmers. The right fellow traveler—when it is too late—too late.

Asta [*softly, quivering*]. Alfred! Alfred!

Borgheim [*looking from one to the other*]. What is the meaning of this? I don't understand——

Rita *comes up from the left at the back.*

Rita [*plaintively*]. Oh, don't go away from me, all of you!

Asta [*going toward her*]. You said you preferred to be alone.

Rita. Yes, but I dare not. It is getting so horribly dark. I seem to see great, open eyes fixed upon me!

Asta [*tenderly and sympathetically*]. What if it were so, Rita? You ought not to be afraid of those eyes.

Rita. How can you say so! Not afraid!

Allmers [*insistently*]. Asta, I beg you—for Heaven's sake—remain here with Rita!

Rita. Yes! And with Alfred, too. Do! Do, Asta!

Asta [*struggling with herself*]. Oh, I want to so much——

Rita. Well, then, do it! For Alfred and I cannot go alone
through the sorrow and heartache.

Allmers [*darkly*]. Say, rather—through the ranklings of
remorse.

Rita. Oh, whatever you like to call it—we cannot bear it
alone, we two. Oh, Asta, I beg and implore you! Stay
here and help us! Take Eyolf's place for us——

Asta [*shrinking*]. Eyolf's——

Rita. Yes, would you not have it so, Alfred?

Allmers. If she can and will.

Rita. You used to call her your little Eyolf. [*Seizes her
hand.*] Henceforth you shall be our Eyolf, Asta! Eyolf, as
you were before.

Allmers [*with concealed emotion*]. Remain—and share
our life with us, Asta. With Rita. With me. With me—your
brother!

Asta [*with decision, snatches her hand away*]. No. I
cannot. [*Turning.*] Mr. Borgheim—what time does the
steamer start?

Borgheim. Now—at once.

Asta. Then I must go on board. Will you go with me?

Borgheim [*with a suppressed outburst of joy*]. Will I?
Yes, yes!

Asta. Then come!

Rita [*slowly*]. Ah! That is how it is. Well, then, you cannot stay with us.

Asta [*throwing her arms round her neck*]. Thanks for
everything, Rita! [*Goes up to* ALLMERS *and grasps his
hand.*] Alfred—good-by! A thousand times, good-by!

Allmers [*softly and eagerly*]. What is this, Asta? It seems
as though you were taking flight.

Asta [*in subdued anguish*]. Yes, Alfred—I am taking
flight.

Allmers. Flight—from me!

Asta [*whispering*]. From you—and from myself.

Allmers [*shrinking back*]. Ah——!

ASTA *rushes down the steps at the back.* BORGHEIM *waves
his hat and follows her.* RITA *leans against the entrance to
the summerhouse.* ALLMERS *goes, in strong inward emotion, up to the railing, and stands there gazing downwards. A pause.*

[*Turns, and says with hard-won composure.*] There comes
the steamer. Look, Rita.

Rita. I dare not look at it.

Allmers. You dare not?

Rita. No. For it has a red eye—and a green one, too. Great, glowing eyes.

Allmers. Oh, those are only the lights, you know.

Rita. Henceforth they are eyes—for me. They stare and stare out of the darkness—and into the darkness.

Allmers. Now she is putting in to shore.

Rita. Where are they mooring her this evening, then?

Allmers [*coming forward*]. At the pier, as usual——

Rita [*drawing herself up*]. How can they moor her there!

Allmers. They must.

Rita. But it was there that Eyolf——! How can they moor her there!

Allmers. Yes, life is pitiless, Rita.

Rita. Men are heartless. They take no thought—either for the living or for the dead.

Allmers. There you are right. Life goes its own way—just as if nothing in the world had happened.

Rita [*gazing straight before her*]. And nothing has happened, either. Not to others. Only to us two.

Allmers [*the pain reawakening*]. Yes, Rita—so it was to no purpose that you bore him in sorrow and anguish. For now he is gone again—and has left no trace behind him.

Rita. Only the crutch was saved.

Allmers [*angrily*]. Be silent! Do not let me hear that word!

Rita [*plaintively*]. Oh, I cannot bear the thought that he is gone from us.

Allmers [*coldly and bitterly*]. You could very well do without him while he was with us. Half the day would often pass without your setting eyes on him.

Rita. Yes, for I knew that I could see him whenever I wanted to.

Allmers. Yes, that is how we have gone and squandered the short time we had with Little Eyolf.

Rita [*listening, in dread*]. Do you hear, Alfred! Now it is ringing again!

Allmers [*looking over the fiord*]. It is the steamer's bell that is ringing. She is just starting.

Rita. Oh, it's not that bell I mean. All day I have heard it ringing in my ears.—Now it is ringing again!

Allmers [*going up to her*]. You are mistaken, Rita.

Rita. No, I hear it so plainly. It sounds like a knell. Slow. Slow. And always the same words.

Allmers. Words? What words?

Rita [*nodding her head in the rhythm*]. "The crútch is —flóating. The crútch is—flóating." Oh, surely you must hear it, too!

Allmers [*shaking his head*]. I hear nothing. And there is nothing to hear.

Rita. Oh, you may say what you will—I hear it so plainly.

Allmers [*looking out over the railing*]. Now they are on board, Rita. Now the steamer is on her way to the town.

Rita. Is it possible you do not hear it? "The crútch is— flóating. The crútch is——"

Allmers [*coming forward*]. You shall not stand there listening to a sound that does not exist. I tell you, Asta and Borgheim are on board. They have started already. Asta is gone.

Rita [*looks timidly at him*]. Then I suppose you will soon be gone, too, Alfred?

Allmers [*quickly*]. What do you mean by that?

Rita. That you will follow your sister.

Allmers. Has Asta told you anything?

Rita. No. But you said yourself it was for Asta's sake that—that we came together.

Allmers. Yes, but you, you yourself, have bound me to you—by our life together.

Rita. Oh, in your eyes I am not—I am not—entrancingly beautiful any more.

Allmers. The law of change may perhaps keep us together, nonetheless.

Rita [*nodding slowly*]. There is a change in me now— I feel the anguish of it.

Allmers. Anguish?

Rita. Yes, for change, too, is a sort of birth.

Allmers. It is—or a resurrection. Transition to a higher life.

Rita [*gazing sadly before her*]. Yes—with the loss of all, all life's happiness.

Allmers. That loss is just the gain.

Rita [*vehemently*]. Oh, phrases! Good God, we are creatures of earth after all.

Allmers. But something akin to the sea and the heavens too, Rita.

Rita. You perhaps. Not I.

Allmers. Oh, yes—you too, more than you yourself suspect.

Rita [*advancing a pace toward him*]. Tell me, Alfred—could you think of taking up your work again?

Allmers. The work that you have hated so.

Rita. I am easier to please now. I am willing to share you with the book.

Allmers. Why?

Rita. Only to keep you here with me—to have you near me.

Allmers. Oh, it is so little I can do to help you, Rita.

Rita. But perhaps I could help you.

Allmers. With my book, do you mean?

Rita. No; but to live your life.

Allmers [*shaking his head*]. I seem to have no life to live.

Rita. Well then, to endure your life.

Allmers [*darkly, looking away from her*]. I think it would be best for both of us that we should part.

Rita [*looking curiously at him*]. Then where would you go? Perhaps to Asta, after all?

Allmers. No—never again to Asta.

Rita. Where then?

Allmers. Up into the solitudes.

Rita. Up among the mountains? Is that what you mean?

Allmers. Yes.

Rita. But all that is mere dreaming, Alfred! You could not live up there.

Allmers. And yet I feel myself drawn to them.

Rita. Why? Tell me!

Allmers. Sit down—and I will tell you something.

Rita. Something that happened to you up there?

Allmers. Yes.

Rita. And that you never told Asta and me?

Allmers. Yes.

Rita. Oh, you are so silent about everything. You ought not to be.

Allmers. Sit down there—and I will tell you about it.

Rita. Yes, yes—tell me! [*She sits on the bench beside the summerhouse.*]

Allmers. I was alone up there, in the heart of the great mountains. I came to a wide, dreary mountain lake; and that lake I had to cross. But I could not—for there was neither a boat nor anyone there.

Rita. Well? And then?

Allmers. Then I went without any guidance into a side valley. I thought that by that way I could push on over the heights and between the peaks—and then down again on the other side of the lake.

Rita. Oh, and you lost yourself, Alfred!

Allmers. Yes; I mistook the direction—for there was no path or track. And all day I went on—and all the next night. And at last I thought I should never see the face of man again.

Rita. Not come home to us? Oh, then, I am sure your thoughts were with us here.

Allmers. No—they were not.

Rita. Not?

Allmers. No. It was so strange. Both you and Eyolf seemed to have drifted far, far away from me—and Asta too.

Rita. Then what did you think of?

Allmers. I did not think. I dragged myself along among the precipices—and reveled in the peace and luxury of death.

Rita [*springing up*]. Oh, don't speak in that way of that horror!

Allmers. I did not feel it so. I had no fear. Here went death and I, it seemed to me, like two good fellow travelers. It all seemed so natural—so simple, I thought. In my family, we don't live to be old——

Rita. Oh, don't say such things, Alfred! You see you came safely out of it, after all.

Allmers. Yes; all of a sudden, I found myself where I wanted to be—on the other side of the lake.

Rita. It must have been a night of terror for you, Alfred. But now that it is over, you will not admit it to yourself.

Allmers. That night sealed my resolution. And it was then that I turned about and came straight homewards. To Eyolf.

Rita [*softly*]. Too late.

Allmers. Yes. And then when—my fellow traveler came and took him—then I felt the horror of it; of it all; of all that, in spite of everything, we dare not tear ourselves away from. So earth-bound are we, both of us, Rita.

Rita [*with a gleam of joy*]. Yes, you are, too, are you not! [*Coming close to him.*] Oh, let us live our life together as long as we can!

Allmers [*shrugging his shoulders*]. Live our life, yes! And have nothing to fill life with. An empty void on all sides—wherever I look.

Rita [*in fear*]. Oh, sooner or later you will go away from me, Alfred! I feel it! I can see it in your face! You will go away from me.

Allmers. With my fellow traveler, do you mean?

Rita. No, I mean worse than that. Of your own free will you will leave me—for you think it's only here, with me, that you have nothing to live for. Is not that what is in your thoughts?

Allmers [*looking steadfastly at her*]. What if it were——? [*A disturbance, and the noise of angry, quarreling voices is heard from down below, in the distance.* ALLMERS *goes to the railing.*]

Rita. What is that? [*With an outburst.*] Oh, you'll see, they have found him!

Allmers. He will never be found.

Rita. But what is it then?

Allmers [*coming forward*]. Only fighting—as usual.

Rita. Down on the beach?

Allmers. Yes. The whole village down there ought to be swept away. Now the men have come home—drunk, as they always are. They are beating the children—do you hear the boys crying! The women are shrieking for help for them——

Rita. Should we not get someone to go down and help them?

Allmers [*harshly and angrily*]. Help them, who did not help Eyolf! Let them go—as they let Eyolf go.

Rita. Oh, you must not talk like that, Alfred! Nor think like that!

Allmers. I cannot think otherwise. All the old hovels ought to be torn down.

Rita. And then what is to become of all the poor people?

Allmers. They must go somewhere else.

Rita. And the children, too?

Allmers. Does it make much difference where they go to the dogs?

Rita [*quietly and reproachfully*]. You are forcing yourself into this harshness, Alfred.

Allmers [*vehemently*]. I have a right to be harsh now! It is my duty.

Rita. Your duty?

Allmers. My duty to Eyolf. He must not lie unavenged. Once for all, Rita—it is as I tell you! Think it over! Have the whole place down there razed to the ground—when I am gone.

Rita [*looks intently at him*]. When you are gone?

Allmers. Yes. For that will at least give you something to fill your life with—and something you must have.

Rita [*firmly and decidedly*]. There you are right—I must. But can you guess what I will set about—when you are gone?

Allmers. Well, what?

Rita [*slowly and with resolution*]. As soon as you are gone from me, I will go down to the beach, and bring all the poor neglected children home with me. All the mischievous boys——

Allmers. What will you do with them here?

Rita. I will take them to my heart.

Allmers. You!

Rita. Yes, I will. From the day you leave me, they shall all be here, all of them, as if they were mine.

Allmers [*shocked*]. In our little Eyolf's place!

Rita. Yes, in our little Eyolf's place. They shall live in Eyolf's rooms. They shall read his books. They shall play with his toys. They shall take it in turns to sit in his chair at table.

Allmers. But this is sheer madness in you! I do not know a creature in the world that is less fitted than you for anything of that sort.

Rita. Then I shall have to educate myself for it; to train myself; to discipline myself.

Allmers. If you are really in earnest about this—about all you say—then there must indeed be a change in you.

Rita. Yes, there is, Alfred—and for that I have you to thank. You have made an empty place within me; and I must try to fill it up with something—with something that is a little like love.

Allmers [*stands for a moment lost in thought; then looks at her*]. The truth is, we have not done much for the poor people down there.

Rita. We have done nothing for them.

Allmers. Scarcely even thought of them.

Rita. Never thought of them in sympathy.

Allmers. We, who had "the gold, and the green forests"——

Rita. Our hands were closed to them. And our hearts too.

Allmers [*nods*]. Then it was perhaps natural enough, after all, that they should not risk their lives to save little Eyolf.

Rita [*softly*]. Think, Alfred! Are you so certain that—that we would have risked ours?

Allmers [*with an uneasy gesture of repulsion*]. You must never doubt that.

Rita. Oh, we are children of earth.

Allmers. What do you really think you can do with all these neglected children?

Rita. I suppose I must try if I cannot lighten and—and ennoble their lot in life.

Allmers. If you can do that—then Eyolf was not born in vain.

Rita. Nor taken from us in vain, either.

Allmers [*looking steadfastly at her*]. Be quite clear about one thing, Rita—it is not love that is driving you to this.

Rita. No, it is not—at any rate, not yet.

Allmers. Well, then what is it?

Rita [*half-evasively*]. You have so often talked to Asta of human responsibility——

Allmers. Of the book that you hated.

Rita. I hate that book still. But I used to sit and listen to what you told her. And now I will try to continue it—in my own way.

Allmers [*shaking his head*]. It is not for the sake of that unfinished book——

Rita. No, I have another reason as well.

Allmers. What is that?

Rita [*softly, with a melancholy smile*]. I want to make my peace with the great, open eyes, you see.

Allmers [*struck, fixing his eyes upon her*]. Perhaps, I could join you in that? And help you, Rita?

Rita. Would you?

Allmers. Yes—if I were only sure I could.

Rita [*hesitatingly*]. But then you would have to remain here.

Allmers [*softly*]. Let us try if it could not be so.

Rita [*almost inaudibly*]. Yes, let us, Alfred.

Both are silent. Then ALLMERS *goes up to the flagstaff and hoists the flag to the top.* RITA *stands beside the summerhouse and looks at him in silence.*

Allmers [*coming forward again*]. We have a heavy day of work before us, Rita.

Rita. You will see—that now and then a Sabbath peace will descend on us.

Allmers [*quietly, with emotion*]. Then, perhaps, we shall know that the spirits are with us.

Rita [*whispering*]. The spirits?

Allmers [*as before*]. Yes, they will perhaps be around us—those whom we have lost.

Rita [*nods slowly*]. Our little Eyolf. And your big Eyolf, too.

Allmers [*gazing straight before him*]. Now and then, perhaps, we may still—on the way through life—have a little, passing glimpse of them.

Rita. Where shall we look for them, Alfred?

Allmers [*fixing his eyes upon her*]. Upwards.

Rita [*nods in approval*]. Yes, yes—upwards.

Allmers. Upwards—toward the peaks. Toward the stars. And toward the great silence.

Rita [*giving him her hand*]. Thanks!

JOHN GABRIEL BORKMAN

Play in Four Acts

(1896)

INTRODUCTION

THE anecdotic history of *John Gabriel Borkman* is even scantier than that of *Little Eyolf*. It is true that two mentions of it occur in Ibsen's letters, but they throw no light whatever upon its spiritual antecedents. Writing to George Brandes from Christiania, on April 24, 1896, Ibsen says: "In your last letter you make the suggestion that I should visit London. If I knew enough English, I might perhaps go. But as I unfortunately do not, I must give up the idea altogether. Besides, I am engaged in preparing for a big new work, and I do not wish to put off the writing of it longer than necessary. It might so easily happen that a roof-tile fell on my head before I had 'found time to make the last verse.' And what then?" On October 3 of the same year, writing to the same correspondent, he again alludes to his work as "a new long play, which must be completed as soon as possible." It was, as a matter of fact, completed with very little delay, for it appeared in Copenhagen on December 15, 1896.

The irresponsible gossip of the time made out that Björnson discerned in the play some personal allusions to himself; but this Björnson emphatically denied. I am not aware that any attempt has been made to identify the originals of the various characters. It need scarcely be pointed out that in the sisters Gunhild and Ella we have the pair of women, one strong and masterful, the other tender and devoted, who run through so many of Ibsen's plays, from *The Feast at Solhoug* onwards—nay, even from *Catilina*. In my Introduction to *The Lady from the Sea* (p. 202) it is pointed out that Ibsen had the character of Foldal clearly in his mind when, in March, 1880, he made the first draft of that play. The character there appears as: "The old married clerk. Has written a play in his youth which was only once acted. Is forever touching it up, and lives in the illusion that it will be published and will make a great success. Takes no steps, however, to bring this about. Nevertheless accounts himself one of the 'literary' class. His wife and children believe blindly in the play." By the time Foldal actually came to life, the faith of his wife and children had sadly dwindled away.

We find in the *Literary Remains* only brief and unimportant fragments of the preliminary studies for this play. They tell us nothing more notable than that Borkman at first bore the incurably prosaic name of Jens, and that he was originally conceived as occupying his leisure by playing Beethoven on the violin, to a pianoforte accompaniment provided by Frida Foldal.

There was scarcely a theater in Scandinavia or Finland at which *John Gabriel Borkman* was not acted in the course of January, 1897. Helsingfors led the way with performances both at the Swedish and at the Finnish Theatres on January 10. Christiania and Stockholm followed on January 25, Copenhagen on January 31; and meanwhile the piece had been presented at many provincial theaters as well. In Christiania, Borkman, Gunhild, and Ella were played by Garmann, Fru Gundersen, and Fröken Reimers respectively; in Copenhagen, by Emil Poulsen, Fru Eckhardt, and Fru Hennings. In the course of 1897 it spread all over Germany, beginning with Frankfort on the Main, where, oddly enough, it was somewhat maltreated by the Censorship. In London, an organization calling itself the New Century Theatre presented *John Gabriel Borkman* at the Strand Theatre on the afternoon of May 3, 1897, with Mr. W. H. Vernon as Borkman, Miss Geneviève Ward as Gunhild, Miss Elizabeth Robins as Ella Rentheim, Mr. Martin Harvey as Erhart, Mr. James Welch as Foldal, and Mrs. Beerbohm Tree as Mrs. Wilton. The first performance in America was given by the Criterion Independent Theatre of New York on November 18, 1897, Mr. E. J. Henley playing Borkman; Mr. John Blair, Erhart; Miss Maude Banks, Gunhild; and Miss Ann Warrington, Ella. For some reason, which I can only conjecture to be the weakness of the third act, the play seems nowhere to have taken a very firm hold on the stage.

Dr. Brahm has drawn attention to the great similarity between the theme of *John Gabriel Borkman* and that of *Pillars of Society*. "In both," he says, "we have a business man of great ability who is guilty of a crime; in both this man is placed between two sisters; and in both he renounces a marriage of inclination for the sake of a marriage that shall further his business interests." The likeness is undeniable; and yet how utterly unlike are the two plays! and how immeasurably superior the later one! It may seem, on a superficial view, that in *John Gabriel Borkman* Ibsen had returned to prose and the common earth after his excursion into poetry and the possibly supernatural, if I may so call it, in *The Master Builder* and *Little Eyolf*. But this is a very superficial view indeed. We have only to compare the whole invention of *John Gabriel Borkman* with the invention of *Pillars of Society*, to realize the difference between the poetry and the prose of drama. The quality of imagination which conceived the story of the House of Bernick is utterly unlike that which conceived the tragedy of the House of Borkman. The difference is not greater between (say) *The Merchant of Venice* and *King Lear*.

The technical feat which Ibsen here achieves of carrying through without a single break the whole action of a four-act play has been much commented on and admired. The imaginary time of the drama is actually shorter than the real time of representation, since the poet does not even leave intervals for the changing of the scenes. This feat, however, is more curious than important. Nothing particular is gained by such a literal observance of the unity of time. For the rest, we feel definitely in *John Gabriel Borkman* what we already felt vaguely in *Little Eyolf* —that the poet's technical staying-power is beginning to fail him. We feel that the initial design was larger and more detailed than the finished work. If the last acts of *The Wild Duck* and *Hedda Gabler* be compared with the last acts of *Little Eyolf* and *Borkman*, it will be seen that in the earlier plays his constructive faculty is working at its highest tension up to the very end, while in the later plays it relaxes toward the close, to make room for pure imagination and lyric beauty. The actual drama is over long before the curtain falls on either play, and in the one case we have Rita and Allmers, in the other Ella and Borkman, looking back over their shattered lives and playing chorus to their own tragedy. For my part, I set the highest value on these choral odes, these mournful antiphones, in which the poet definitely triumphs over the mere playwright. They seem to me noble and beautiful in themselves, and as truly artistic, if not as theatrical, as any abrupter catastrophe could be. But I am not quite sure that they are exactly the conclusions the poet originally

projected, and still less am I satisfied that they are reached
by precisely the paths which he at first designed to pursue.

The traces of a change of scheme in *John Gabriel Borkman* seem to me almost unmistakable. The first two acts
laid the foundation for a larger and more complex superstructure than is ultimately erected. Ibsen seems to have
designed that Hinkel, the man who "betrayed" Borkman
in the past, should play some efficient part in the alienation
of Erhart from his family and home. Otherwise, why this
insistence on a "party" at the Hinkels', which is apparently
to serve as a sort of "send off" for Erhart and Mrs. Wilton?
It appears in the third act that the "party" was imaginary.
"Erhart and I were the whole party," says Mrs. Wilton,
"and little Frida, of course." We might, then, suppose it
to have been a mere blind to enable Erhart to escape from
home; but, in the first place, as Erhart does not live at
home, there is no need for any such pretext; in the second
place, it appears that the trio do actually go to the
Hinkels' house (since Mrs. Borkman's servant finds them
there), and do actually make it their starting point. Erhart
comes and goes with the utmost freedom in Mrs. Wilton's
own house; what possible reason can they have for not
setting out from there? No reason is shown or hinted. We
cannot even imagine that the Hinkels have been instru-
mental in bringing Erhart and Mrs. Wilton together; it is
expressly stated that Erhart made her acquaintance and
saw a great deal of her in town, before she moved out
into the country. The whole conception of the party at the
Hinkels' is, as it stands, mysterious and a little cumber-
some. We are forced to conclude, I think, that something
more was at one time intended to come of it, and that,
when the poet abandoned the idea, he did not think it
worth-while to remove the scaffolding. To this change
of plan, too, we may possibly trace what I take to be the
one serious flaw in the play—the comparative weakness
of the second half of the third act. The scene of Erhart's
rebellion against the claims of mother, aunt, and father
strikes one as the symmetrical working out of a problem
rather than a passage of living drama.

All this means, of course, that there is a certain looseness
of fiber in *John Gabriel Borkman* which we do not find
in the best of Ibsen's earlier works. But in point of intel-
lectual power and poetic beauty it yields to none of its
predecessors. The conception of the three leading figures

is one of the great things of literature; the second act, with the exquisite humor of the Foldal scene, and the dramatic intensity of the encounter between Borkman and Ella, is perhaps the finest single act Ibsen ever wrote, in prose at all events; and the last scene is a thing of rare and exalted beauty. One could wish that the poet's last words to us had been those haunting lines with which Gunhild and Ella join hands over Borkman's body:

> We twin sisters—over him we both have loved.
> We two shadows—over the dead man.[1]

Among many verbal difficulties which this play presents, the greatest, perhaps, has been to find an equivalent for the word "opreisning," which occurs again and again in the first and second acts. No one English word that I could discover would fit in all the different contexts; so I have had to employ three: "redemption," "restoration," and in one place "rehabilitation." The reader may bear in mind that these three terms represent one idea in the original.

Borkman in Act II uses a very odd expression—"over-skurkens moral," which I have rendered "the morals of the higher rascality." I cannot but suspect (though for this I have no authority) that in the word "overskurk," which might be represented in German by "Ueberschurke," Borkman is parodying the expression "Uebermensch," of which so much has been heard of late. When I once suggested this to Ibsen, he neither affirmed nor denied it. I understood him to say, however, that in speaking of "over-skurken" he had a particular man in view. Somewhat pusillanimously, perhaps, I pursued my inquiries no further.

---

[1] In the first draft this passage runs thus:

Ella Rentheim. The cold has killed him.
Mrs. Borkman. Ah, Ella, the cold had killed him long ago.
Ella Rentheim. Us too.
Mrs. Borkman. You are right there.
Ella Rentheim. We are three dead people—we three here.
Mrs. Borkman. We are. So perhaps we two can join hands, Ella.
Ella Rentheim [*quietly*]. Over the third. Yes.

How the poet has transfigured the passage in rewriting it!

PERSONS

JOHN GABRIEL BORKMAN, *formerly Managing Director of a Bank*

MRS. GUNHILD BORKMAN, *his wife*

ERHART BORKMAN, *their son, a student*

MISS ELLA RENTHEIM, *Mrs. Borkman's twin sister*

MRS. FANNY WILTON

VILHELM FOLDAL, *subordinate clerk in a Government office*

FRIDA FOLDAL, *his daughter*

MRS. BORKMAN'S MAID

The action passes one winter evening, at the manor house of the Rentheim family, in the neighborhood of Christiania.

JOHN GABRIEL BORKMAN

ACT FIRST

MRS. BORKMAN'S *drawing room, furnished with old-fashioned, faded splendor. At the back, an open sliding door leads into a garden room, with windows and a glass door. Through it a view over the garden; twilight with driving snow. On the right, a door leading from the hall. Farther forward, a large old-fashioned iron stove, with the fire lighted. On the left, toward the back, a single smaller door. In front, on the same side, a window, covered with thick curtains. Between the window and the door a horsehair sofa, with a table in front of it covered with a cloth. On the table, a lighted lamp with a shade. Beside the stove a high-backed armchair.*

MRS. GUNHILD BORKMAN *sits on the sofa, crocheting. She is an elderly lady, of cold, distinguished appearance, with stiff carriage and immobile features. Her abundant hair is very gray. Delicate transparent hands. Dressed in a gown of heavy dark silk, which has originally been handsome, but is now somewhat worn and shabby. A woolen shawl over her shoulders.*

She sits for a time erect and immovable at her crocheting. Then the bells of a passing sledge are heard.

MRS. BORKMAN [*listens; her eyes sparkle with gladness and she involuntarily whispers*]. Erhart! At last!

She rises and draws the curtain a little aside to look out. Appears disappointed, and sits down to her work again, on the sofa. Presently THE MAID *enters from the hall with a visiting card on a small tray.*

[*Quickly.*] Has Mr. Erhart come after all?

The Maid. No, ma'am. But there's a lady——

Mrs. Borkman [*laying aside her crocheting*]. Oh, Mrs. Wilton, I suppose——

The Maid [*approaching*]. No, it's a strange lady——

Mrs. Borkman [*taking the card*]. Let me see—— [*Reads it; rises hastily and looks intently at the girl.*] Are you sure this is for me?

The Maid. Yes, I understand it was for you, ma'am.

Mrs. Borkman. Did she say she wanted to see Mrs. Borkman?

The Maid. Yes, she did.

Mrs. Borkman [*shortly, resolutely*]. Good. Then say I am at home.

THE MAID *opens the door for the strange lady and goes out.* MISS ELLA RENTHEIM *enters. She resembles her sister; but her face has rather a suffering than a hard expression. It still shows signs of great beauty, combined with strong character. She has a great deal of hair, which is drawn back from the forehead in natural ripples, and is snow white. She is dressed in black velvet, with a hat and a fur-lined cloak of the same material.*

The two sisters stand silent for a time, and look searchingly at each other. Each is evidently waiting for the other to speak first.

Ella Rentheim [*who has remained near the door*]. You are surprised to see me, Gunhild.

Mrs. Borkman [*standing erect and immovable between the sofa and the table, resting her finger tips upon the cloth*]. Have you not made a mistake? The bailiff lives in the side wing, you know.

Ella Rentheim. It is not the bailiff I want to see today.

Mrs. Borkman. Is it me you want, then?

Ella Rentheim. Yes. I have a few words to say to you.

Mrs. Borkman [*coming forward into the middle of the room*]. Well—then sit down.

Ella Rentheim. Thank you. I can quite well stand for the present.

Mrs. Borkman. Just as you please. But at least loosen your cloak.

Ella Rentheim [*unbuttoning her cloak*]. Yes, it is very warm here.

Mrs. Borkman. I am always cold.

Ella Rentheim [*stands looking at her for a time with her arms resting on the back of the armchair*]. Well, Gunhild, it is nearly eight years now since we saw each other last.

Mrs. Borkman [*coldly*]. Since last we spoke to each other at any rate.

Ella Rentheim. True, since we spoke to each other. I daresay you have seen me now and again—when I came on my yearly visit to the bailiff.

Mrs. Borkman. Once or twice, I have.

Ella Rentheim. I have caught one or two glimpses of you, too—there, at the window.

Mrs. Borkman. You must have seen me through the curtains then. You have good eyes. [*Harshly and cuttingly.*] But the last time we spoke to each other—it was here in this room——

Ella Rentheim [*trying to stop her*]. Yes, yes; I know, Gunhild!

Mrs. Borkman. —the week before he—before he was let out.

Ella Rentheim [*moving toward the back*]. Oh, don't speak about that.

Mrs. Borkman [*firmly, but in a low voice*]. It was the week before he—was set at liberty.

Ella Rentheim [*coming down*]. Oh, yes, yes, yes! I shall never forget that time! But it is too terrible to think of! Only to recall it for a moment—oh!

Mrs. Borkman [*gloomily*]. And yet one's thoughts can never get away from it! [*Vehemently; clenching her hands together.*] No, I can't understand it! I never shall! I can't understand how such a thing—how anything so horrible can come upon one single family! And then—that it should be our family! So old a family as ours! Think of its choosing us out!

Ella Rentheim. Oh, Gunhild—there were many, many families besides ours that that blow fell upon.

Mrs. Borkman. Oh, yes; but those others don't trouble me very much. For in their case it was only a matter of a little money—or some papers. But for us——! For me! And then for Erhart! My little boy—as he then was! [*In rising excitement.*] The shame that fell upon us two innocent ones! The dishonor! The hateful, terrible dishonor! And then the utter ruin too!

Ella Rentheim [*cautiously*]. Tell me, Gunhild, how does he bear it?

Mrs. Borkman. Erhart, do you mean?

Ella Rentheim. No—he himself. How does he bear it?

Mrs. Borkman [*scornfully*]. Do you think I ever ask about that?

Ella Rentheim. Ask? Surely you do not require to ask——

Mrs. Borkman [*looks at her in surprise*]. You don't suppose I ever have anything to do with him? That I ever meet him? That I see anything of him?

Ella Rentheim. Not even that!

Mrs. Borkman [*as before*]. The man who was in gaol, in gaol for five years! [*Covers her face with her hands.*] Oh, the crushing shame of it! [*With increased vehemence.*] And then to think of all that the name of John Gabriel Borkman used to mean! No, no, no—I can never see him again! Never!

Ella Rentheim [*looks at her for a while*]. You have a hard heart, Gunhild.

Mrs. Borkman. Toward him, yes.

Ella Rentheim. After all, he is your husband.

Mrs. Borkman. Did he not say in court that it was I who began his ruin? That I spent money so recklessly?

Ella Rentheim [*tentatively*]. But is there not some truth in that?

Mrs. Borkman. Why, it was he himself that made me do it! He insisted on our living in such an absurdly lavish style——

Ella Rentheim. Yes, I know. But that is just where you should have restrained him; and apparently you didn't.

Mrs. Borkman. How was I to know that it was not his own money he gave me to squander? And that he himself used to squander, too—ten times more than I did!

Ella Rentheim [*quietly*]. Well, I daresay his position forced him to do that—to some extent at any rate.

Mrs. Borkman [*scornfully*]. Yes, it was always the same story—we were to "cut a figure." And he did "cut a figure" to some purpose! He used to drive about with a four-in-hand as if he were a king. And he had people bowing and scraping to him just as to a king. [*With a laugh.*] And they always called him by his Christian names—all the country over—as if he had been the king himself. "John Gabriel," "John Gabriel." Everyone knew what a great man "John Gabriel" was!

Ella Rentheim [*warmly and emphatically*]. He was a great man then.

Mrs. Borkman. Yes, to all appearance. But he never breathed a single word to me as to his real position—never gave a hint as to where he got his means from.

Ella Rentheim. No, no; and other people did not dream of it either.

Mrs. Borkman. I don't care about the other people. But it was his duty to tell me the truth. And that he never did! He kept on lying to me—lying abominably——

Ella Rentheim [*interrupting*]. Surely not, Gunhild. He kept things back perhaps, but I am sure he did not lie.

Mrs. Borkman. Well, well; call it what you please; it makes no difference. And then it all fell to pieces—the whole thing.

Ella Rentheim [*to herself*]. Yes, everything fell to pieces for him—and for others.

Mrs. Borkman [*drawing herself up menacingly*]. But I tell you this, Ella, I do not give in yet! I shall redeem myself yet—you may make up your mind to that!

Ella Rentheim [*eagerly*]. Redeem yourself! What do you mean by that?

Mrs. Borkman. Redeem my name, and honor, and fortune! Redeem my ruined life—that is what I mean! I have someone in reserve, let me tell you—one who will wash away every stain that he has left.

Ella Rentheim. Gunhild! Gunhild!

Mrs. Borkman [*with rising excitement*]. There is an avenger living, I tell you! One who will make up to me for all his father's sins!

Ella Rentheim. Erhart, you mean.

Mrs. Borkman. Yes, Erhart, my own boy! He will redeem the family, the house, the name. All that can be redeemed. —And perhaps more besides.

Ella Rentheim. And how do you think that is to be done?

Mrs. Borkman. It must be done as best it can; I don't know how. But I know that it must and shall be done. [*Looks searchingly at her.*] Come now, Ella; isn't that really what you have had in mind too, ever since he was a child?

Ella Rentheim. No, I can't exactly say that.

Mrs. Borkman. No? Then why did you take charge of him when the storm broke upon—upon this house?

Ella Rentheim. You could not look after him yourself at that time, Gunhild.

Mrs. Borkman. No, no. I could not. And his father—he had a valid enough excuse—while he was there—in safe-keeping——

Ella Rentheim [*indignant*]. Oh, how can you say such things!—You!

Mrs. Borkman [*with a venomous expression*]. And how could you make up your mind to take charge of the child of a—a John Gabriel! Just as if he had been your own? To take the child away from me—home with you—and keep him there year after year, until the boy was nearly grown up. [*Looking suspiciously at her*.] What was your real reason, Ella? Why did you keep him with you?

Ella Rentheim. I came to love him so dearly——

Mrs. Borkman. More than I—his mother?

Ella Rentheim [*evasively*]. I don't know about that. And then, you know, Erhart was rather delicate as a child——

Mrs. Borkman. Erhart—delicate!

Ella Rentheim. Yes, I thought so—at that time at any rate. And you know the air of the west coast is so much milder than here.

Mrs. Borkman [*smiling bitterly*]. H'm—is it indeed? [*Breaking off*.] Yes, it is true you have done a great deal for Erhart. [*With a change of tone*.] Well of course, you could afford it. [*Smiling*.] You were so lucky, Ella; you managed to save all your money.

Ella Rentheim [*hurt*]. I did not manage anything about it, I assure you. I had no idea—until long, long afterwards —that the securities belonging to me—that they had been left untouched.

Mrs. Borkman. Well, well; I don't understand anything about these things! I only say you were lucky. [*Looking inquiringly at her*.] But when you, of your own accord, undertook to educate Erhart for me—what was your motive in that?

Ella Rentheim [*looking at her*]. My motive?

Mrs. Borkman. Yes, some motive you must have had. What did you want to do with him? To make of him, I mean?

Ella Rentheim [*slowly*]. I wanted to smooth the way for Erhart to happiness in life.

Mrs. Borkman [*contemptuously*]. Pooh—people situated as we are have something else than happiness to think of.

Ella Rentheim. What, then?

Mrs. Borkman [*looking steadily and earnestly at her*]. Erhart has in the first place to make so brilliant a position for himself, that no trace shall be left of the shadow his father has cast upon my name—and my son's.

Ella Rentheim [*searchingly*]. Tell me, Gunhild, is this what Erhart himself demands of his life?

Mrs. Borkman [*slightly taken aback*]. Yes, I should hope so!

Ella Rentheim. Is it not rather what you demand of him?

Mrs. Borkman [*curtly*]. Erhart and I always make the same demands upon ourselves.

Ella Rentheim [*sadly and slowly*]. You are so very certain of your boy, then, Gunhild?

Mrs. Borkman [*with veiled triumph*]. Yes, that I am —thank Heaven. You may be sure of that!

Ella Rentheim. Then I should think in reality you must be happy after all; in spite of all the rest.

Mrs. Borkman. So I am—so far as that goes. But then, every moment, all the rest comes rushing in upon me like a storm.

Ella Rentheim [*with a change of tone*]. Tell me—you may as well tell me at once—for that is really what I have come for——

Mrs. Borkman. What?

Ella Rentheim. Something I felt I must talk to you about.—Tell me—Erhart does not live out here with—with you others?

Mrs. Borkman [*harshly*]. Erhart cannot live out here with me. He has to live in town——

Ella Rentheim. So he wrote to me.

Mrs. Borkman. He must, for the sake of his studies. But he comes out to me for a little while every evening.

Ella Rentheim. Well, may I see him then? May I speak to him at once?

Mrs. Borkman. He has not come yet; but I expect him every moment.

Ella Rentheim. Why, Gunhild, surely he must have come. I can hear his footsteps overhead.

Mrs. Borkman [*with a rapid upward glance*]. Up in the long gallery?

Ella Rentheim. Yes. I have heard him walking up and down there ever since I came.

Mrs. Borkman [*looking away from her*]. That is not Erhart, Ella.

Ella Rentheim [*surprised*]. Not Erhart? [*Divining.*] Who is it then?

Mrs. Borkman. It is he.

Ella Rentheim [*softly, with suppressed pain*]. Borkman? John Gabriel Borkman?

Mrs. Borkman. He walks up and down like that—backwards and forwards—from morning to night—day out and day in.

Ella Rentheim. I have heard something of this——

Mrs. Borkman. I daresay. People find plenty to say about us, no doubt.

Ella Rentheim. Erhart has spoken of it in his letters. He said that his father generally remained by himself—up there—and you alone down here.

Mrs. Borkman. Yes; that is how it has been, Ella, ever since they let him out, and sent him home to me. All these long eight years.

Ella Rentheim. I never believed it could really be so. It seemed impossible!

Mrs. Borkman [*nods*]. It is so; and it can never be otherwise.

Ella Rentheim [*looking at her*]. This must be a terrible life, Gunhild.

Mrs. Borkman. Worse than terrible—almost unendurable.

Ella Rentheim. Yes, it must be.

Mrs. Borkman. Always to hear his footsteps up there—from early morning till far into the night. And everything sounds so clear in this house!

Ella Rentheim. Yes, it is strange how clear the sound is.

Mrs. Borkman. I often feel as if I had a sick wolf pacing his cage up there in the gallery, right over my head. [*Listens and whispers.*] Hark! Do you hear! Backwards and forwards, up and down, goes the wolf.

Ella Rentheim [*tentatively*]. Is no change possible, Gunhild?

Mrs. Borkman [*with a gesture of repulsion*]. He has never made any movement toward a change.

Ella Rentheim. Could you not make the first movement, then?

Mrs. Borkman [*indignantly*]. I! After all the wrong he has done me! No, thank you! Rather let the wolf go on prowling up there.

Ella Rentheim. This room is too hot for me. You must let me take off my things after all.

Mrs. Borkman. Yes, I asked you to.

ELLA RENTHEIM *takes off her hat and cloak and lays them on a chair beside the door leading to the hall.*

Ella Rentheim. Do you never happen to meet him, away from home?

Mrs. Borkman [*with a bitter laugh*]. In society, do you mean?

Ella Rentheim. I mean, when he goes out walking. In the woods, or——

Mrs. Borkman. He never goes out.

Ella Rentheim. Not even in the twilight?

Mrs. Borkman. Never.

Ella Rentheim [*with emotion*]. He cannot bring himself to go out?

Mrs. Borkman. I suppose not. He has his great cloak and his hat hanging in the cupboard—the cupboard in the hall, you know——

Ella Rentheim [*to herself*]. The cupboard we used to hide in when we were little——

Mrs. Borkman [*nods*]. And now and then—late in the evening—I can hear him come down as though to go out. But he always stops when he is halfway downstairs, and turns back—straight back to the gallery.

Ella Rentheim [*quietly*]. Do none of his old friends ever come up to see him?

Mrs. Borkman. He has no old friends.

Ella Rentheim. He had so many—once.

Mrs. Borkman. H'm! He took the best possible way to get rid of them. He was a dear friend to his friends, was John Gabriel.

Ella Rentheim. Oh, yes, that is true, Gunhild.

Mrs. Borkman [*vehemently*]. All the same, I call it mean, petty, base, contemptible of them, to think so much of the paltry losses they may have suffered through him. They were only money losses, nothing more.

Ella Rentheim [*not answering her*]. So he lives up there quite alone. Absolutely by himself.

Mrs. Borkman. Yes, practically so. They tell me an old clerk or copyist or something comes out to see him now and then.

Ella Rentheim. Ah, indeed; no doubt it is a man called Foldal. I know they were friends as young men.

Mrs. Borkman. Yes, I believe they were. But I know nothing about him. He was quite outside our circle—when we had a circle——

Ella Rentheim. So he comes out to see Borkman now?

Mrs. Borkman. Yes, he condescends to. But of course he only comes when it is dark.

Ella Rentheim. This Foldal—he was one of those that suffered when the bank failed.

Mrs. Borkman [*carelessly*]. Yes, I believe I heard he had lost some money. But no doubt it was something quite trifling.

Ella Rentheim [*with slight emphasis*]. It was all he possessed.

Mrs. Borkman [*smiling*]. Oh, well; what he possessed must have been little enough—nothing to speak of.

Ella Rentheim. And he did not speak of it—Foldal I mean—during the investigation.

Mrs. Borkman. At all events, I can assure you Erhart has made ample amends for any loss he may have suffered.

Ella Rentheim [*with surprise*]. Erhart! How can Erhart have done that?

Mrs. Borkman. He has taken an interest in Foldal's youngest daughter. He has taught her things, and put her in the way of getting employment, and someday providing for herself. I am sure that is a great deal more than her father could ever have done for her.

Ella Rentheim. Yes, I daresay her father can't afford to do much.

Mrs. Borkman. And then Erhart has arranged for her to have lessons in music. She has made such progress already that she can come up to—to him in the gallery, and play to him.

Ella Rentheim. So he is still fond of music?

Mrs. Borkman. Oh, yes, I suppose he is. Of course he has the piano you sent out here—when he was expected back——

Ella Rentheim. And she plays to him on it?

Mrs. Borkman. Yes, now and then—in the evenings. That is Erhart's doing too.

Ella Rentheim. Has the poor girl to come all the long way out here, and then go back to town again?

Mrs. Borkman. No, she doesn't need to. Erhart has arranged for her to stay with a lady who lives near us—a Mrs. Wilton——

Ella Rentheim [*with interest*]. Mrs. Wilton?

Mrs. Borkman. A very rich woman. You don't know her.

Ella Rentheim. I have heard her name. Mrs. Fanny Wilton, is it not——?

Mrs. Borkman. Yes, quite right.

Ella Rentheim. Erhart has mentioned her several times. Does she live out here now?

Mrs. Borkman. Yes, she has taken a villa here; she moved out from town sometime ago.

Ella Rentheim [*with a slight hesitation*]. They say she is divorced from her husband.

Mrs. Borkman. Her husband has been dead for several years.

Ella Rentheim. Yes, but they were divorced. He got a divorce.

Mrs. Borkman. He deserted her, that is what he did. I am sure the fault wasn't hers.

Ella Rentheim. Do you know her at all intimately, Gunhild?

Mrs. Borkman. Oh, yes, pretty well. She lives close by here; and she looks in every now and then.

Ella Rentheim. And do you like her?

Mrs. Borkman. She is unusually intelligent; remarkably clear in her judgments.

Ella Rentheim. In her judgments of people, do you mean?

Mrs. Borkman. Yes, principally of people. She has made quite a study of Erhart; looked deep into his character—into his soul. And the result is she idolizes him, as she could not help doing.

Ella Rentheim [*with a touch of finesse*]. Then perhaps she knows Erhart still better than she knows you?

Mrs. Borkman. Yes, Erhart saw a good deal of her in town, before she came out here.

Ella Rentheim [*without thinking*]. And in spite of that she moved out of town?

Mrs. Borkman [*taken aback, looking keenly at her*]. In spite of that! What do you mean?

Ella Rentheim [*evasively*]. Oh, nothing particular.

Mrs. Borkman. You said it so strangely—you did mean something by it, Ella!

Ella Rentheim [*looking her straight in the eyes*]. Yes, that is true, Gunhild! I did mean something by it.

Mrs. Borkman. Well, then, say it right out.

Ella Rentheim. First let me tell you, I think I too have a certain claim upon Erhart. Do you think I haven't?

Mrs. Borkman [*glancing round the room*]. No doubt— after all the money you have spent upon him.

Ella Rentheim. Oh, not on that account, Gunhild. But because I love him.

Mrs. Borkman [*smiling scornfully*]. Love my son? Is it possible? You? In spite of everything?

Ella Rentheim. Yes, it is possible—in spite of everything. And it is true. I love Erhart—as much as I can love anyone—now—at my time of life.

Mrs. Borkman. Well, well, suppose you do: what then?

Ella Rentheim. Why, then, I am troubled as soon as I see anything threatening him.

Mrs. Borkman. Threatening Erhart! Why, what should threaten him? Or who?

Ella Rentheim. You in the first place—in your way.

Mrs. Borkman [*vehemently*]. I!

Ella Rentheim. And then this Mrs. Wilton, too, I am afraid.

Mrs. Borkman [*looks at her for a moment in speechless surprise*]. And you can think such things of Erhart! Of my own boy! He, who has his great mission to fulfill!

Ella Rentheim [*lightly*]. Oh, his mission!

Mrs. Borkman [*indignantly*]. How dare you say that so scornfully?

Ella Rentheim. Do you think a young man of Erhart's age, full of health and spirits—do you think he is going to sacrifice himself for—for such a thing as a "mission"?

Mrs. Borkman [*firmly and emphatically*]. Erhart will! I know he will.

Ella Rentheim [*shaking her head*]. You neither know it nor believe it, Gunhild.

Mrs. Borkman. I don't believe it!

Ella Rentheim. It is only a dream that you cherish. For

if you hadn't that to cling to, you feel that you would utterly despair.

Mrs. Borkman. Yes, indeed I should despair. [*Vehemently.*] And I daresay that is what you would like to see, Ella!

Ella Rentheim [*with head erect*]. Yes, I would rather see that then see you "redeem" yourself at Erhart's expense.

Mrs. Borkman [*threateningly*]. You want to come between us? Between mother and son? You?

Ella Rentheim. I want to free him from your power—your will—your despotism.

Mrs. Borkman [*triumphantly*]. You are too late! You had him in your nets all those years—until he was fifteen. But now I have won him again, you see!

Ella Rentheim. Then I will win him back from you! [*Hoarsely, half whispering.*] We two have fought a life-and-death battle before, Gunhild—for a man's soul!

Mrs. Borkman [*looking at her in triumph*]. Yes, and I won the victory.

Ella Rentheim [*with a smile of scorn*]. Do you still think that victory was worth the winning?

Mrs. Borkman [*darkly*]. No; Heaven knows you are right there.

Ella Rentheim. You need look for no victory worth the winning this time either.

Mrs. Borkman. Not when I am fighting to preserve a mother's power over my son!

Ella Rentheim. No; for it is only power over him that you want.

Mrs. Borkman. And you?

Ella Rentheim [*warmly*]. I want his affection—his soul —his whole heart!

Mrs. Borkman [*with an outburst*]. That you shall never have in this world!

Ella Rentheim [*looking at her*]. You have seen to that?

Mrs. Borkman [*smiling*]. Yes, I have taken that liberty. Could you not see that in his letters?

Ella Rentheim [*nods slowly*]. Yes. I could see you— the whole of you—in his letters of late.

Mrs. Borkman [*gallingly*]. I have made the best use of these eight years. I have had him under my own eye, you see.

Ella Rentheim [*controlling herself*]. What have you said to Erhart about me? Is it the sort of thing you can tell me?

Mrs. Borkman. Oh, yes, I can tell you well enough.

Ella Rentheim. Then please do.

Mrs. Borkman. I have only told him the truth.

Ella Rentheim. Well?

Mrs. Borkman. I have impressed upon him, every day of his life, that he must never forget that it is you we have to thank for being able to live as we do—for being able to live at all.

Ella Rentheim. Is that all?

Mrs. Borkman. Oh, that is the sort of thing that rankles; I feel that in my own heart.

Ella Rentheim. But that is very much what Erhart knew already.

Mrs. Borkman. When he came home to me, he imagined that you did it all out of goodness of heart. [*Looks malignly at her.*] Now he does not believe that any longer, Ella.

Ella Rentheim. Then what does he believe now?

Mrs. Borkman. He believes what is truth. I asked him how he accounted for the fact that Aunt Ella never came here to visit us——

Ella Rentheim [*interrupting*]. He knew my reasons already!

Mrs. Borkman. He knows them better now. You had got him to believe that it was to spare me and—and him up there in the gallery——

Ella Rentheim. And so it was.

Mrs. Borkman. Erhart does not believe that for a moment, now.

Ella Rentheim. What have you put in his head?

Mrs. Borkman. He thinks, what is the truth, that you are ashamed of us—that you despise us. And do you pretend that you don't? Were you not once planning to take him quite away from me? Think, Ella; you cannot have forgotten.

Ellen Rentheim [*with a gesture of negation*]. That was at the height of the scandal—when the case was before the courts. I have no such designs now.

Mrs. Borkman. And it would not matter if you had. For in that case what would become of his mission? No, thank you. It is me that Erhart needs—not you. And therefore he is as good as dead to you—and you to him.

Ella Rentheim [*coldly, with resolution*]. We shall see. For now I shall remain out here.

Mrs. Borkman [*stares at her*]. Here? In this house?

Ella Rentheim. Yes, here.

Mrs. Borkman. Here—with us? Remain all night?

Ella Rentheim. I shall remain here all the rest of my days if need be.

Mrs. Borkman [*collecting herself*]. Very well, Ella; the house is yours——

Ella Rentheim. Oh, nonsense——

Mrs. Borkman. Everything is yours. The chair I am sitting in is yours. The bed I lie and toss in at night belongs to you. The food we eat comes to us from you.

Ella Rentheim. It can't be arranged otherwise, you know. Borkman can hold no property of his own; for someone would at once come and take it from him.

Mrs. Borkman. Yes, I know. We must be content to live upon your pity and charity.

Ella Rentheim [*coldly*]. I cannot prevent you from looking at it in that light, Gunhild.

Mrs. Borkman. No, you cannot. When do you want us to move out?

Ella Rentheim [*looking at her*]. Move out?

Mrs. Borkman [*in great excitement*]. Yes; you don't imagine that I will go on living under the same roof with you! I tell you, I would rather go to the workhouse or tramp the roads!

Ella Rentheim. Good. Then let me take Erhart with me——

Mrs. Borkman. Erhart? My own son? My child?

Ella Rentheim. Yes; for then I would go straight home again.

Mrs. Borkman [*after reflecting a moment, firmly*]. Erhart himself shall choose between us.

Ella Rentheim [*looking doubtfully and hesitatingly at her*]. He choose? Dare you risk that, Gunhild?

Mrs. Borkman [*with a hard laugh*]. Dare I? Let my boy choose between his mother and you? Yes, indeed I dare!

Ella Rentheim [*listening*]. Is there someone coming? I thought I heard——

Mrs. Borkman. Then it must be Erhart.

There is a sharp knock at the door leading in from the hall, which is immediately opened. MRS. WILTON *enters, in evening dress, and with outer wraps. She is followed by* THE MAID, *who has not had time to announce her, and looks bewildered. The door remains half open.* MRS. WILTON *is a strikingly handsome, well-developed woman in the thirties. Broad, red, smiling lips, sparkling eyes. Luxuriant dark hair.*

Mrs. Wilton. Good evening, my dearest Mrs. Borkman!

Mrs. Borkman [*rather dryly*]. Good evening, Mrs. Wilton. [*To* THE MAID, *pointing toward the garden room.*] Take out the lamp that is in there and light it.

THE MAID *takes the lamp and goes out with it.*

Mrs. Wilton [*observing* ELLA RENTHEIM]. Oh, I beg your pardon—you have a visitor.

Mrs. Borkman. Only my sister, who has just arrived from——

ERHART BORKMAN *flings the half-open door wide open and rushes in. He is a young man with bright cheerful eyes. He is well-dressed; his mustache is beginning to grow.*

Erhart [*radiant with joy; on the threshold*]. What is this! Is Aunt Ella here? [*Rushing up to her, and seizing her hands.*] Aunt, Aunt! Is it possible? Are you here?

Ella Rentheim [*throws her arms round his neck*]. Erhart! My dear, dear boy! Why, how big you have grown! Oh, how good it is to see you again!

Mrs. Borkman [*sharply*]. What does this mean, Erhart? Were you hiding out in the hall?

Mrs. Wilton [*quickly*]. Erhart—Mr. Borkman came in with me.

Mrs. Borkman [*looking hard at him*]. Indeed, Erhart! You don't come to your mother first.

Erhart. I had just to look in at Mrs. Wilton's for a moment—to call for little Frida.

Mrs. Borkman. Is that Miss Foldal with you too?

Mrs. Wilton. Yes, we have left her in the hall.

Erhart [*addressing someone through the open door*]. You can go right upstairs, Frida.

Pause. ELLA RENTHEIM *observes* ERHART. *He seems embarrassed and a little impatient; his face has assumed a nervous and colder expression.*

THE MAID *brings the lighted lamp into the garden room, goes out again and closes the door behind her.*

Mrs. Borkman [*with forced politeness*]. Well, Mrs. Wilton, if you will give us the pleasure of your company this evening, won't you——

Mrs. Wilton. Many thanks, my dear lady, but I really can't. We have another invitation. We're going down to the Hinkels'.

Mrs. Borkman [*looking at her*]. We? Whom do you mean by we?

Mrs. Wilton [*laughing*]. Oh, I ought really to have said I. But I was commissioned by the ladies of the house to bring Mr. Borkman with me—if I happened to see him.

Mrs. Borkman. And you did happen to see him, it appears.

Mrs. Wilton. Yes, fortunately. He was good enough to look in at my house—to call for Frida.

Mrs. Borkman [*dryly*]. But, Erhart, I did not know that you knew that family—those Hinkels?

Erhart [*irritated*]. No, I don't exactly know them. [*Adds rather impatiently.*] You know better than anybody, Mother, what people I know and don't know.

Mrs. Wilton. Oh, it doesn't matter! They soon put you at your ease in that house! They are such cheerful, hospitable people—the house swarms with young ladies.

Mrs. Borkman [*with emphasis*]. If I know my son rightly, Mrs. Wilton, they are no fit company for him.

Mrs. Wilton. Why, good gracious, dear lady, he is young, too, you know!

Mrs. Borkman. Yes, fortunately he's young. He would need to be young.

Erhart [*concealing his impatience*]. Well, well, well, Mother, it's quite clear I can't go to the Hinkels' this evening. Of course I shall remain here with you and Aunt Ella.

Mrs. Borkman. I knew you would, my dear Erhart.

Ella Rentheim. No, Erhart, you must not stop at home on my account——

Erhart. Yes, indeed, my dear Aunt; I can't think of going. [*Looking doubtfully at* Mrs. Wilton.] But how shall we manage? Can I get out of it? You have said "Yes" for me, haven't you?

Mrs. Wilton [*gaily*]. What nonsense! Not get out of it! When I make my entrance into the festive halls—just imagine it!—deserted and forlorn—then I must simply say "No" for you.

Erhart [*hesitatingly*]. Well, if you really think I can get out of it——

Mrs. Wilton [*putting the matter lightly aside*]. I am quite used to saying both yes and no—on my own account. And you can't possibly think of leaving your aunt the moment she has arrived! For shame, Monsieur Erhart! Would that be behaving like a good son?

Mrs. Borkman [*annoyed*]. Son?

Mrs. Wilton. Well, adopted son then, Mrs. Borkman.

Mrs. Borkman. Yes, you may well add that.

Mrs. Wilton. Oh, it seems to me we have often more cause to be grateful to a foster mother than to our own mother.

Mrs. Borkman. Has that been your experience?

Mrs. Wilton. I knew very little of my own mother, I am sorry to say. But if I had had a good foster mother, perhaps I shouldn't have been so—so naughty, as people say I am. [*Turning toward* ERHART.] Well, then, we stop peaceably at home like a good boy, and drink tea with mamma and auntie! [*To the ladies.*] Good-by, good-by, Mrs. Borkman! Good-by, Miss Rentheim.

The ladies bow silently. She goes toward the door.

Erhart [*following her*]. Shan't I go a little bit of the way with you?

Mrs. Wilton [*in the doorway, motioning him back*]. You shan't go a step with me. I am quite accustomed to taking my walks alone. [*Stops on the threshold, looks at him and nods.*] But now beware, Mr. Borkman—I warn you!

Erhart. What am I to be aware of?

Mrs. Wilton [*gaily*]. Why, as I go down the road— deserted and forlorn, as I said before—I shall try if I can't cast a spell upon you.

Erhart [*laughing*]. Oh, indeed! Are you going to try that again?

Mrs. Wilton [*half seriously*]. Yes, just you beware! As I go down the road, I will say in my own mind—right from the very center of my will—I will say: "Mr. Erhart Borkman, take your hat at once!"

Mrs. Borkman. And you think he will take it?

Mrs. Wilton [*laughing*]. Good heavens, yes, he'll snatch up his hat instantly. And then I will say: "Now put on your overcoat, like a good boy, Erhart Borkman! And your galoshes! Be sure you don't forget the galoshes! And then follow me! Do as I bid you, as I bid you, as I bid you!"

Erhart [*with forced gaiety*]. Oh, you may rely on that.

Mrs. Wilton [*raising her forefinger*]. As I bid you! As I bid you! Good night! [*She laughs and nods to the ladies, and closes the door behind her.*]

Mrs. Borkman. Does she really play tricks of that sort?

Erhart. Oh, not at all. How can you think so! She only says it in fun. [*Breaking off.*] But don't let us talk about Mrs. Wilton. [*He forces* ELLA RENTHEIM *to seat herself in the armchair beside the stove, then stands and looks at her.*] To think of your having taken all this long journey, Aunt Ella! And in winter too!

Ella Rentheim. I found I had to, Erhart.

Erhart. Indeed? Why so?

Ella Rentheim. I had to come to town after all, to consult the doctors.

Erhart. Oh, I'm glad of that!

Ella Rentheim [*smiling*]. Are you glad of that?

Erhart. I mean I am glad you made up your mind to it at last.

Mrs. Borkman [*on the sofa, coldly*]. Are you ill, Ella?

Ella Rentheim [*looking hardly at her*]. You know quite well that I am ill.

Mrs. Borkman. I knew you were not strong, and hadn't been for years.

Erhart. I told you before I left you that you ought to consult a doctor.

Ella Rentheim. There is no one in my neighborhood that I have any real confidence in. And, besides, I did not feel it so much at that time.

Erhart. Are you worse, then, Aunt?

Ella Rentheim. Yes, my dear boy; I am worse now.

Erhart. But there's nothing dangerous?

Ella Rentheim. Oh, that depends how you look at it.

Erhart [*emphatically*]. Well, then, I tell you what it is, Aunt Ella; you mustn't think of going home again for the present.

Ella Rentheim. No, I am not thinking of it.

Erhart. You must remain in town; for here you can have your choice of all the best doctors.

Ella Rentheim. That was what I thought when I left home.

Erhart. And then you must be sure and find a really nice place to live—quiet, comfortable rooms.

Ella Rentheim. I went this morning to the old ones, where I used to stay before.

Erhart. Oh, well, you were comfortable enough there.

Ella Rentheim. Yes, but I shall not be staying there after all.

Erhart. Indeed? Why not?

Ella Rentheim. I changed my mind after coming out here.

Erhart [*surprised*]. Really? Changed your mind?

Mrs. Borkman [*crocheting; without looking up*]. Your aunt will live here, in her own house, Erhart.

Erhart [*looking from one to the other alternately*]. Here, with us? With us? Is this true, Aunt?

Ella Rentheim. Yes, that is what I have made up my mind to do.

Mrs. Borkman [*as before*]. Everything here belongs to your aunt, you know.

Ella Rentheim. I intend to remain here, Erhart—just now—for the present. I shall set up a little establishment of my own, over in the bailiff's wing.

Erhart. Ah, that's a good idea. There are plenty of rooms there. [*With sudden vivacity.*] But, by-the-by, Aunt —aren't you very tired after your journey?

Ella Rentheim. Oh, yes, rather tired.

Erhart. Well, then, I think you ought to go quite early to bed.

Ella Rentheim [*looks at him smilingly*]. I mean to.

Erhart [*eagerly*]. And then we could have a good long talk tomorrow—or some other day, of course—about this and that—about things in general—you and mother and I. Wouldn't that be much the best plan, Aunt Ella?

Mrs. Borkman [*with an outburst, rising from the sofa*]. Erhart, I can see you are going to leave me!

Erhart [*starts*]. What do you mean by that?

Mrs. Borkman. You are going down to—to the Hinkels'?

Erhart [*involuntarily*]. Oh, that! [*Collecting himself.*] Well, you wouldn't have me sit here and keep Aunt Ella up half the night? Remember, she's an invalid, Mother.

Mrs. Borkman. You are going to the Hinkels', Erhart!

Erhart [*impatiently*]. Well, really, Mother, I don't think I can well get out of it. What do you say, Aunt?

Ella Rentheim. I should like you to feel quite free, Erhart.

Mrs. Borkman [*goes up to her menacingly*]. You want to take him away from me!

Ella Rentheim [*rising*]. Yes, if only I could, Gunhild!

Music is heard from above.

Erhart [*writhing as if in pain*]. Oh, I can't endure this! [*Looking round.*] What have I done with my hat? [*To* ELLA RENTHEIM.] Do you know the air that she is playing up there?

Ella Rentheim. No. What is it?

Erhart. It's the *Danse Macabre*—the Dance of Death! Don't you know the Dance of Death, Aunt?

Ella Rentheim [*smiling sadly*]. Not yet, Erhart.

Erhart [*to* MRS. BORKMAN]. Mother—I beg and implore you—let me go!

Mrs. Borkman [*looks hardly at him*]. Away from your mother? So that is what you want to do?

Erhart. Of course, I'll come out again—tomorrow perhaps.

Mrs. Borkman [*with passionate emotions*]. You want to go away from me! To be with those strange people! With —with—no, I will not even think of it!

Erhart. There are bright lights down there, and young, happy faces; and there's music there, Mother!

Mrs. Borkman [*pointing upwards*]. There is music here, too, Erhart.

Erhart. Yes, it's just that music that drives me out of the house.

Ella Rentheim. Do you grudge your father a moment of self-forgetfulness?

Erhart. No, I don't. I'm very, very glad that he should have it—if only *I* don't have to listen.

Mrs. Borkman [*looking solemnly at him*]. Be strong, Erhart! Be strong, my son! Do not forget that you have your great mission.

Erhart. Oh, Mother—do spare me these phrases! I wasn't born to be a "missionary."—Good night, Aunt dear! Good night, Mother! [*He goes hastily out through the hall.*]

Mrs. Borkman [*after a short silence*]. It has not taken you long to recapture him, Ella, after all.

Ella Rentheim. I wish I could believe it.

Mrs. Borkman. But you shall see you won't be allowed to keep him long.

Ella Rentheim. Allowed? By you, do you mean?

Mrs. Borkman. By me or—by her, the other one——

Ella Rentheim. Then rather she than you.

Mrs. Borkman [*nodding slowly*]. That I understand. I say the same. Rather she than you.

Ella Rentheim. Whatever should become of him in the end——

Mrs. Borkman. It wouldn't greatly matter, I should say.

Ella Rentheim [*taking her outdoor things upon her arm*]. For the first time in our lives, we twin sisters are of one mind. Good night, Gunhild. [*She goes out by the hall. The music sounds louder from above.*]

Mrs. Borkman [*stands still for a moment, starts, shrinks together, and whispers involuntarily*]. The wolf is whining again—the sick wolf. [*She stands still for a moment, then flings herself down on the floor, writhing in agony and whispering.*] Erhart! Erhart—be true to me! Oh, come home and help your mother! For I can bear this life no longer!

ACT SECOND

The great gallery on the first floor of the Rentheim house. The walls are covered with old tapestries, representing hunting scenes, shepherds and shepherdesses, all in faded colors. A folding door to the left, and farther forward a piano. In the left-hand corner, at the back, a door, cut in the tapestry, and covered with tapestry, without any frame. Against the middle of the right wall, a large writing table of carved oak, with many books and papers. Farther forward on the same side, a sofa with a table and chairs in front of it. The furniture is all of a stiff Empire style. Lighted lamps on both tables.

JOHN GABRIEL BORKMAN *stands with his hands behind his back, beside the piano, listening to* FRIDA FOLDAL, *who is playing the last bars of the "Danse Macabre."*

BORKMAN *is of middle height, a well-knit, powerfully built man, well on in the sixties. His appearance is distinguished, his profile finely cut, his eyes piercing, his hair and beard curly and grayish-white. He is dressed in a slightly old-fashioned black coat, and wears a white necktie.* FRIDA FOLDAL *is a pretty, pale girl of fifteen, with a somewhat*

*weary and overstrained expression. She is cheaply dressed
in light colors.*

The music ceases. A pause.

BORKMAN. Can you guess where I first heard tones like
these?

Frida [*looking up at him*]. No, Mr. Borkman.

Borkman. It was down in the mines.

Frida [*not understanding*]. Indeed? Down in the mines?

Borkman. I am a miner's son, you know. Or perhaps you
did not know?

Frida. No, Mr. Borkman.

Borkman. A miner's son. And my father used sometimes
to take me with him into the mines. The metal sings down
there.

Frida. Really? Sings?

Borkman [*nodding*]. When it is loosened. The hammer
strokes that loosen it are the midnight bell clanging to set it
free; and that is why the metal sings—in its own way—for
gladness.

Frida. Why does it do that, Mr. Borkman?

Borkman. It wants to come up into the light of day and
serve mankind. [*He paces up and down the gallery, always with his hands behind his back.*]

Frida [*sits waiting a little, then looks at her watch and
rises*]. I beg your pardon, Mr. Borkman; but I am afraid
I must go.

Borkman [*stopping before her*]. Are you going already?

Frida [*putting her music in its case*]. I really must.
[*Visibly embarrassed.*] I have an engagement this evening.

Borkman. For a party?

Frida. Yes.

Borkman. And you are to play before the company?

Frida [*biting her lips*]. No; at least I am only to play for
dancing.

Borkman. Only for dancing?

Frida. Yes; there is to be a dance after supper.

Borkman [*stands and looks at her*]. Do you like playing
dance music? At parties, I mean?

Frida [*putting on her outdoor things*]. Yes, when I can
get an engagement. I can always earn a little in that way.

Borkman [*with interest*]. Is that the principal thing in
your mind as you sit playing for the dancers?

Frida. No; I'm generally thinking how hard it is that I mayn't join in the dance myself.

Borkman [*nodding*]. That is just what I wanted to know. [*Moving restlessly about the room.*] Yes, yes, yes. That you must not join in the dance, that is the hardest thing of all. [*Stopping.*] But there is one thing that should make up to you for that, Frida.

Frida [*looking inquiringly at him*]. What is that, Mr. Borkman?

Borkman. The knowledge that you have ten times more music in you than all the dancers together.

Frida [*smiling evasively*]. Oh, that's not at all so certain.

Borkman [*holding up his forefinger warningly*]. You must never be so mad as to have doubts of yourself!

Frida. But since no one knows it——

Borkman. So long as you know it yourself, that is enough. Where is it you are going to play this evening?

Frida. Over at Mr. Hinkel's.

Borkman [*with a swift, keen glance at her*]. Hinkel's, you say!

Frida. Yes.

Borkman [*with a cutting smile*]. Does that man give parties? Can he get people to visit him?

Frida. Yes, they have a great many people about them, Mrs. Wilton says.

Borkman [*vehemently*]. But what sort of people? Can you tell me that?

Frida [*a little nervously*]. No, I really don't know. Yes, by-the-by, I know that young Mr. Borkman is to be there this evening.

Borkman [*taken aback*]. Erhart? My son?

Frida. Yes, he is going there.

Borkman. How do you know that?

Frida. He said so himself—an hour ago.

Borkman. Is he out here today?

Frida. Yes, he has been at Mrs. Wilton's all the afternoon.

Borkman [*inquiringly*]. Do you know if he called here too? I mean, did he see anyone downstairs?

Frida. Yes, he looked in to see Mrs. Borkman.

Borkman [*bitterly*]. Aha—I might have known it.

Frida. There was a strange lady calling upon her, I think.

Borkman. Indeed? Was there? Oh, yes, I suppose people do come now and then to see Mrs. Borkman.

Frida. If I meet young Mr. Borkman this evening, shall I ask him to come up and see you too?

Borkman [*harshly*]. You shall do nothing of the sort! I won't have it on any account. The people who want to see me can come of their own accord. I ask no one.

Frida. Oh, very well; I shan't say anything then. Good night, Mr. Borkman.

Borkman [*pacing up and down and growling*]. Good night.

Frida. Do you mind if I run down by the winding stair? It's the shortest way.

Borkman. Oh, by all means; take whatever stair you please, so far as I am concerned. Good night to you!

Frida. Good night, Mr. Borkman. [*She goes out by the little tapestry door in the back on the left.*]

BORKMAN, *lost in thought, goes up to the piano, and is about to close it, but changes his mind. Looks round the great empty room, and sets to pacing up and down it from the corner beside the piano to the corner at the back on the right—pacing backward and forward uneasily and incessantly. At last he goes up to the writing table, listens in the direction of the folding door, hastily snatches up a hand glass, looks at himself in it, and straightens his necktie.*

A knock at the folding door. BORKMAN *hears it, looks rapidly toward the door, but says nothing. In a little there comes another knock, this time louder.*

Borkman [*standing beside the writing table with his left hand resting upon it, and his right thrust in the breast of his coat*]. Come in!

VILHELM FOLDAL *comes softly into the room. He is a bent and worn man with mild blue eyes and long, thin gray hair straggling down over his coat collar. He has a portfolio under his arm, a soft felt hat, and large horn spectacles, which he pushes up over his forehead.*

[*Changes his attitude and looks at* FOLDAL *with a half-disappointed, half-pleased expression.*] Oh, is it only you?

Foldal. Good evening, John Gabriel. Yes, you see it is me.

Borkman [*with a stern glance*]. I must say you are rather a late visitor.

Foldal. Well, you know, it's a good bit of a way, especially when you have to trudge it on foot.

Borkman. But why do you always walk, Vilhelm? The tramway passes your door.

Foldal. It's better for you to walk—and then you always save twopence. Well, has Frida been playing to you lately?

Borkman. She has just this moment gone. Did you not meet her outside?

Foldal. No, I have seen nothing of her for a long time; not since she went to live with this Mrs. Wilton.

Borkman [*seating himself on the sofa and waving his hand toward a chair*]. You may sit down, Vilhelm.

Foldal [*seating himself on the edge of a chair*]. Many thanks. [*Looks mournfully at him.*] You can't think how lonely I feel since Frida left home.

Borkman. Oh, come—you have plenty left.

Foldal. Yes, God knows I have—five of them. But Frida was the only one who at all understood me. [*Shaking his head sadly.*] The others don't understand me a bit.

Borkman [*gloomily, gazing straight before him, and drumming on the table with his fingers*]. No, that's just it. That is the curse we exceptional, chosen people have to bear. The common herd—the average man and woman—they do not understand us, Vilhelm.

Foldal [*with resignation*]. If it were only the lack of understanding—with a little patience, one could manage to wait for that awhile yet. [*His voice choked with tears.*] But there is something still bitterer.

Borkman [*vehemently*]. There is nothing bitterer than that.

Foldal. Yes, there is, John Gabriel. I have gone through a domestic scene tonight—just before I started.

Borkman. Indeed? What about?

Foldal [*with an outburst*]. My people at home—they despise me.

Borkman [*indignantly*]. Despise——!

Foldal [*wiping his eyes*]. I have long known it; but today it came out unmistakably.

Borkman [*after a short silence*]. You made an unwise choice, I fear, when you married.

Foldal. I had practically no choice in the matter. And, you see, one feels a need for companionship as one begins to get on in years. And so crushed as I then was—so utterly broken down——

Borkman [*jumping up in anger*]. Is this meant for me? A reproach——!

Foldal [*alarmed*]. No, no, for Heaven's sake, John Gabriel——!

Borkman. Yes, you are thinking of the disaster to the bank, I can see you are!

Foldal [*soothingly*]. But I don't blame you for that! Heaven forbid!

Borkman [*growling, resumes his seat*]. Well, that is a good thing, at any rate.

Foldal. Besides, you mustn't think it is my wife that I complain of. It is true she has not much polish, poor thing; but she is a good sort of woman all the same. No, it's the children.

Borkman. I thought as much.

Foldal. For the children—well, they have more culture, and therefore they expect more of life.

Borkman [*looking at him sympathetically*]. And so your children despise you, Vilhelm?

Foldal [*shrugging his shoulders*]. I haven't made much of a career, you see—there is no denying that.

Borkman [*moving nearer to him, and laying his hand upon his arm*]. Do they not know, then, that in your young days you wrote a tragedy?

Foldal. Yes, of course they know that. But it doesn't seem to make much impression on them.

Borkman. Then they don't understand these things. For your tragedy is good. I am firmly convinced of that.

Foldal [*brightening up*]. Yes, don't you think there are some good things in it, John Gabriel? Good God, if I could only manage to get it placed——! [*Opens his portfolio, and begins eagerly turning over the contents.*] Look here! Just let me show you one or two alterations I have made.

Borkman. Have you it with you?

Foldal. Yes, I thought I would bring it. It's so long now since I have read it to you. And I thought perhaps it might amuse you to hear an act or two.

Borkman [*rising, with a negative gesture*]. No, no, we will keep that for another time.

Foldal. Well, well, as you please.

BORKMAN *paces up and down the room.* FOLDAL *puts the manuscript up again.*

Borkman [*stopping in front of him*]. You are quite right in what you said just now—you have not made any career. But I promise you this, Vilhelm, that when once the hour of my restoration strikes——

Foldal [*making a movement to rise*]. Oh, thanks, thanks!

Borkman [*waving his hand*]. No, please be seated. [*With rising excitement.*] When the hour of my restoration strikes—when they see that they cannot get on without me—when they come to me, here in the gallery, and crawl to my feet, and beseech me to take the reins of the bank again——! The new bank, that they have founded and can't carry on—— [*Placing himself beside the writing table in the same attitude as before, and striking his breast.*] Here I shall stand, and receive them! And it shall be known far and wide, all the country over, what conditions John Gabriel Borkman imposes before he will—— [*Stopping suddenly and staring at* FOLDAL.] You're looking so doubtfully at me! Perhaps you do not believe that they will come? That they must, must, must come to me someday? Do you not believe it?

Foldal. Yes, Heaven knows I do, John Gabriel.

Borkman [*seating himself again on the sofa*]. I firmly believe it. I am immovably convinced—I know that they will come. If I had not been certain of that I would have put a bullet through my head long ago.

Foldal [*anxiously*]. Oh, no, for Heaven's sake——!

Borkman [*exultantly*]. But they will come! They will come sure enough! You shall see! I expect them any day, any moment. And you see, I hold myself in readiness to receive them.

Foldal [*with a sigh*]. If only they would come quickly.

Borkman [*restlessly*]. Yes, time flies: the years slip away; life—— Ah, no—I dare not think of it! [*Looking at him.*] Do you know what I sometimes feel like?

Foldal. What?

Borkman. I feel like a Napoleon who has been maimed in his first battle.

Foldal [*placing his hand upon his portfolio*]. I have that feeling too.

Borkman. Oh, well, that is on a smaller scale, of course.

Foldal [*quietly*]. My little world of poetry is very precious to me, John Gabriel.

Borkman [*vehemently*]. Yes, but think of me, who could have created millions! All the mines I should have controlled! New veins innumerable! And the waterfalls! And the quarries! And the trade routes, and steamship lines all the wide world over! I would have organized it all— I alone!

Foldal. Yes, I know, I know. There was nothing in the world you would have shrunk from.

Borkman [*clenching his hands together*]. And now I have to sit here, like a wounded eagle, and look on while others pass me in the race, and take everything away from me, piece by piece!

Foldal. That is my fate too.

Borkman [*not noticing him*]. Only to think of it; so near to the goal as I was! If I had only had another week to look about me! All the deposits would have been covered. All the securities I had dealt with so daringly should have been in their places again as before. Vast companies were within a hairsbreadth of being floated. Not a soul should have lost a halfpenny.

Foldal. Yes, yes; you were on the very verge of success.

Borkman [*with suppressed fury*]. And then treachery overtook me! Just at the critical moment! [*Looking at him.*] Do you know what I hold to be the most infamous crime a man can be guilty of?

Foldal. No, tell me.

Borkman. It is not murder. It is not robbery or housebreaking. It is not even perjury. For all these things people do to those they hate, or who are indifferent to them, and do not matter.

Foldal. What is the worst of all then, John Gabriel?

Borkman [*with emphasis*]. The most infamous of crimes is a friend's betrayal of his friend's confidence.

Foldal [*somewhat doubtfully*]. Yes, but you know——

Borkman [*firing up*]. What are you going to say? I see it in your face. But it is of no use. The people who had their securities in the bank should have got them all back again—every farthing. No; I tell you the most infamous crime a man can commit is to misuse a friend's letters; to publish to all the world what has been confided to him alone, in the closest secrecy, like a whisper in an empty, dark, double-locked room. The man who can do such things is infected and poisoned in every fiber with the morals of the higher rascality. And such a friend was mine—and it was he who crushed me.

Foldal. I can guess whom you mean.

Borkman. There was not a nook or cranny of my life that I hesitated to lay open to him. And then, when the moment came, he turned against me the weapons I myself had placed in his hands.

Foldal. I have never been able to understand why he—— Of course, there were whispers of all sorts at the time.

Borkman. What were the whispers? Tell me. You see I know nothing. For I had to go straight into—into isolation. What did people whisper, Vilhelm?

Foldal. You were to have gone into the Cabinet, they said.

Borkman. I was offered a portfolio, but I refused it.

Foldal. Then it wasn't there you stood in his way?

Borkman. Oh, no; that was not the reason he betrayed me.

Foldal. Then I really can't understand——

Borkman. I may as well tell you, Vilhelm——

Foldal. Well?

Borkman. There was—in fact, there was a woman in the case.

Foldal. A woman in the case? Well, but, John Gabriel——

Borkman [*interrupting*]. Well, well—let us say no more of these stupid old stories. After all, neither of us got into the Cabinet, neither he nor I.

Foldal. But he rose high in the world.

Borkman. And I fell into the abyss.

Foldal. Oh, it's a terrible tragedy——

Borkman [*nodding to him*]. Almost as terrible as yours, I fancy, when I come to think of it.

Foldal [*naïvely*]. Yes, at least as terrible.

Borkman [*laughing quietly*]. But looked at from another point of view, it is really a sort of comedy as well.

Foldal. A comedy? The story of your life?

Borkman. Yes, it seems to be taking a turn in that direction. For let me tell you——

Foldal. What?

Borkman. You say you did not meet Frida as you came in?

Foldal. No.

Borkman. At this moment, as we sit here, she is playing waltzes for the guests of the man who betrayed and ruined me.

Foldal. I hadn't the least idea of that.

Borkman. Yes, she took her music, and went straight from me to—to the great house.

Foldal [*apologetically*]. Well, you see, poor child——

Borkman. And can you guess for whom she is playing—among the rest?

Foldal. No.

Borkman. For my son.

Foldal. What?

Borkman. What do you think of that, Vilhelm? My son is down there in the whirl of the dance this evening. Am I not right in calling it a comedy?

Foldal. But in that case you may be sure he knows nothing about it.

Borkman. What does he not know?

Foldal. You may be sure he doesn't know how he—that man——

Borkman. Do not shrink from his name. I can quite well bear it now.

Foldal. I'm certain your son doesn't know the circumstances, John Gabriel.

Borkman [*gloomily, sitting and beating the table*]. Yes, he knows, as surely as I am sitting here.

Foldal. Then how can he possibly be a guest in that house?

Borkman [*shaking his head*]. My son probably does not see things with my eyes. I'll take my oath he is on my enemies' side! No doubt he thinks, as they do, that Hinkel only did his confounded duty when he went and betrayed me.

Foldal. But, my dear friend, who can have got him to see things in that light?

Borkman. Who? Do you forget who has brought him up? First his aunt, from the time he was six or seven years old; and now, of late years, his mother!

Foldal. I believe you are doing them an injustice.

Borkman [*firing up*]. I never do anyone injustice! Both of them have gone and poisoned his mind against me, I tell you!

Foldal [*soothingly*]. Well, well, well, I suppose they have.

Borkman [*indignantly*]. Oh, these women! They wreck and ruin life for us! Play the devil with our whole destiny —our triumphal progress.

Foldal. Not all of them!

Borkman. Indeed? Can you tell me of a single one that is good for anything?

Foldal. No, that is the trouble. The few that I know are good for nothing.

Borkman [*with a snort of scorn*]. Well then, what is the good of it? What is the good of such women existing—if you never know them?

Foldal [*warmly*]. Yes, John Gabriel, there is good in it, I assure you. It is such a blessed, beneficent thought that here or there in the world, somewhere, faraway—the true woman exists after all.

Borkman [*moving impatiently on the sofa*]. Oh, do spare me that poetical nonsense.

Foldal [*looks at him, deeply wounded*]. Do you call my holiest faith poetical nonsense?

Borkman [*harshly*]. Yes, I do! That is what has always prevented you from getting on in the world. If you would get all that out of your head, I could still help you on in life—help you to rise.

Foldal [*boiling inwardly*]. Oh, you can't do that.

Borkman. I can, when once I come into power again.

Foldal. That won't be for many a day.

Borkman [*vehemently*]. Perhaps you think that day will never come? Answer me!

Foldal. I don't know what to answer.

Borkman [*rising, cold and dignified, and waving his hand toward the door*]. Then I no longer have any use for you.

Foldal [*starting up*]. No use——!

Borkman. Since you do not believe that the tide will turn for me——

Foldal. How can I believe in the teeth of all reason? You would have to be legally rehabilitated——

Borkman. Go on! go on!

Foldal. It's true I never passed my examination; but I have read enough law to know that——

Borkman [*quickly*]. It is impossible, you mean?

Foldal. There is no precedent for such a thing.

Borkman. Exceptional men are above precedents.

Foldal. The law knows nothing of such distinctions.

Borkman [*harshly and decisively*]. You are no poet, Vilhelm.

Foldal [*unconsciously folding his hands*]. Do you say that in sober earnest?

Borkman [*dismissing the subject, without answering*]. We are only wasting each other's time. You had better not come here again.

Foldal. Then you really want me to leave you?

Borkman [*without looking at him*]. I have no longer any use for you.

Foldal [*softly, taking his portfolio*]. No, no, no; I daresay not.

Borkman. Here you have been lying to me all the time.

Foldal [*shaking his head*]. Never lying, John Gabriel.

Borkman. Have you not sat here feeding me with hope, and trust, and confidence—that was all a lie?

Foldal. It wasn't a lie so long as you believed in my vocation. So long as you believed in me, I believed in you.

Borkman. Then we have been all the time deceiving each other. And perhaps deceiving ourselves—both of us.

Foldal. But isn't that just the essence of friendship, John Gabriel?

Borkman [*smiling bitterly*]. Yes, you are right there. Friendship means—deception. I have learnt that once before.

Foldal [*looking at him*]. I have no poetic vocation! And you could actually say it to me so bluntly.

Borkman [*in a gentler tone*]. Well, you know, I don't pretend to know much about these matters.

Foldal. Perhaps you know more than you think.

Borkman. I?

Foldal [*softly*]. Yes, you. For I myself have had my doubts, now and then, I may tell you. The horrible doubt that I may have bungled my life for the sake of a delusion.

Borkman. If you have no faith in yourself, you are on the downward path indeed.

Foldal. That was why I found such comfort in coming here to lean upon your faith in me. [*Taking his hat.*] But now you have become a stranger to me.

Borkman. And you to me.

Foldal. Good night, John Gabriel.

Borkman. Good night, Vilhelm.

FOLDAL *goes out to the left.* BORKMAN *stands for a moment gazing at the closed door; makes a movement as though to call* FOLDAL *back, but changes his mind, and begins to pace the floor with his hands behind his back. Then he stops at the table beside the sofa and puts out the lamp. The room becomes half dark. After a short pause, there comes a knock at the tapestry door.*

[*At the table, starts, turns, and asks in a loud voice*]. Who is that knocking?

No answer; another knock.

[*Without moving.*] Who is it? Come in!

ELLA RENTHEIM, *with a lighted candle in her hand, appears in the doorway. She wears her black dress, as before, with her cloak thrown loosely round her shoulders.*

[*Staring at her.*] Who are you? What do you want with me?

Ella Rentheim [*closes the door and advances*]. It is I, Borkman. [*She puts down the candle on the piano and remains standing beside it.*]

Borkman [*stands as though thunderstruck, stares fixedly at her, and says in a half whisper*]. Is it—is it Ella? Is it Ella Rentheim?

Ella Rentheim. Yes, it's "your" Ella, as you used to call me in the old days; many, many years ago.

Borkman [*as before*]. Yes, it is you, Ella, I can see you now.

Ella Rentheim. Can you recognize me?

Borkman. Yes, now I begin to——

Ella Rentheim. The years have told on me, and brought winter with them, Borkman. Do you not think so?

Borkman [*in a forced voice*]. You are a good deal changed—just at the first glance.

Ella Rentheim. There are no dark curls on my neck now—the curls you once loved so to twist round your fingers.

Borkman [*quickly*]. True! I can see now, Ella, you have done your hair differently.

Ella Rentheim [*with a sad smile*]. Precisely; it is the way I do my hair that makes the difference.

Borkman [*changing the subject*]. I had no idea that you were in this part of the world.

Ella Rentheim. I have only just arrived.

Borkman. Why have you come all this way now, in winter?

Ella Rentheim. That you shall hear.

Borkman. Is it me you have come to see?

Ella Rentheim. You among others. But if I am to tell you my errand, I must begin far back.

Borkman. You look tired.

Ella Rentheim. Yes, I am tired.

Borkman. Won't you sit down? There, on the sofa.

Ella Rentheim. Yes, thank you; I need rest.

She crosses to the right and seats herself in the farthest forward corner of the sofa. BORKMAN *stands beside the table with his hands behind his back looking at her. A short silence.*

It seems an endless time since we two met, Borkman, face to face.

Borkman [*gloomily*]. It is a long, long time. And terrible things have passed since then.

Ella Rentheim. A whole lifetime has passed—a wasted lifetime.

Borkman [*looking keenly at her*]. Wasted!

Ella Rentheim. Yes, I say wasted—for both of us.

Borkman [*in a cold, business tone*]. I cannot regard my life as wasted, yet.

Ella Rentheim. And what about mine?

Borkman. There you have yourself to blame, Ella.

Ella Rentheim [*with a start*]. And you can say that?

Borkman. You could quite well have been happy without me.

Ella Rentheim. Do you believe that?

Borkman. If you had made up your mind to.

Ella Rentheim [*bitterly*]. Oh, yes, I know well enough there was someone else ready to marry me.

Borkman. But you rejected him.

Ella Rentheim. Yes, I did.

Borkman. Time after time you rejected him. Year after year——

Ella Rentheim [*scornfully*]. Year after year I rejected happiness, I suppose you think?

Borkman. You might perfectly well have been happy with him. And then I should have been saved.

Ella Rentheim. You?

Borkman. Yes, you would have saved me, Ella.

Ella Rentheim. How do you mean?

Borkman. He thought I was at the bottom of your obstinacy—of your perpetual refusals. And then he took his revenge. It was so easy for him; he had all my frank, confiding letters in his keeping. He made his own use of them; and then it was all over with me—for the time, that is to say. So you see it is all your doing, Ella!

Ella Rentheim. Oh, indeed, Borkman. If we look into the matter, it appears that it is I who owe you reparation.

Borkman. It depends how you look at it. I know quite well all that you have done for us. You bought in this house, and the whole property, at the auction. You placed the house entirely at my disposal—and your sister's. You took charge of Erhart, and cared for him in every way——

Ella Rentheim. As long as I was allowed to——

Borkman. By your sister, you mean. I have never mixed myself up in these domestic affairs. As I was saying, I know all the sacrifices you have made for me and for your sister. But you were in a position to do so, Ella; and you must not forget that it was I who placed you in that position.

Ella Rentheim [*indignantly*]. There you make a great mistake, Borkman! It was the love of my inmost heart for Erhart—and for you too—that made me do it!

Borkman [*interrupting*]. My dear Ella, do not let us get upon questions of sentiment and that sort of thing. I mean, of course, that if you acted generously, it was I that put it in your power to do so.

Ella Rentheim [*smiling*]. H'm! In my power——

Borkman [*warmly*]. Yes, put it in your power, I say! On the eve of the great decisive battle—when I could not afford to spare either kith or kin—when I had to grasp at—when I did grasp at the millions that were entrusted to me—then I spared all that was yours, every farthing, although I could have taken it, and made use of it, as I did of all the rest!

Ella Rentheim [*coldly and quietly*]. That is quite true, Borkman.

Borkman. Yes, it is. And that was why, when they came and took me, they found all your securities untouched in the strong room of the bank.

Ella Rentheim [*looking at him*]. I have often and often

wondered what was your real reason for sparing all my property? That, and that alone?

Borkman. My reason?

Ella Rentheim. Yes, your reason. Tell me.

Borkman [*harshly and scornfully*]. Perhaps you think it was that I might have something to fall back upon, if things went wrong?

Ella Rentheim. Oh, no, I am sure you did not think of that in those days.

Borkman. Never! I was so absolutely certain of victory.

Ella Rentheim. Well then, why was it that——?

Borkman [*shrugging his shoulders*]. Upon my soul, Ella, it is not so easy to remember one's motives of twenty years ago. I only know that when I used to grapple, silently and alone, with all the great projects I had in my mind, I had something like the feeling of a man who is starting on a balloon voyage. All through my sleepless nights I was inflating my giant balloon, and preparing to soar away into perilous, unknown regions.

Ella Rentheim [*smiling*]. You, who never had the least doubt of victory?

Borkman [*impatiently*]. Men are made so, Ella. They both doubt and believe at the same time. [*Looking straight before him.*] And suppose that was why I would not take you and yours with me in the balloon.

Ella Rentheim [*eagerly*]. Why, I ask you? Tell me why!

Borkman [*without looking at her*]. One shrinks from risking what one holds dearest on such a voyage.

Ella Rentheim. You had risked what was dearest to you on that voyage. Your whole future life——

Borkman. Life is not always what one holds dearest.

Ella Rentheim [*breathlessly*]. Was that how you felt at that time?

Borkman. I fancy it was.

Ella Rentheim. I was the dearest thing in the world to you?

Borkman. I seem to remember something of the sort.

Ella Rentheim. And yet years and years had passed since you had deserted me—and married—married another!

Borkman. Deserted you, you say? You must know very well that it was higher motives—well then, other motives that compelled me. Without his support I could not have done anything.

Ella Rentheim [*controlling herself*]. So you deserted me from—higher motives.

Borkman. I could not get on without his help. And he made you the price of helping me.

Ella Rentheim. And you paid the price. Paid it in full— without haggling.

Borkman. I had no choice. I had to conquer or fall.

Ella Rentheim [*in a trembling voice, looking at him*]. Can what you tell me be true—that I was then the dearest thing in the world to you?

Borkman. Both then and afterwards—long, long after.

Ella Rentheim. But you bartered me away nonetheless; drove a bargain with another man for your love. Sold my love for a—for a directorship.

Borkman [*gloomily and bowed down*]. I was driven by inexorable necessity, Ella.

Ella Rentheim [*rises from the sofa, quivering with passion*]. Criminal!

Borkman [*starts, but controls himself*]. I have heard that word before.

Ella Rentheim. Oh, don't imagine I'm thinking of any-thing you may have done against the law of the land! The use you made of all those vouchers and securities, or what-ever you call them—do you think I care a straw about that! If I could have stood at your side when the crash came——

Borkman [*eagerly*]. What then, Ella?

Ella Rentheim. Trust me, I should have borne it all so gladly along with you. The shame, the ruin—I would have helped you to bear it all—all!

Borkman. Would you have had the will—the strength?

Ella Rentheim. Both the will and the strength. For then I did not know of your great, your terrible crime.

Borkman. What crime? What are you speaking of?

Ella Rentheim. I am speaking of that crime for which there is no forgiveness.

Borkman [*staring at her*]. You must be out of your mind.

Ella Rentheim [*approaching him*]. You are a murderer! You have committed the one mortal sin!

Borkman [*falling back toward the piano*]. You are raving, Ella!

Ella Rentheim. You have killed the love-life in me. [*Still nearer him.*] Do you understand what that means? The

Bible speaks of a mysterious sin for which there is no for-giveness. I have never understood what it could be; but now I understand. The great, unpardonable sin is to murder the love life in a human soul.

Borkman. And you say I have done that?

Ella Rentheim. You have done that. I have never rightly understood until this evening what had really happened to me. That you deserted me and turned to Gunhild in-stead—I took that to be mere common fickleness on your part, and the result of heartless scheming on hers. I al-most think I despised you a little, in spite of everything. But now I see it! You deserted the woman you loved! Me, me, me! What you held dearest in the world you were ready to barter away for gain. That is the double murder you have committed! The murder of your own soul and of mine!

Borkman [*with cold self-control*]. How well I recognize your passionate, ungovernable spirit, Ella. No doubt it is natural enough that you should look at the thing in this light. Of course, you are a woman, and therefore it would seem that your own heart is the one thing you know or care about in the world.

Ella Rentheim. Yes, yes it is.

Borkman. Your own heart is the only thing that exists for you.

Ella Rentheim. The only thing! The only thing! You are right there.

Borkman. But you must remember that I am a man. As a woman, you were the dearest thing in the world to me. But if the worst comes to the worst, one woman can al-ways take the place of another.

Ella Rentheim [*looks at him with a smile*]. Was that your experience when you had made Gunhild your wife?

Borkman. No. But the great aims I had in life helped me to bear even that. I wanted to have at my command all the sources of power in this country. All the wealth that lay hidden in the soil, and the rocks, and the forests, and the sea—— I wanted to gather it all into my hands, to make myself master of it all, and so to promote the well-being of many, many thousands.

Ella Rentheim [*lost in recollection*]. I know it. Think of all the evenings we spent in talking over your projects.

Borkman. Yes, I could talk to you, Ella.

Ella Rentheim. I jested with your plans, and asked whether you wanted to awaken all the sleeping spirits of the mine.

Borkman [*nodding*]. I remember that phrase. [*Slowly.*] All the sleeping spirits of the mine.

Ella Rentheim. But you did not take it as a jest. You said: "Yes, yes, Ella, that is just what I want to do."

Borkman. And so it was. If only I could get my foot into the stirrup—— And that depended on that one man. He could and would secure me the control of the bank—if I on my side——

Ella Rentheim. Yes, just so! If you on your side would renounce the woman you loved—and who loved you beyond words in return.

Borkman. I knew his consuming passion for you. I knew that on no other condition would he——

Ella Rentheim. And so you struck the bargain.

Borkman [*vehemently*]. Yes, I did, Ella! For the love of power is uncontrollable in me, you see! So I struck the bargain; I had to. And he helped me halfway up toward the beckoning heights that I was bent on reaching. And I mounted and mounted; year by year I mounted——

Ella Rentheim. And I was as though wiped out of your life.

Borkman. And after all he hurled me into the abyss again. On account of you, Ella.

Ella Rentheim [*after a short thoughtful silence*]. Borkman, does it not seem to you as if there had been a sort of curse on our whole relation?

Borkman [*looking at her*]. A curse?

Ella Rentheim. Yes. Don't you think so?

Borkman [*uneasily*]. Yes. But why is it? [*With an outburst.*] Oh, Ella, I begin to wonder which is in the right—you or I!

Ella Rentheim. It is you who have sinned. You have done to death all the gladness of life in me.

Borkman [*anxiously*]. Do not say that, Ella!

Ella Rentheim. All a woman's gladness at any rate. From the day when your image began to dwindle in my mind, I have lived my life as though under an eclipse. During all these years it has grown harder and harder for me—and at last utterly impossible—to love any living creature. Human beings, animals, plants: I shrank from all—from all but one——

Borkman. What one?

Ella Rentheim. Erhart, of course.

Borkman. Erhart?

Ella Rentheim. Erhart—your son, Borkman.

Borkman. Has he really been so close to your heart?

Ella Rentheim. Why else should I have taken him to me, and kept him as long as ever I could? Why?

Borkman. I thought it was out of pity, like all the rest that you did.

Ella Rentheim [*in strong inward emotion*]. Pity! Ha, ha! I have never known pity, since you deserted me. I was incapable of feeling it. If a poor starved child came into my kitchen, shivering, and crying, and begging for a morsel of food, I let the servants look to it. I never felt any desire to take the child to myself, to warm it at my own hearth, to have the pleasure of seeing it eat and be satisfied. And yet I was not like that when I was young; that I remember clearly! It is you that have created an empty, barren desert within me—and without me too!

Borkman. Except only for Erhart.

Ella Rentheim. Yes, except for your son. But I am hardened to every other living thing. You have cheated me of a mother's joy and happiness in life—and of a mother's sorrows and tears as well. And perhaps that is the heaviest part of the loss to me.

Borkman. Do you say that, Ella?

Ella Rentheim. Who knows? It may be that a mother's sorrows and tears were what I needed most. [*With still deeper emotion.*] But at that time I could not resign myself to my loss; and that was why I took Erhart to me. I won him entirely. Won his whole warm, trustful childish heart—until—— Oh!

Borkman. Until what?

Ella Rentheim. Until his mother—his mother in the flesh, I mean—took him from me again.

Borkman. He had to leave you in any case; he had to come to town.

Ella Rentheim [*wringing her hands*]. Yes, but I cannot bear the solitude—the emptiness! I cannot bear the loss of your son's heart!

Borkman [*with an evil expression in his eyes*]. H'm—I doubt whether you have lost it, Ella. Hearts are not so easily lost to a certain person—in the room below.

Ella Rentheim. I have lost Erhart here, and she has won

him back again. Or if not she, someone else. That is plain enough in the letters he writes me from time to time.

Borkman. Then it is to take him back with you that you have come here?

Ella Rentheim. Yes, if only it were possible——!

Borkman. It is possible enough, if you have set your heart upon it. For you have the first and strongest claims upon him.

Ella Rentheim. Oh, claims, claims! What is the use of claims? If he is not mine of his own free will, he is not mine at all. And have him I must! I must have my boy's heart, whole and undivided—now!

Borkman. You must remember that Erhart is well into his twenties. You could scarcely reckon on keeping his heart very long undivided, as you express it.

Ella Rentheim [*with a melancholy smile*]. It would not need to be for so very long.

Borkman. Indeed? I should have thought that when you want a thing, you want it to the end of your days.

Ella Rentheim. So I do. But that need not mean for very long.

Borkman [*taken aback*]. What do you mean by that?

Ella Rentheim. I suppose you know I have been in bad health for many years past?

Borkman. Have you?

Ella Rentheim. Do you not know that?

Borkman. No, I cannot say I did——

Ella Rentheim [*looking at him in surprise*]. Has Erhart not told you so?

Borkman. I really don't remember at the moment.

Ella Rentheim. Perhaps he has not spoken of me at all?

Borkman. Oh, yes, I believe he has spoken of you. But the fact is, I so seldom see anything of him—scarcely ever. There is a certain person below that keeps him away from me. Keeps him away, you understand?

Ella Rentheim. Are you quite sure of that, Borkman?

Borkman. Yes, absolutely sure. [*Changing his tone.*] And so you have been in bad health, Ella?

Ella Rentheim. Yes, I have. And this autumn I grew so much worse that I had to come to town and take better medical advice.

Borkman. And you have seen the doctors already?

Ella Rentheim. Yes, this morning.

Borkman. And what did they say to you?

Ella Rentheim. They gave me full assurance of what I had long suspected.

Borkman. Well?

Ella Rentheim [*calmly and quietly*]. My illness will never be cured, Borkman.

Borkman. Oh, you must not believe that, Ella.

Ella Rentheim. It is a disease that there is no help or cure for. The doctors can do nothing with it. They must just let it take its course. They cannot possibly check it; at most, they can allay the suffering. And that is always something.

Borkman. Oh, but it will take a long time to run its course. I am sure it will.

Ella Rentheim. I may perhaps last out the winter, they told me.

Borkman [*without thinking*]. Oh, well, the winter is long.

Ella Rentheim [*quietly*]. Long enough for me, at any rate.

Borkman [*eagerly, changing the subject*]. But what in all the world can have brought on this illness? You, who have always lived such a healthy and regular life? What can have brought it on?

Ella Rentheim [*looking at him*]. The doctors thought that perhaps at one time in my life I had had to go through some great stress of emotion.

Borkman [*firing up*]. Emotion! Aha, I understand! You mean that it is my fault?

Ella Rentheim [*with increasing inward agitation*]. It is too late to go into that matter now! But I must have my heart's own child again before I go! It is so unspeakably sad for me to think that I must go away from all that is called life—away from sun, and light, and air—and not leave behind me one single human being who will think of me—who will remember me lovingly and mournfully—as a son remembers and thinks of the mother he has lost.

Borkman [*after a short pause*]. Take him, Ella, if you can win him.

Ella Rentheim [*with animation*]. Do you give your consent? Can you?

Borkman [*gloomily*]. Yes. And it is no great sacrifice either. For in any case he is not mine.

Ella Rentheim. Thank you, thank you all the same for the sacrifice! But I have one thing more to beg of you— a great thing for me, Borkman.

Borkman. Well, what is it?

Ella Rentheim. I daresay you will think it childish of me—you will not understand——

Borkman. Go on—tell me what it is.

Ella Rentheim. When I die—as I must soon—I shall have a fair amount to leave behind me.

Borkman. Yes, I suppose so.

Ella Rentheim. And I intend to leave it all to Erhart.

Borkman. Well, you have really no one nearer to you than he.

Ella Rentheim [*warmly*]. No, indeed, I have no one nearer me than he.

Borkman. No one of your own family. You are the last.

Ella Rentheim [*nodding slowly*]. Yes, that is just it. When I die, the name of Rentheim dies with me. And that is such a torturing thought to me. To be wiped out of existence—even to your very name——

Borkman [*firing up*]. Ah, I see what you are driving at!

Ella Rentheim [*passionately*]. Do not let this be my forte. Let Erhart bear my name after me!

Borkman [*looking harshly at her*]. I understand you well enough. You want to save my son from having to bear his father's name. That is your meaning.

Ella Rentheim. No, no, not that! I myself would have borne it proudly and gladly along with you! But a mother who is at the point of death—— There is more binding force in a name than you think or believe, Borkman.

Borkman [*coldly and proudly*]. Well and good, Ella. I am man enough to bear my own name alone.

Ella Rentheim [*seizing and pressing his hand*]. Thank you, thank you! Now there has been a full settlement between us! Yes, yes, let it be so! You have made all the atonement in your power. For when I have gone from the world, I shall leave Erhart Rentheim behind me!

The tapestry door is thrown open. MRS. BORKMAN, *with the large shawl over her head, stands in the doorway.*

Mrs. Borkman [*in violent agitation*]. Never to his dying day shall Erhart be called by that name!

Ella Rentheim [*shrinking back*]. Gunhild!

Borkman [*harshly and threateningly*]. I allow no one to come up to my room!

Mrs. Borkman [*advancing a step*]. I do not ask your permission.

Borkman [*going toward her*]. What do you want with me?

Mrs. Borkman. I will fight with all my might for you. I will protect you from the powers of evil.

Ella Rentheim. The worst "powers of evil" are in yourself, Gunhild!

Mrs. Borkman [*harshly*]. So be it then. [*Menacingly, with upstretched arm.*] But this I tell you—he shall bear his father's name! And bear it aloft in honor again. And I will be his mother! I alone! My son's heart shall be mine—mine, and no other's. [*She goes out by the tapestry door and shuts it behind her.*]

Ella Rentheim [*shaken and shattered*]. Borkman, Erhart's life will be wrecked in this storm. There must be an understanding between you and Gunhild. We must go down to her at once.

Borkman [*looking at her*]. We? I, too, do you mean?

Ella Rentheim. Both you and I.

Borkman [*shaking his head*]. She is hard, I tell you. Hard as the metal I once dreamed of hewing out of the rocks.

Ella Rentheim. Then try it now!

BORKMAN *does not answer, but stands looking doubtfully at her.*

ACT THIRD

MRS. BORKMAN'S *drawing room. The lamp is still burning on the table beside the sofa in front. The garden room at the back is quite dark.*

MRS. BORKMAN, *with the shawl still over her head, enters, in violent agitation, by the hall door, goes up to the window, draws the curtain a little aside, and looks out; then she seats herself beside the stove, but immediately springs up again, goes to the bellpull and rings. Stands beside the sofa, and waits a moment. No one comes. Then she rings again, this time more violently.*

THE MAID *presently enters from the hall. She looks sleepy and out of temper, and appears to have dressed in great haste.*

MRS. BORKMAN [*impatiently*]. What has become of you, Malena? I have rung for you twice!

The Maid. Yes, ma'am, I heard you.

Mrs. Borkman. And yet you didn't come?

The Maid [*sulkily*]. I had to put some clothes on first, I suppose.

Mrs. Borkman. Yes, you must dress yourself properly, and then you must run at once and fetch my son.

The Maid [*looking at her in astonishment*]. You want me to fetch Mr. Erhart?

Mrs. Borkman. Yes; tell him he must come home to me at once; I want to speak to him.

The Maid [*grumbling*]. Then I'd better go to the bailiff's and call up the coachman.

Mrs. Borkman. Why?

The Maid. To get him to harness the sledge. The snow's dreadful tonight.

Mrs. Borkman. Oh, that doesn't matter; only make haste and go. It's just round the corner.

The Maid. Why, ma'am, you can't call that just round the corner!

Mrs. Borkman. Of course it is. Don't you know Mr. Hinkel's villa?

The Maid [*with malice*]. Oh, indeed! It's there Mr. Erhart is this evening?

Mrs. Borkman [*taken aback*]. Why, where else should he be?

The Maid [*with a slight smile*]. Well, I only thought he might be where he usually is.

Mrs. Borkman. Where do you mean?

The Maid. At that Mrs. Wilton's, as they call her.

Mrs. Borkman. Mrs. Wilton's? My son isn't so often there.

The Maid [*half muttering*]. I've heard say as he's there every day of his life.

Mrs. Borkman. That's all nonsense, Malena. Go straight to Mr. Hinkel's and try to get hold of him.

The Maid [*with a toss of her head*]. Oh, very well; I'm going.

*She is on the point of going out by the hall, but just at
that moment the hall door is opened, and* ELLA RENTHEIM
and BORKMAN *appear on the threshold.*

Mrs. Borkman [*staggers a step backward*]. What does
this mean?

The Maid [*terrified, instinctively folding her hands*].
Lord save us!

Mrs. Borkman [*whispers to* THE MAID]. Tell him he
must come this instant.

The Maid [*softly*]. Yes, ma'am.

ELLA RENTHEIM *and, after her,* BORKMAN *enter the room.*
THE MAID *sidles behind them to the door, goes out, and
closes it after her. A short silence.*

Mrs. Borkman [*having recovered her self-control, turns
to* ELLA]. What does he want down here in my room?

Ella Rentheim. He wants to come to an understanding
with you, Gunhild.

Mrs. Borkman. He has never tried that before.

Ella Rentheim. He is going to, this evening.

Mrs. Borkman. The last time we stood face to face—
it was in the Court, when I was summoned to give an
account——

Borkman [*approaching*]. And this evening it is *I* who
will give an account of myself.

Mrs. Borkman [*looking at him*]. You?

Borkman. Not of what I have done amiss. All the world
knows that.

Mrs. Borkman [*with a bitter sigh*]. Yes, that is true; all
the world knows that.

Borkman. But it does not know why I did it; why I had
to do it. People do not understand that I had to, because
I was myself—because I was John Gabriel Borkman—
myself, and not another. And that is what I will try to
explain to you.

Mrs. Borkman [*shaking her head*]. It is of no use.
Temptations and promptings acquit no one.

Borkman. They may acquit one in one's own eyes.

Mrs. Borkman [*with a gesture of repulsion*]. Oh, let all
that alone! I have thought over that black business of yours
enough and to spare.

Borkman. I, too. During those five endless years in my
cell—and elsewhere—I had time to think it over. And

during the eight years up there in the gallery I have had still more ample time. I have retried the whole case—by myself. Time after time I have retried it. I have been my own accuser, my own defender, and my own judge. I have been more impartial than anyone else could be—that I venture to say. I have paced up and down the gallery there, turning every one of my actions upside down and inside out. I have examined them from all sides as unsparingly, as pitilessly, as any lawyer of them all. And the final judgment I have always come to is this: the one person I have sinned against is—myself.

Mrs. Borkman. And what about me? What about your son?

Borkman. You and he are included in what I mean when I say myself.

Mrs. Borkman. And what about the hundreds of others, then—the people you are said to have ruined?

Borkman [*more vehemently*]. I had power in my hands! And then I felt the irresistible vocation within me! The prisoned millions lay all over the country, deep in the bowels of the earth, calling aloud to me! They shrieked to me to free them! But no one else heard their cry—I alone had ears for it.

Mrs. Borkman. Yes, to the branding of the name of Borkman.

Borkman. If the others had had the power, do you think they would not have acted exactly as I did?

Mrs. Borkman. No one, no one but you would have done it!

Borkman. Perhaps not. But that would have been because they had not my brains. And if they had done it, it would not have been with my aims in view. The act would have been a different act. In short, I have acquitted myself.

Ella Rentheim [*softly and appealingly*]. Oh, can you say that so confidently, Borkman?

Borkman [*nodding*]. Acquitted myself on that score. But then comes the great, crushing self-accusation.

Mrs. Borkman. What is that?

Borkman. I have skulked up there and wasted eight precious years of my life! The very day I was set free, I should have gone forth into the world—out into the steel-hard, dreamless world of reality! I should have begun at the bottom and swung myself up to the heights anew—

higher than ever before—in spite of all that lay between.

Mrs. Borkman. Oh, it would only have been the same thing over again; take my word for that.

Borkman [*shakes his head, and looks at her with a sententious air*]. It is true that nothing new happens; but what has happened does not repeat itself either. It is the eye that transforms the action. The eye, born anew, transforms the old action. [*Breaking off.*] But you do not understand this.

Mrs. Borkman [*curtly*]. No, I do not understand it.

Borkman. Ah, that is just the curse—I have never found one single soul to understand me.

Ella Rentheim [*looking at him*]. Never, Borkman?

Borkman. Except one—perhaps. Long, long ago. In the days when I did not think I needed understanding. Since then, at any rate, no one has understood me! There has been no one alive enough to my needs to be afoot and rouse me—to ring the morning bell for me—to call me up to manful work anew. And to impress upon me that I had done nothing inexpiable.

Mrs. Borkman [*with a scornful laugh*]. So, after all, you require to have that impressed on you from without?

Borkman [*with increasing indignation*]. Yes, when the whole world hisses in chorus that I have sunk never to rise again, there come moments when I almost believe it myself. [*Raising his head.*] But then my inmost assurance rises again triumphant; and that acquits me.

Mrs. Borkman [*looking harshly at him*]. Why have you never come and asked me for what you call understanding?

Borkman. What use would it have been to come to you?

Mrs. Borkman [*with a gesture of repulsion*]. You have never loved anything outside yourself; that is the secret of the whole matter.

Borkman [*proudly*]. I have loved power.

Mrs. Borkman. Yes, power!

Borkman. The power to create human happiness in wide, wide circles around me!

Mrs. Borkman. You had once the power to make me happy. Have you used it to that end?

Borkman [*without looking at her*]. Someone must generally go down in a shipwreck.

Mrs. Borkman. And your own son! Have you used your power—have you lived and labored—to make him happy?

Borkman. I do not know him.

Mrs. Borkman. No, that is true. You do not even know him.

Borkman [*harshly*]. You, his mother, have taken care of that!

Mrs. Borkman [*looking at him with a lofty air*]. Oh, you do not know what I have taken care of!

Borkman. You?

Mrs. Borkman. Yes, I. I alone.

Borkman. Then tell me.

Mrs. Borkman. I have taken care of your memory.

Borkman [*with a short dry laugh*]. My memory? Oh, indeed! It sounds almost as if I were dead already.

Mrs. Borkman [*with emphasis*]. And so you are.

Borkman [*slowly*]. Yes, perhaps you are right. [*Firing up.*] But no, no! Not yet! I have been close to the verge of death. But now I have awakened. I have come to myself. A whole life lies before me yet. I can see it awaiting me, radiant and quickening. And you—you shall see it too.

Mrs. Borkman [*raising her hand*]. Never dream of life again! Lie quiet where you are.

Ella Rentheim [*shocked*]. Gunhild! Gunhild, how can you——!

Mrs. Borkman [*not listening to her*]. I will raise the monument over your grave.

Borkman. The pillar of shame, I suppose you mean?

Mrs. Borkman [*with increasing excitement*]. Oh, no, it shall be no pillar of metal or stone. And no one shall be suffered to carve any scornful legend on the monument I shall raise. There shall be, as it were, a quickset hedge of trees and bushes, close, close around your tomb. They shall hide away all the darkness that has been. The eyes of men and the thoughts of men shall no longer dwell on John Gabriel Borkman!

Borkman [*hoarsely and cuttingly*]. And this labor of love you will perform?

Mrs. Borkman. Not by my own strength. I cannot think of that. But I have brought up one to help me, who shall live for this alone. His life shall be so pure and high and bright, that your burrowing in the dark shall be as though it had never been!

Borkman [*darkly and threateningly*]. If it is Erhart you mean, say so at once!

Mrs. Borkman [*looking him straight in the eyes*]. Yes, it is Erhart; my son; he whom you are ready to renounce in atonement for your own acts.

Borkman [*with a look toward* ELLA]. In atonement for my blackest sin.

Mrs. Borkman [*repelling the idea*]. A sin toward a stranger only. Remember the sin toward me! [*Looking triumphantly at them both.*] But he will not obey you! When I cry out to him in my need, he will come to me! It is with me that he will remain! With me, and never with anyone else. [*Suddenly listens, and cries.*] I hear him! He is here, he is here! Erhart!

ERHART BORKMAN *hastily tears open the hall door, and enters the room. He is wearing an overcoat and has his hat on.*

Erhart [*pale and anxious*]. Mother! What in Heaven's name——! [*Seeing* BORKMAN, *who is standing beside the doorway leading into the garden room, he starts and takes off his hat. After a moment's silence, he asks.*] What do you want with me, Mother? What has happened?

Mrs. Borkman [*stretching out her arms toward him*]. I want to see you, Erhart! I want to have you with me, always!

Erhart [*stammering*]. Have me——? Always? What do you mean by that?

Mrs. Borkman. I will have you, I say! There is someone who wants to take you from me!

Erhart [*recoiling a step*]. Ah—so you know?

Mrs. Borkman. Yes. Do you know it, too?

Erhart [*surprised, looking at her*]. Do *I* know it? Yes, of course.

Mrs. Borkman. Aha, so you have planned it all out! Behind my back! Erhart! Erhart!

Erhart [*quickly*]. Mother, tell me what it is you know!

Mrs. Borkman. I know everything. I know that your aunt has come here to take you from me.

Erhart. Aunt Ella!

Ella Rentheim. Oh, listen to me a moment, Erhart!

Mrs. Borkman [*continuing*]. She wants me to give you up to her! She wants to stand in your mother's place to you, Erhart. She wants you to be her son, and not mine, from this time forward. She wants you to inherit everything from her; to renounce your own name and take hers instead!

Erhart. Aunt Ella, is this true?

Ella Rentheim. Yes, it is true.

Erhart. I knew nothing of this. Why do you want to have me with you again?

Ella Rentheim. Because I feel that I am losing you here.

Mrs. Borkman [*hardly*]. You are losing him to me—yes. And that is just as it should be.

Ella Rentheim [*looking beseechingly at him*]. Erhart, I cannot afford to lose you. For, I must tell you, I am a lonely—dying woman.

Erhart. Dying——?

Ella Rentheim. Yes, dying. Will you come and be with me to the end? Attach yourself wholly to me? Be to me, as though you were my own child——?

Mrs. Borkman [*interrupting*]. And forsake your mother, and perhaps your mission in life as well? Will you, Erhart?

Ella Rentheim. I am condemned to death. Answer me, Erhart.

Erhart [*warmly, with emotion*]. Aunt Ella, you have been unspeakably good to me. With you I grew up in as perfect happiness as any boy can ever have known——

Mrs. Borkman. Erhart, Erhart!

Ella Rentheim. Oh, how glad I am that you can still say that!

Erhart. But I cannot sacrifice myself to you now. It is not possible for me to devote myself wholly to taking a son's place toward you.

Mrs. Borkman [*triumphing*]. Ah, I knew it! You shall not have him! You shall not have him, Ella!

Ella Rentheim [*sadly*]. I see it. You have won him back.

Mrs. Borkman. Yes, yes! Mine he is, and mine he shall remain! Erhart, say it is so, dear; we two have still a long way to go together, have we not?

Erhart [*struggling with himself*]. Mother, I may as well tell you plainly——

Mrs. Borkman [*eagerly*]. What?

Erhart. I am afraid it is only a very little way you and I can go together.

Mrs. Borkman [*stands as though thunderstruck*]. What do you mean by that?

Erhart [*plucking up spirit*]. Good heavens, Mother, I am young, after all! I feel as if the close air of this room must stifle me in the end.

Mrs. Borkman. Close air? Here—with me?

Erhart. Yes, here with you, Mother.

Ella Rentheim. Then come with me, Erhart.

Erhart. Oh, Aunt Ella, it's not a whit better with you. It's different, but no better—no better for me. It smells of rose leaves and lavender there too; it is as airless there as here.

Mrs. Borkman [*shaken, but having recovered her composure with an effort*]. Airless in your mother's room, you say!

Erhart [*in growing impatience*]. Yes, I don't know how else to express it. All this morbid watchfulness and—and idolization, or whatever you like to call it—— I can't endure it any longer!

Mrs. Borkman [*looking at him with deep solemnity*]. Have you forgotten what you have consecrated your life to, Erhart?

Erhart [*with an outburst*]. Oh, say rather what you have consecrated my life to. You, you have been my will. You have never given me leave to have any of my own. But now I cannot bear this yoke any longer. I am young; remember that, Mother. [*With a polite, considerate glance toward* BORKMAN.] I cannot consecrate my life to making atonement for another—whoever that other may be.

Mrs. Borkman [*seized with a growing anxiety*]. Who is it that has transformed you, Erhart?

Erhart [*struck*]. Who? Can you not conceive that it is I myself?

Mrs. Borkman. No, no, no! You have come under some strange power. You are not in your mother's power any longer; nor in your—your foster mother's either.

Erhart [*with labored defiance*]. I am in my own power, Mother! And working my own will!

Borkman [*advancing toward* ERHART]. Then perhaps my hour has come at last.

ERHART [*distantly and with measured politeness*]. How so? How do you mean, sir?

Mrs. Borkman [*scornfully*]. Yes, you may well ask that.

Borkman [*continuing undisturbed*]. Listen, Erhart—will you not cast in your lot with your father? Is it not through any other man's life that a man who has fallen can be raised up again. These are only empty fables that have been told to you down here in the airless room. If you were to set yourself to live your life like all the saints together, it would be of no use whatever to me.

Erhart [*with measured respectfulness*]. That is very true indeed.

Borkman. Yes, it is. And it would be of no use either if I should resign myself to wither away in abject penitence. I have tried to feed myself upon hopes and dreams, all through these years. But I am not the man to be content with that; and now I mean to have done with dreaming.

Erhart [*with a slight bow*]. And what will—what will you do, sir?

Borkman. I will work out my own redemption, that is what I will do. I will begin at the bottom again. It is only through his present and his future that a man can atone for his past. Through work, indefatigable work, for all that, in my youth, seemed to give life its meaning—and that now seems a thousand times greater than it did then. Erhart, will you join with me and help me in this new life?

Mrs. Borkman [*raising her hand warningly*]. Do not do it, Erhart!

Ella Rentheim [*warmly*]. Yes, yes, do it! Oh, help him, Erhart!

Mrs. Borkman. And you advise him to do that? You, the lonely, dying woman.

Ella Rentheim. I don't care about myself.

Mrs. Borkman. No, so long as it is not I that take him from you.

Ella Rentheim. Precisely so, Gunhild.

Borkman. Will you, Erhart?

Erhart [*wrung with pain*]. Father, I cannot now. It is utterly impossible!

Borkman. What do you want to do then?

Erhart [*with a sudden glow*]. I am young! I want to live, for once in a way, as well as other people! I want to live my own life!

Ella Rentheim. You cannot give up two or three little months to brighten the close of a poor waning life?

Erhart. I cannot, Aunt, however much I may wish to.

Ella Rentheim. Not for the sake of one who loves you so dearly?

Erhart. I solemnly assure you, Aunt Ella, I cannot.

Mrs. Borkman [*looking sharply at him*]. And your mother has no power over you either, any more?

Erhart. I will always love you, Mother; but I cannot go on living for you alone. This is no life for me.

Borkman. Then come and join with me, after all! For life, life means work, Erhart. Come, we two will go forth into life and work together!

Erhart [*passionately*]. Yes, but I don't want to work now! For I am young! That's what I never realized before; but now the knowledge is tingling through every vein in my body. I will not work! I will only live, live, live!

Mrs. Borkman [*with a cry of divination*]. Erhart, what will you live for?

Erhart [*with sparkling eyes*]. For happiness, Mother!

Mrs. Borkman. And where do you think you can find that?

Erhart. I have found it, already!

Mrs. Borkman [*shrieks*]. Erhart!

ERHART *goes quickly to the hall door and throws it open.*

Erhart [*calls out*]. Fanny, you can come in now!

MRS. WILTON, *in outdoor wraps, appears on the threshold.*

Mrs. Borkman [*with uplifted hands*]. Mrs. Wilton!

Mrs. Wilton [*hesitating a little, with an inquiring glance at* ERHART]. Do you want me to——?

Erhart. Yes, now you can come in. I have told them everything.

MRS. WILTON *comes forward into the room.* ERHART *closes the door behind her. She bows formally to* BORKMAN, *who returns her bow in silence. A short pause.*

Mrs. Wilton [*in a subdued but firm voice*]. So the word has been spoken—and I suppose you all think I have brought a great calamity upon this house?

Mrs. Borkman [*slowly, looking hard at her*]. You have crushed the last remnant of interest in life for me. [*With an outburst.*] But all this—all this is utterly impossible!

Mrs. Wilton. I can quite understand that it must appear impossible to you, Mrs. Borkman.

Mrs. Borkman. Yes, you can surely see for yourself that it is impossible. Or what——?

Mrs. Wilton. I should rather say that it seems highly improbable. But it's so, nonetheless.

Mrs. Borkman [*turning*]. Are you really in earnest about this, Erhart?

Erhart. This means happiness for me, Mother—all the

beauty and happiness of life. That is all I can say to you.

Mrs. Borkman [*clenching her hands together; to* Mrs.
WILTON]. Oh, how you have cajoled and deluded my
unhappy son!

Mrs. Wilton [*raising her head proudly*]. I have done
nothing of the sort.

Mrs. Borkman. You have not, you say!

Mrs. Wilton. No. I have neither cajoled nor deluded him.
Erhart came to me of his own free will. And of my own
free will I went out halfway to meet him.

Mrs. Borkman [*measuring her scornfully with her eye*].
Yes, indeed! That I can easily believe.

Mrs. Wilton [*with self-control*]. Mrs. Borkman, there
are forces in human life that you seem to know very little
about.

Mrs. Borkman. What forces, may I ask?

Mrs. Wilton. The forces which ordain that two people
shall join their lives together, indissolubly—and fearlessly.

Mrs. Borkman [*with a smile*]. I thought you were already indissolubly bound—to another.

Mrs. Wilton [*shortly*]. That other has deserted me.

Mrs. Borkman. But he is still living, they say.

Mrs. Wilton. He's dead to me.

Erhart [*insistently*]. Yes, Mother, he is dead to Fanny.
And besides, this other makes no difference to me!

Mrs. Borkman [*looking sternly at him*]. So you know all
this—about the other.

Erhart. Yes, Mother, I know quite well—all about it!

Mrs. Borkman. And yet you can say that it makes no
difference to you?

Erhart [*with defiant petulance*]. I can only tell you that
it is happiness I must have! I am young! I want to live, live,
live!

Mrs. Borkman. Yes, you are young, Erhart. Too young
for this.

Mrs. Wilton [*firmly and earnestly*]. You must not think,
Mrs. Borkman, that I haven't said the same to him. I have
laid my whole life before him. Again and again I have
reminded him that I am seven years older than he——

Erhart [*interrupting*]. Oh, nonsense, Fanny—I knew
that all the time.

Mrs. Wilton. But nothing—nothing was of any use.

Mrs. Borkman. Indeed? Nothing? Then why did you not

dismiss him without more ado? Close your door to him?
You should have done that, and done it in time!

Mrs. Wilton [*looks at her, and says in a low voice*]. I
could not do that, Mrs. Borkman.

Mrs. Borkman. Why could you not?

Mrs. Wilton. Because for me too this meant happiness.

Mrs. Borkman [*scornfully*]. H'm, happiness, happiness——

Mrs. Wilton. I have never before known happiness in
life. And I cannot possibly drive happiness away from
me, merely because it comes so late.

Mrs. Borkman. And how long do you think this happiness will last?

Erhart [*interrupting*]. Whether it lasts or does not last,
Mother, it doesn't matter now!

Mrs. Borkman [*in anger*]. Blind boy that you are! Do
you not see where all this is leading you?

Erhart. I don't want to look into the future. I don't want
to look around me in any direction; I am only determined
to live my own life—at last!

Mrs. Borkman [*with deep pain*]. And you call this life,
Erhart!

Erhart. Don't you see how lovely she is!

Mrs. Borkman [*wringing her hands*]. And I have to bear
this load of shame as well!

Borkman [*at the back, harshly and cuttingly*]. Ho—you
are used to bearing things of that sort, Gunhild!

Ella Rentheim [*imploringly*]. Borkman!

Erhart [*similarly*]. Father!

Mrs. Borkman. Day after day I shall have to see my own
son linked to a—a——

Erhart [*interrupting her harshly*]. You shall see nothing
of the kind, Mother! You may make your mind easy on
that point. I shall not remain here.

Mrs. Wilton [*quickly and with decision*]. We are going
away, Mrs. Borkman.

Mrs. Borkman [*turning pale*]. Are you going away, too?
Together, no doubt?

Mrs. Wilton [*nodding*]. Yes, I am going abroad, to the
South. I am taking a young girl with me. And Erhart is
going along with us.

Mrs. Borkman. With you—and a young girl?

Mrs. Wilton. Yes. It is little Frida Foldal, whom I have

had living with me. I want her to go abroad and get more instruction in music.

Mrs. Borkman. So you are taking her with you?

Mrs. Wilton. Yes; I can't well send her out into the world alone.

Mrs. Borkman [*suppressing a smile*]. What do you say to this, Erhart?

Erhart [*with some embarrassment, shrugging his shoulders*]. Well, Mother, since Fanny will have it so——

Mrs. Borkman [*coldly*]. And when does this distinguished party set out, if one may ask?

Mrs. Wilton. We are going at once—tonight. My covered sledge is waiting on the road, outside the Hinkels'.

Mrs. Borkman [*looking her over from head to foot*]. Aha! so that was what the party meant?

Mrs. Wilton [*smiling*]. Yes, Erhart and I were the whole party. And little Frida, of course.

Mrs. Borkman. And where is she now?

Mrs. Wilton. She is sitting in the sledge waiting for us.

Erhart [*in painful embarrassment*]. Mother, surely you can understand? I would have spared you all this—you and everyone.

Mrs. Borkman [*looks at him, deeply pained*]. You would have gone away from me without saying good-by?

Erhart. Yes, I thought that would be best; best for all of us. Our boxes were packed and everything settled. But of course when you sent for me, I—— [*Holding out his hands to her.*] Good-by, Mother.

Mrs. Borkman [*with a gesture of repulsion*]. Don't touch me!

Erhart [*gently*]. Is that your last word?

Mrs. Borkman [*sternly*]. Yes.

Erhart [*turning*]. Good-by to you, then, Aunt Ella.

Ella Rentheim [*pressing his hands*]. Good-bye, Erhart! And live your life—and be as happy—as happy as ever you can.

Erhart. Thanks, Aunt. [*Bowing to* BORKMAN.] Good-by, Father. [*Whispers to* MRS. WILTON.] Let us get away, the sooner the better.

Mrs. Wilton [*in a low voice*]. Yes, let us.

Mrs. Borkman [*with a malignant smile*]. Mrs. Wilton, do you think you are acting quite wisely in taking that girl with you?

Mrs. Wilton [*returning the smile, half ironically, half*

seriously]. Men are so unstable, Mrs. Borkman. And women too. When Erhart is done with me—and I with him—then it will be well for us both that he, poor fellow, should have someone to fall back upon.

Mrs. Borkman. But you yourself?

Mrs. Wilton. Oh, I shall know what to do, I assure you. Good-by to you all!

She bows and goes out by the hall door. ERHART *stands for a moment as though wavering; then he turns and follows her.*

Mrs. Borkman [*dropping her folded hands*]. Childless.

Borkman [*as though awakening to a resolution*]. [*He goes hastily toward the door.*] Then out into the storm alone! My hat! My cloak!

Ella Rentheim [*in terror, stopping him*]. John Gabriel, where are you going?

Borkman. Out into the storm of life, I tell you. Let me go, Ella!

Ella Rentheim [*holding him back*]. No, no, I won't let you out! You are ill. I can see it in your face!

Borkman. Let me go, I tell you! [*He tears himself away from her, and goes out by the hall.*]

Ella Rentheim [*in the doorway*]. Help me to hold him, Gunhild!

Mrs. Borkman [*coldly and sharply, standing in the middle of the room*]. I will not try to hold anyone in all the world. Let them go away from me—both the one and the other! As far—as far as ever they please. [*Suddenly, with a piercing shriek.*] Erhart, don't leave me!

She rushes with outstretched arms toward the door. ELLA RENTHEIM *stops her.*

ACT FOURTH

An open space outside the main building, which lies to the right. A projecting corner of it is visible, with a door approached by a flight of low stone steps. The background consists of steep fir-clad slopes, quite close at hand. On the left are small scattered trees, forming the margin of a wood. The snowstorm has ceased; but the newly fallen snow lies deep around. The fir branches droop under heavy

*loads of snow. The night is dark, with drifting clouds. Now
and then the moon gleams out faintly. Only a dim light is
reflected from the snow.*

BORKMAN, MRS. BORKMAN *and* ELLA RENTHEIM *are standing upon the steps,* BORKMAN *leaning wearily against the
wall of the house. He has an old-fashioned cape thrown
over his shoulders, holds a soft gray felt hat in one hand
and a thick knotted stick in the other.* ELLA RENTHEIM
carries her cloak over her arm. MRS. BORKMAN'S *great
shawl has slipped down over her shoulders, so that her hair
is uncovered.*

ELLA RENTHEIM [*barring the way for* MRS. BORKMAN].
Don't go after him, Gunhild!

Mrs. Borkman [*in fear and agitation*]. Let me pass, I
say! He must not go away from me!

Ella Rentheim. It is utterly useless, I tell you! You will
never overtake him.

Mrs. Borkman. Let me go, Ella! I will cry aloud after
him all down the road. And he must hear his mother's cry!

Ella Rentheim. He cannot hear you. You may be sure he
is in the sledge already.

Mrs. Borkman. No, no; he can't be in the sledge yet!

Ella Rentheim. The doors are closed upon him long ago,
believe me.

Mrs. Borkman [*in despair*]. If he is in the sledge, then he
is there with her, with her—her!

Borkman [*laughing gloomily*]. Then he probably won't
hear his mother's cry.

Mrs. Borkman. No, he will not hear it. [*Listening.*] Hark!
what is that?

Ella Rentheim [*also listening*]. It sounds like sledge
bells.

Mrs. Borkman [*with a suppressed scream*]. It is her
sledge!

Ella Rentheim. Perhaps it's another.

Mrs. Borkman. No, no, it is Mrs. Wilton's covered sledge!
I know the silver bells! Hark! Now they are driving right
past here, at the foot of the hill!

Ella Rentheim [*quickly*]. Gunhild, if you want to cry out
to him, now is the time! Perhaps after all——! [*The tinkle
of the bells sounds close at hand, in the wood.*] Make haste,
Gunhild! Now they are right under us!

Mrs. Borkman [*stands for a moment undecided, then she stiffens and says sternly and coldly*]. No. I will not cry out to him. Let Erhart Borkman pass away from me—far, far away—to what he calls life and happiness.

The sound dies away in the distance.

Ella Rentheim [*after a moment*]. Now the bells are out of hearing.

Mrs. Borkman. They sounded like funeral bells.

Borkman [*with a dry suppressed laugh*]. Oho—it is not for me they are ringing tonight!

Mrs. Borkman. No, but for me—and for him who has gone from me.

Ella Rentheim [*nodding thoughtfully*]. Who knows if, after all, they may not be ringing in life and happiness for him, Gunhild.

Mrs. Borkman [*with sudden animation, looking hard at her*]. Life and happiness, you say!

Ella Rentheim. For a little while at any rate.

Mrs. Borkman. Could you endure to let him know life and happiness, with her?

Ella Rentheim [*with warmth and feeling*]. Indeed I could, with all my heart and soul!

Mrs. Borkman [*coldly*]. Then you must be richer than I am in the power of love.

Ella Rentheim [*looking far away*]. Perhaps it is the lack of love that keeps that power alive.

Mrs. Borkman [*fixing her eyes on her*]. If that is so, then I shall soon be as rich as you, Ella. [*She turns and goes into the house.*]

Ella Rentheim [*stands for a time looking with a troubled expression at* BORKMAN; *then lays her hand cautiously upon his shoulder*]. Come, John—you must come in, too.

Borkman [*as if awakening*]. I?

Ella Rentheim. Yes, this winter air is too keen for you; I can see that, John. So come—come in with me—into the house, into the warmth.

Borkman [*angrily*]. Up to the gallery again, I suppose.

Ella Rentheim. No, rather into the room below.

Borkman [*his anger flaming forth*]. Never will I set foot under that roof again!

Ella Rentheim. Where will you go then? So late, and in the dark, John?

Borkman [*putting on his hat*]. First of all, I will go out and see to all my buried treasures.

Ella Rentheim [*looking anxiously at him*]. John—I don't understand you.

Borkman [*with laughter, interrupted by coughing*]. Oh, it is not hidden plunder I mean; don't be afraid of that, Ella. [*Stopping, and pointing outwards.*] Do you see that man there? Who is it?

VILHELM FOLDAL, *in an old cape, covered with snow, with his hatbrim turned down, and a large umbrella in his hand, advances toward the corner of the house, laboriously stumbling through the snow. He is noticeably lame in his left foot.*

Vilhelm! What do you want with me again?

Foldal [*looking up*]. Good heavens, are you out on the steps, John Gabriel? [*Bowing.*] And Mrs. Borkman, too, I see.

Borkman [*shortly*]. This is not Mrs. Borkman.

Foldal. Oh, I beg your pardon. You see, I have lost my spectacles in the snow. But how is it that you, who never put your foot out of doors——?

Borkman [*carelessly and gaily*]. It is high time I should come out into the open air again, don't you see? Nearly three years in detention—five years in prison—eight years in the gallery up there——

Ella Rentheim [*distressed*]. Borkman, I beg you——

Foldal. Ah, yes, yes, yes!

Borkman. But I want to know what has brought you here.

Foldal [*still standing at the foot of the steps*]. I wanted to come up to you, John Gabriel. I felt I must come to you, in the gallery. Ah me, that gallery——!

Borkman. Did you want to come up to me after I had shown you the door?

Foldal. Oh, I couldn't let that stand in the way.

Borkman. What have you done to your foot? I see you are limping.

Foldal. Yes, what do you think—I have been run over.

Ella Rentheim. Run over!

Foldal. Yes, by a covered sledge.

Borkman. Oho!

Foldal. With two horses. They came down the hill at

a tearing gallop. I couldn't get out of the way quick enough; and so——

Ella Rentheim. And so they ran over you?

Foldal. They came right down upon me, madam—or miss. They came right upon me and sent me rolling over and over in the snow—so that I lost my spectacles and got my umbrella broken. [*Rubbing his leg.*] And my ankle a little hurt, too.

Borkman [*laughing inwardly*]. Do you know who were in that sledge, Vilhelm?

Foldal. No, how could I see? It was a covered sledge, and the curtains were down. And the driver didn't stop a moment after he had sent me spinning. But it doesn't matter a bit, for—— [*With an outburst.*] Oh, I am so happy, so happy!

Borkman. Happy?

Foldal. Well, I don't exactly know what to call it. But I think happy is the nearest word. For something so wonderful has happened! And that is why I couldn't help—I had to come out and share my happiness with you, John Gabriel.

Borkman [*harshly*]. Well, share away then!

Ella Rentheim. Oh, but first take your friend indoors with you, Borkman.

Borkman [*sternly*]. I have told you I will not go into the house.

Ella Rentheim. But don't you hear, he has been run over!

Borkman. Oh, we are all of us run over, sometime or other in life. The thing is to jump up again, and let no one see you are hurt.

Foldal. That is a profound saying, John Gabriel. But I can easily tell you my story out here, in a few words.

Borkman [*more mildly*]. Yes, please do, Vilhelm.

Foldal. Well, now you shall hear! Only think, when I got home this evening after I had been with you, what did I find but a letter. Can you guess who it was from?

Borkman. Possibly from your little Frida?

Foldal. Precisely! Think of your hitting on it at once! Yes, it was a long—a pretty long letter from Frida. A footman had brought it. And can you imagine what was in it?

Borkman. Perhaps it was to say good-by to her mother and you?

Foldal. Exactly! How good you are at guessing, John Gabriel! Yes, she tells me that Mrs. Wilton has taken such a fancy to her, and she is to go abroad with her and study music. And Mrs. Wilton has engaged a first-rate teacher who is to accompany them on the journey—and to read with Frida, too. For unfortunately she has been a good deal neglected in some branches, you see.

Borkman [*shaken with inward laughter*]. Of course, of course—I see it all quite clearly, Vilhelm.

Foldal [*eagerly continuing*]. And only think, she knew nothing about the arrangement until this evening; at that party, you know, h'm! And yet she found time to write to me. And the letter is such a beautiful one—so warm and affectionate, I assure you. There is not a trace of contempt for her father in it. And then what a delicate thought it was to say good-by to us by letter—before she started. [*Laughing.*] But of course I can't let her go like that.

Borkman [*looks inquiringly at him*]. How so?

Foldal. She tells me that they start early tomorrow morning; quite early.

Borkman. Oh indeed—tomorrow? Does she tell you that?

Foldal [*laughing and rubbing his hands*]. Yes; but I know a trick worth two of that, you see! I am going straight up to Mrs. Wilton's——

Borkman. This evening?

Foldal. Oh, it's not so very late yet. And even if the house is shut up, I shall ring; without hesitation. For I must and will see Frida before she starts. Good night, good night! [*Makes a movement to go.*]

Borkman. Stop a moment, my poor Vilhelm; you may spare yourself that heavy bit of road.

Foldal. Oh, you are thinking of my ankle——

Borkman. Yes; and in any case you won't get in at Mrs. Wilton's.

Foldal. Yes, indeed I will. I'll go on ringing and knocking till someone comes and lets me in. For I must and will see Frida.

Ella Rentheim. Your daughter has gone already, Mr. Foldal.

Foldal [*stands as though thunderstruck*]. Has Frida gone already! Are you quite sure? Who told you?

Borkman. We had it from her future teacher.

Foldal. Indeed? And who is he?

Borkman. A certain Mr. Erhart Borkman.

Foldal [*beaming with joy*]. Your son, John Gabriel! Is he going with them?

Borkman. Yes; it is he that is to help Mrs. Wilton with little Frida's education.

Foldal. Oh, Heaven be praised! Then the child is in the best of hands. But is it quite certain that they have started with her already?

Borkman. They took her away in that sledge which ran over you on the road.

Foldal [*clasping his hands*]. To think that my little Frida was in that magnificent sledge!

Borkman [*nodding*]. Yes, yes, Vilhelm, your daughter has come to drive in her carriage. And Master Erhart, too. Tell me, did you notice the silver bells?

Foldal. Yes, indeed. Silver bells did you say? Were they silver? Real, genuine silver bells?

Borkman. You may be quite sure of that. Everything was genuine—both outside and in.

Foldal [*in quiet emotion*]. Isn't it strange how fortune can sometimes befriend one? It is my—my little gift of song that has transmuted itself into music in Frida. So after all, it is not for nothing that I was born a poet. For now she is going forth into the great wide world, that I once yearned so passionately to see. Little Frida sets out in a splendid covered sledge with silver bells on the harness——

Borkman. And runs over her father.

Foldal [*happily*]. Oh, pooh! What does it matter about me, if only the child——! Well, so I am too late, then, after all. I must just go home again and comfort her mother. I left her crying in the kitchen.

Borkman. Crying?

Foldal [*smiling*]. Yes, would you believe it, she was crying her eyes out when I came away.

Borkman. And you are laughing, Vilhelm?

Foldal. Yes, *I* am, of course. But she, poor thing, she doesn't know any better, you see. Well, good-by! It's a good thing I have the tramway so handy. Good-by, good-by, John Gabriel. Good-by, Madam. [*He bows and limps laboriously out by the way he came.*]

Borkman [*stands silent for a moment, gazing before him*]. Good-by, Vilhelm! It is not the first time in your life that you've been run over, old friend.

Ella Rentheim [*looking at him with suppressed anxiety*]. You are so pale, John, so very pale.

Borkman. That is the effect of the prison air up yonder.

Ella Rentheim. I have never seen you like this before.

Borkman. No, for I suppose you have never seen an escaped convict before.

Ella Rentheim. Oh, do come into the house with me, John!

Borkman. It is no use trying to lure me in. I have told you——

Ella Rentheim. But when I beg and implore you——? For your own sake——

THE MAID *opens the door, and stands in the doorway.*

The Maid. I beg pardon. Mrs. Borkman told me to lock the front door now.

Borkman [*in a low voice, to* ELLA]. You see, they want to lock me up again!

Ella Rentheim [*to* THE MAID]. Mr. Borkman is not quite well. He wants to have a little fresh air before coming in.

The Maid. But Mrs. Borkman told me to——

Ella Rentheim. I shall lock the door. Just leave the key in the lock.

The Maid. Oh, very well; I'll leave it. [*She goes into the house again.*]

Borkman [*stands silent for a moment, and listens; then goes hastily down the steps and out into the open space*]. Now I am outside the walls, Ella! Now they will never get hold of me again!

Ella Rentheim [*who has gone down to him*]. But you are a free man in there, too, John. You can come and go just as you please.

Borkman [*softly, as though in terror*]. Never under a roof again! It is so good to be out here in the night. If I went up into the gallery now, ceiling and walls would shrink together and crush me—crush me flat as a fly.

Ella Rentheim. But where will you go, then?

Borkman. I will simply go on, and on, and on. I will try if I cannot make my way to freedom, and life, and human beings again. Will you go with me, Ella?

Ella Rentheim. I? Now?

Borkman. Yes, at once!

Ella Rentheim. But how far?

Borkman. As far as ever I can.

Ella Rentheim. Oh, but think what you are doing! Out in this raw, cold winter night——

Borkman [*speaking very hoarsely*]. Oho—my lady is concerned about her health? Yes, yes—I know it is delicate.

Ella Rentheim. It is your health I am concerned about.

Borkman. Hohoho! A dead man's health! I can't help laughing at you, Ella! [*He moves onwards.*]

Ella Rentheim [*following him: holding him back*]. What did you call yourself?

Borkman. A dead man, I said. Don't you remember, Gunhild told me to lie quiet where I was?

Ella Rentheim [*with resolution, throwing her cloak around her*]. I will go with you, John.

Borkman. Yes, we two belong to each other, Ella. [*Advancing.*] So come!

They have gradually passed into the low wood on the left. It conceals them little by little, until they are quite lost to sight. The house and the open space disappear. The landscape, consisting of wooded slopes and ridges, slowly changes and grows wilder and wilder.

Ella Rentheim's Voice [*is heard in the wood to the right*]. Where are we going, John? I don't recognize this place.

Borkman's Voice [*higher up*]. Just follow my footprints in the snow!

Ella Rentheim's Voice. But why need we climb so high?

Borkman's Voice [*nearer at hand*]. We must go up the winding path.

Ella Rentheim [*still hidden*]. Oh, but I can't go much farther.

Borkman [*on the verge of the wood to the right*]. Come, come! We are not far from the view now. There used to be a seat there.

Ella Rentheim [*appearing among the trees*]. Do you remember it?

Borkman. You can rest there.

They have emerged upon a small high-lying, open plateau in the wood. The mountain rises abruptly behind them. To the left, far below, an extensive fiord landscape, with high ranges in the distance, towering one above the other. On the plateau, to the left, a dead fir tree with a bench under it. The snow lies deep upon the plateau.

BORKMAN *and, after him,* ELLA RENTHEIM *enter from the right and wade with difficulty through the snow.*

[*Stopping at the verge of the steep declivity on the left.*] Come here, Ella, and you shall see.

Ella Rentheim [*coming up to him*]. What do you want to show me, John?

Borkman [*pointing outwards*]. Do you see how free and open the country lies before us—away to the far horizon?

Ella Rentheim. We have often sat on this bench before, and looked out into a much, much farther distance.

Borkman. It was a dreamland we then looked out over.

Ella Rentheim [*nodding sadly*]. It was the dreamland of our life, yes. And now that land is buried in snow. And the old tree is dead.

Borkman [*not listening to her*]. Can you see the smoke of the great steamships out on the fiord?

Ella Rentheim. No.

Borkman. I can. They come and they go. They weave a network of fellowship all round the world. They shed light and warmth over the souls of men in many thousands of homes. That was what I dreamed of doing.

Ella Rentheim [*softly*]. And it remained a dream.

Borkman. It remained a dream, yes. [*Listening.*] And hark, down by the river, dear! The factories are working! My factories! All those that I would have created! Listen! Do you hear them humming? The night shift is on—so they are working night and day. Hark! hark! the wheels are whirling and the bands are flashing—round and round and round. Can't you hear, Ella?

Ella Rentheim. No.

Borkman. I can hear it.

Ella Rentheim [*anxiously*]. I think you are mistaken, John.

Borkman [*more and more fired*]. Oh, but all these—they are only like the outworks around the kingdom, I tell you!

Ella Rentheim. The kingdom, you say? What kingdom?

Borkman. My kingdom, of course! The kingdom I was on the point of conquering when I—when I died.

Ella Rentheim [*shaken, in a low voice*]. Oh, John, John!

Borkman. And now there it lies—defenseless, masterless —exposed to all the robbers and plunderers. Ella, do you see the mountain chains there—far away? They soar, they tower aloft, one behind the other! That is my vast, my infinite, inexhaustible kingdom!

Ella Rentheim. Oh, but there comes an icy blast from that kingdom, John!

Borkman. That blast is the breath of life to me. That blast comes to me like a greeting from subject spirits. I seem to touch them, the prisoned millions; I can see the veins of metal stretch out their winding, branching, luring arms to me. I saw them before my eyes like living shapes, that night when I stood in the strong room with the candle in my hand. You begged to be liberated, and I tried to free you. But my strength failed me; and the treasure sank back into the deep again. [*With outstretched hands.*] But I will whisper it to you here in the stillness of the night: I love you, as you lie there spellbound in the deeps and the darkness! I love you, unborn treasures, yearning for the light! I love you, with all your shining train of power and glory! I love you, love you, love you!

Ella Rentheim [*in suppressed but rising agitation*]. Yes, your love is still down there, John. It has always been rooted there. But here, in the light of day, here there was a living, warm, human heart that throbbed and glowed for you. And this heart you crushed. Oh, worse than that! Ten times worse! You sold it for—for——

Borkman [*trembles; a cold shudder seems to go through him*]. For the kingdom—and the power—and the glory—you mean?

Ella Rentheim. Yes, that is what I mean. I have said it once before tonight: you have murdered the love life in the woman who loved you. And whom you loved in return, so far as you could love anyone. [*With uplifted arm.*] And therefore I prophesy to you, John Gabriel Borkman —you will never touch the price you demanded for the murder. You will never enter in triumph into your cold, dark kingdom!

Borkman [*staggers to the bench and seats himself heavily*]. I almost fear your prophecy will come true, Ella.

Ella Rentheim [*going up to him*]. You must not fear it, John. That is the best thing that can happen to you.

Borkman [*with a shriek; clutching at his breast*]. Ah——! [*Feebly.*] Now it let me go again.

Ella Rentheim [*shaking him*]. What was it, John?

Borkman [*sinking down against the back of the seat*]. It was a hand of ice that clutched at my heart.

Ella Rentheim. John! Did you feel the ice-hand again!

Borkman [*murmurs*]. No. No ice-hand. It was a metal hand. [*He sinks right down upon the bench.*]

Ella Rentheim [*tears off her cloak and throws it over him*]. Lie still where you are! I will go and bring help for you.

She goes a step or two toward the right; then she stops, returns, and carefully feels his pulse and touches his face.

[*Softly and firmly.*] No. It is best so, John Borkman. Best so for you. [*She spreads the cloak closer around him, and sinks down in the snow in front of the bench. A short silence.*]

MRS. BORKMAN, *wrapped in a mantle, comes through the wood on the right.* THE MAID *goes before her carrying a lantern.*

The Maid [*throwing the light upon the snow*]. Yes, yes, ma'am, here are their tracks.

Mrs. Borkman [*peering around*]. Yes, here they are! They are sitting there on the bench. [*Calls.*] Ella!

Ella Rentheim [*rising*]. Are you looking for us?

Mrs. Borkman [*sternly*]. Yes, you see I have to.

Ella Rentheim [*pointing*]. Look, there he lies, Gunhild.

Mrs. Borkman. Sleeping?

Ella Rentheim. A long, deep sleep, I think.

Mrs. Borkman [*with an outburst*]. Ella! [*Controls herself and asks in a low voice.*] Did he do it—of his own accord?

Ella Rentheim. No.

Mrs. Borkman [*relieved*]. Not by his own hand then?

Ella Rentheim. No. It was an ice-cold metal hand that gripped him by the heart.

Mrs. Borkman [*to* THE MAID]. Go for help. Get the men to come up from the farm.

The Maid. Yes, I will, ma'am. [*To herself.*] Lord save us! [*She goes out through the woods to the right.*]

Mrs. Borkman [*standing behind the bench*]. So the night air has killed him——

Ella Rentheim. So it appears.

Mrs. Borkman. ——strong man that he was.

Ella Rentheim [*coming in front of the bench*]. Will you not look at him, Gunhild?

Mrs. Borkman [*with a gesture of repulsion*]. No, no, no. [*Lowering her voice.*] He was a miner's son, John Gabriel Borkman. He could not live in the fresh air.

Ella Rentheim. It was rather the cold that killed him.

Mrs. Borkman [*shakes her head*]. The cold, you say? The cold—that had killed him long ago.

Ella Rentheim [*nodding to her*]. Yes—and changed us two into shadows.

Mrs. Borkman. You are right there.

Ella Rentheim [*with a painful smile*]. A dead man and two shadows—that is what the cold has made of us.

Mrs. Borkman. Yes, the coldness of heart.—And now I think we two may hold out our hands to each other, Ella.

Ella Rentheim. I think we may, now.

Mrs. Borkman. We twin sisters—over him we have both loved.

Ella Rentheim. We two shadows—over the dead man.

Mrs. Borkman *behind the bench, and* Ella Rentheim *in front of it, take each other's hand.*

WHEN WE DEAD AWAKEN

A Dramatic Epilogue

(1899)

INTRODUCTION

FROM *Pillars of Society* to *John Gabriel Borkman,* Ibsen's
plays had followed each other at regular intervals of two
years, save when his indignation over the abuse heaped
upon *Ghosts* reduced to a single year the interval between
that play and *An Enemy of the People. John Gabriel
Borkman* having appeared in 1896, its successor was expected in 1898; but Christmas came and brought no
rumor of a new play. In a man now seventy, this breach of
a long-established habit seemed ominous. The new Na-
tional Theatre in Christiania was opened in September of
the following year; and when I then met Ibsen (for the
last time) he told me that he was actually at work on a
new play, which he thought of calling a "Dramatic Epilogue." "He wrote *When We Dead Awaken,*" says Dr.
Elias, "with such labor and such passionate agitation, so
spasmodically and so feverishly, that those around him
were almost alarmed. He must get on with it, he must get
on! He seemed to hear the beating of dark pinions over
his head. He seemed to feel the grim Visitant, who had
accompanied Alfred Allmers on the mountain paths, already standing behind him with uplifted hands. His rel-
atives are firmly convinced that he knew quite clearly
that this would be his last play, that he was to write no
more. And soon the blow fell."

The *Literary Remains* contain some preliminary jottings
for *When We Dead Awaken,* and a rejected draft of the
final scene. From the jottings it appears that the play was
to have been called *The Resurrection Day,* and that Ibsen
originally thought of introducing at least two characters
whom he ultimately suppressed—the Physician at the
Baths, "a youngish, intelligent man," and "the Tattling
Lady from the capital" who "is considered immensely
amusing by the patients," and is "malicious out of thought-
lessness." At the end of a rough scenario of the first act
there occurs the following curious reflection: "In this
country it is only the mountains which have any resonance

[literally "give an echo"] not the people." In the draft of the last scene, Rubek, Irene, Ulfheim and Maia are all assembled outside Ulfheim's hut. The fragment begins thus:

> *Maia* (*interrupting*). Is it not strange that we four should meet here in the middle of the wild mountains?
> *Rubek.* You with an eagle-shooter, and I with—(*to Irene*)—with what shall I say?
> *Irene.* With a shot eagle.
> *Maia.* Shot?
> *Irene.* Winged, madam.

Ulfheim unlocks the hut, and produces from it champagne and glasses, which he fills.

> *Ulfheim* (*to Maia*). What shall we drink to, honored lady?
> *Maia.* Let us drink to freedom! [*She empties her glass at one draught.*]
> *Rubek.* Yes, let us drink to freedom. [*He drinks.*]
> *Irene.* And to the courage which dares to use it. [*She takes a sip from her glass and pours the rest on the ground.*]

After Ulfheim and Maia have departed, Rubek and Irene have a last conversation which ends thus:

> *Irene.* The craving for life is dead in me. Now I have arisen, and I see that life lies a corpse. The whole of life lies on its bier—[*The clouds droop slowly down in the form of a clammy mist*]. See how the shroud is drooping over us, too! But I will not die over again. Arnold! Save me! Save me, if you can and if you will!
> *Rubek.* Above the mists I see the mountain peak. It stands there glittering in the sunrise. We must climb to it—through the night mists, up into the light of morning.

The mists droop closer and closer over the scene. RUBEK *and* IRENE *descend into the mist-veil and are gradually lost to sight.*

The SISTER OF MERCY'S *head, spying, comes in sight in a rift in the mist.*

High up above the sea of the mist, the peak shines in the morning sun.

And that is the end.

When We Dead Awaken *was published very shortly before Christmas, 1899. Ibsen had still a year of comparative health before him. We find him, in March, 1900, writing to Count Prozor: "I cannot say yet whether or not*

I shall write another drama; but if I continue to retain the vigor of body and mind which I at present enjoy, I do not imagine that I shall be able to keep permanently away from the old battlefields. However, if I were to make my appearance again, it would be with new weapons and in new armor." Was he hinting at the desire, which he had long ago confessed to Professor Herford, that his last work should be a drama in verse? Whatever his dream, it was not to be realized. His last letter (defending his attitude of philosophic impartiality with regard to the South African war) is dated December 9, 1900. With the dawn of the new century, the curtain descended upon the mind of the great dramatic poet of the age which had passed away.

When We Dead Awaken was acted during 1900 at most of the leading theaters in Scandinavia and Germany. In some German cities (notably in Frankfort on the Main) it even attained a considerable number of representations. I cannot learn, however, that it has anywhere held the stage. It was produced in London, by the Stage Society, at the Imperial Theatre, on January 25 and 26, 1903. Mr. G. S. Titheradge played Rubek, Miss Henrietta Watson, Irene, Miss Mabel Hackney, Maia, and Mr. Laurence Irving, Ulfheim. In New York it was acted at the Knickerbocker Theatre, the part of Irene being taken by Miss Florence Kahn, and that of Rubek by Mr. Frederick Lewis.

In the above-mentioned letter to Count Prozor, Ibsen confirmed that critic's conjecture that "the series which ends with the Epilogue really began with *The Master Builder.*" As the last confession, so to speak, of a great artist, the Epilogue will always be read with interest. It contains, moreover, many flashes of the old genius, many strokes of the old incommunicable magic. One may say with perfect sincerity that there is more fascination in the dregs of Ibsen's mind than in the "first sprightly running" of more commonplace talents. But to his sane admirers the interest of the play must always be melancholy, because it is purely pathological. To deny this is, in my opinion, to cast a slur over all the poet's previous work, and in great measure to justify the criticisms of his most violent detractors. For *When We Dead Awaken* is very like the sort of play that haunted the "anti-Ibsenite" imagination in the year 1893 or thereabouts. It is a piece of self-caricature, a series of echoes from all the earlier plays, an exaggeration of manner to the pitch of mannerism. More-over, in his treatment of his symbolic motives, Ibsen did exactly what he had hitherto, with perfect justice, plumed himself upon never doing: he sacrificed the surface reality to the underlying meaning. Take, for instance, the history of Rubek's statue and its development into a group. In actual sculpture this development is a grotesque impossi-bility. In conceiving it we are deserting the domain of reality, and plunging into some fourth dimension where the properties of matter are other than those we know. This is an abandonment of the fundamental principle which Ibsen over and over again emphatically expressed —namely, that any symbolism his work might be found to contain was entirely incidental, and subordinate to the truth and consistency of his picture of life. Even when he dallied with the supernatural, as in *The Master Builder* and *Little Eyolf*, he was always careful, as I have tried to show, not to overstep decisively the boundaries of the natural. Here on the other hand, without any suggestion of the su-pernatural, we are confronted with the wholly impossible, the inconceivable. How remote is this alike from his prin-ciples of art and from the consistent, unvarying practice of his better years! So great is the chasm between *John Gabriel Borkman* and *When We Dead Awaken* that one could almost suppose his mental breakdown to have preceded instead of followed the writing of the latter play. Certainly it is one of the premonitions of the coming end. It is Ibsen's *Count Robert of Paris*. To pretend to rank it with his masterpieces is to show a very imperfect sense of the nature of their mastery.

CHARACTERS

PROFESSOR ARNOLD RUBEK, *a sculptor*
MRS. MAIA RUBEK, *his wife*
THE INSPECTOR, *at the Baths*
ULFHEIM, *a landed proprietor*
A STRANGER LADY
A SISTER OF MERCY
SERVANTS, VISITORS *to the Baths, and* CHILDREN

The First Act passes at a bathing establishment on the coast; the Second and Third Acts in the neighborhood of a health resort, high in the mountains.

Progress is low → high
Each act is set on higher level

WHEN WE DEAD AWAKEN

ACT FIRST

Outside the Bath Hotel. A portion of the main building can be seen to the right. An open, parklike place with a fountain, groups of fine old trees, and shrubbery. To the left, a little pavilion almost covered with ivy and Virginia creeper. A table and chair outside it. At the back a view over the fiord, right out to sea, with headlands and small islands in the distance. It is a calm, warm and sunny summer morning.

PROFESSOR RUBEK *and* MRS. MAIA RUBEK *are sitting in basket chairs beside a covered table on the lawn outside the hotel, having just breakfasted. They have champagne and seltzer water on the table, and each has a newspaper.* PROFESSOR RUBEK *is an elderly man of distinguished appearance, wearing a black velvet jacket, and otherwise in light summer attire.* MAIA *is quite young, with a vivacious expression and lively, mocking eyes, yet with a suggestion of fatigue. She wears an elegant traveling dress.*

MAIA [*sits for some time as though waiting for the* PROFESSOR *to say something, then lets her paper drop with a deep sigh*]. Oh dear, dear, dear——!

Professor Rubek [*looks up from his paper*]. Well, Maia? What is the matter with you?

Maia. Just listen how silent it is here.

Professor Rubek [*smiles indulgently*]. And you can hear that?

Maia. What?

Professor Rubek. The silence?

Maia. Yes, indeed I can.

Professor Rubek. Well, perhaps you are right, *mein Kind.* One can really hear the silence.

Maia. Heaven knows you can—when it's so absolutely overpowering as it is here——

Professor Rubek. Here at the Baths, you mean?

Maia. Wherever you go at home here, it seems to me. Of course there was noise and bustle enough in the town. But I don't know how it is—even the noise and bustle seemed to have something dead about it.

Professor Rubek [*with a searching glance*]. You don't seem particularly glad to be at home again, Maia?

Maia [*looks at him*]. Are you glad?

Professor Rubek [*evasively*]. I——?

Maia. Yes, you, who have been so much, much farther away than I. Are you entirely happy, now that you are at home again?

Professor Rubek. No—to be quite candid—perhaps not entirely happy——

Maia [*with animation*]. There, you see! Didn't I know it!

Professor Rubek. I have perhaps been too long abroad. I have drifted quite away from all this—this home life.

Maia [*eagerly, drawing her chair nearer him*]. There, you see, Rubek! We had much better get away again! As quickly as ever we can.

Professor Rubek [*somewhat impatiently*]. Well, well, that is what we intend to do, my dear Maia. You know that.

Maia. But why not now—at once? Only think how cozy and comfortable we could be down there, in our lovely new house——

Professor Rubek [*smiles indulgently*]. We ought by rights to say: our lovely new home.

Maia [*shortly*]. I prefer to say house—let us keep to that.

Professor Rubek [*his eyes dwelling on her*]. You are really a strange little person.

Maia. Am I so strange?

Professor Rubek. Yes, I think so.

Maia. But why, pray? Perhaps because I'm not desperately in love with mooning about up here——?

Professor Rubek. Which of us was it that was absolutely bent on our coming north this summer?

Maia. I admit, it was I.

Professor Rubek. It was certainly not I, at any rate.

Maia. But good heavens, who could have dreamed that everything would have altered so terribly at home here? And in so short a time, too! Why, it is only just four years since I went away——

Professor Rubek. Since you were married, yes.

Maia. Married? What has that to do with the matter?

Professor Rubek [*continuing*]. —since you became the Frau Professor, and found yourself mistress of a charming home—I beg your pardon—a very handsome house, I ought to say. And a villa on the Lake of Taunitz, just at the point that has become most fashionable, too—— In fact it is all very handsome and distinguished, Maia, there's no denying that. And spacious too. We need not always be getting in each other's way——

Maia [*lightly*]. No, no, no—there's certainly no lack of house room, and that sort of thing——

Professor Rubek. Remember, too, that you have been living in altogether more spacious and distinguished surroundings—in more polished society than you were accustomed to at home.

Maia [*looking at him*]. Ah, so you think it is *I* that have changed?

Professor Rubek. Indeed I do, Maia.

Maia. I alone? Not the people here?

Professor Rubek. Oh, yes, they too—a little perhaps. And not at all in the direction of amiability. That I readily admit.

Maia. I should think you must admit it, indeed.

Professor Rubek [*changing the subject*]. Do you know how it affects me when I look at the life of the people around us here?

Maia. No. Tell me.

Professor Rubek. It makes me think of that night we spent in the train, when we were coming up here——

Maia. Why, you were sound asleep all the time.

Professor Rubek. Not quite. I noticed how silent it became at all the little roadside stations. I heard the silence —like you, Maia——

Maia. H'm,—like me, yes.

Professor Rubek. —and that assured me that we had crossed the frontier—that we were really at home. For the train stopped at all the little stations—although there was nothing doing at all.

Maia. Then why did it stop—though there was nothing to be done?

Professor Rubek. Can't say. No one got out or in; but all the same the train stopped a long, endless time. And at every station I could make out that there were two railway men walking up and down the platform—one with a lantern in his hand—and they said things to each other in the night, low, and toneless, and meaningless.

Maia. Yes, that is quite true. There are always two men walking up and down, and talking——

Professor Rubek. —of nothing. [*Changing to a livelier tone.*] But just wait till tomorrow. Then we shall have the great luxurious steamer lying in the harbor. We'll go on board her, and sail all round the coast—northward ho!—right to the polar sea.

Maia. Yes, but then you will see nothing of the country—and of the people. And that was what you particularly wanted.

Professor Rubek [*short and snappishly*]. I have seen more than enough.

Maia. Do you think a sea voyage will be better for you?

Professor Rubek. It is always a change.

Maia. Well well, if only it is the right thing for you——

Professor Rubek. For me? The right thing? There is nothing in the world the matter with me.

Maia [*rises and goes up to him*]. Yes, there is, Rubek. I am sure you must feel it yourself.

Professor Rubek. Why, my dearest Maia—what should be amiss with me?

Maia [*behind him, bending over the back of his chair*]. That you must tell me. You have begun to wander about without a moment's peace. You cannot rest anywhere—neither at home nor abroad. You have become quite misanthropic of late.

Professor Rubek [*with a touch of sarcasm*]. Dear me—have you noticed that?

Maia. No one that knows you can help noticing it. And then it seems to me so sad that you have lost all pleasure in your work.

Professor Rubek. That too, eh?

Maia. You that used to be so indefatigable—working from morning to night!

Professor Rubek [*gloomily*]. Used to be, yes——

Maia. But ever since you got your great masterpiece out of hand——

Professor Rubek [*nods thoughtfully*]. "The Resurrection Day"——

Maia. —the masterpiece that has gone round the whole world, and made you so famous——

Professor Rubek. Perhaps that is just the misfortune, Maia.

Maia. How so?

Professor Rubek. When I had finished this masterpiece of mine—[*Makes a passionate movement with his hand.*] —for "The Resurrection Day" is a masterpiece! Or was one in the beginning. No, it is one still. It must, must, must be a masterpiece!

Maia [*looks at him in astonishment*]. Why, Rubek—all the world knows that.

Professor Rubek [*short, repellently*]. All the world knows nothing! Understands nothing!

Maia. Well, at any rate it can divine something——

Professor Rubek. Something that isn't there at all, yes. Something that never was in my mind. Ah, yes, that they can all go into ecstasies over! [*Growling to himself.*] What is the good of working oneself to death for the mob and the masses—for "all the world"!

Maia. Do you think it is better, then—do you think it is worthy of you, to do nothing at all but a portrait bust now and then?

Professor Rubek [*with a sly smile*]. They are not exactly portrait busts that I turn out, Maia.

Maia. Yes, indeed they are—for the last two or three years—ever since you finished your great group and got it out of the house——

Professor Rubek. All the same, they are no mere portrait busts, I assure you.

Maia. What are they, then?

Professor Rubek. There is something equivocal, something cryptic, lurking in and behind these busts—a secret something, that the people themselves cannot see——

Maia. Indeed?

Professor Rubek [*decisively*]. I alone can see it. And it amuses me unspeakably.—On the surface I give them the "striking likeness," as they call it, that they all stand and gape at in astonishment—[*Lowers his voice.*]—but at bottom they are all respectable, pompous horsefaces, and self-opinionated donkey muzzles, and lop-eared, low-browed dog skulls and fatted swine snouts—and sometimes dull, brutal bull fronts as well——

Maia [*indifferently*]. All the dear domestic animals, in fact.

Professor Rubek. Simply the dear domestic animals, Maia. All the animals which men have bedeviled in their own image—and which have bedeviled men in return. [*Empties his champagne glass and laughs.*] And it is these double-faced works of art that our excellent plutocrats come and order of me. And pay for in all good faith—and in good round figures too—almost their weight in gold, as the saying goes.

Maia [*fills his glass*]. Come, Rubek! Drink and be happy.

Professor Rubek [*passes his hand several times across his forehead and leans back in his chair*]. I am happy, Maia. Really happy—in a way. [*Short silence.*] For after all there is a certain happiness in feeling oneself free and independent on every hand—in having at one's command everything one can possibly wish for—all outward things, that is to say. Do you not agree with me, Maia?

Maia. Oh yes, I agree. All that is well enough in its way. [*Looking at him.*] But do you remember what you promised me the day we came to an understanding on—on that troublesome point——

Professor Rubek [*nods*]. —On the subject of our marriage, yes. It was no easy matter for you, Maia.

Maia [*continuing unruffled*]. —and agreed that I was to go abroad with you, and live there for good and all—and enjoy myself.—Do you remember what you promised me that day?

Professor Rubek [*shaking his head*]. No, I can't say that I do. Well, what did I promise?

Maia. You said you would take me up to a high mountain and show me all the glory of the world.

Professor Rubek [*with a slight start*]. Did I promise you that, too?

Maia. Me, too? Who else, pray?

Professor Rubek [*indifferently*]. No, no, I only meant did I promise to show you——?

Maia. —all the glory of the world? Yes, you did. And all that glory should be mine, you said.

Professor Rubek. That is a sort of figure of speech that I was in the habit of using once upon a time.

Maia. Only a figure of speech?

Professor Rubek. Yes, a schoolboy phrase—the sort of thing I used to say when I wanted to lure the neighbors' children out to play with me, in the woods and on the mountains.

Maia [*looking hard at him*]. Perhaps you only wanted to lure me out to play, as well?

Professor Rubek [*passing it off as a jest*]. Well, has it not been a tolerably amusing game, Maia?

Maia [*coldly*]. I did not go with you only to play.

Professor Rubek. No, no, I daresay not.

Maia. And you never took me up with you to any high mountain, or showed me——

Professor Rubek [*with irritation*]. —all the glory of the world? No, I did not. For, let me tell you something: you are not really born to be a mountain climber, little Maia.

Maia [*trying to control herself*]. Yet at one time you seemed to think I was.

Professor Rubek. Four or five years ago, yes. [*Stretching himself in his chair.*] Four or five years—it's a long, long time, Maia.

Maia [*looking at him with a bitter expression*]. Has the time seemed so very long to you, Rubek?

Professor Rubek. I am beginning now to find it a trifle long. [*Yawning.*] Now and then, you know.

Maia [*returning to her place*]. I shall not bore you any longer. [*She resumes her seat, takes up the newspaper, and begins turning over the leaves. Silence on both sides.*]

Professor Rubek [*leaning on his elbows across the table, and looking at her teasingly*]. Is the Frau Professor offended?

Maia [*coldly, without looking up*]. No, not at all.

Visitors *to the baths, most of them ladies, begin to pass, singly and in groups, through the park from the right, and out to the left.*

Waiters *bring refreshments from the hotel, and go off behind the pavilion.*

The Inspector, *wearing gloves and carrying a stick, comes from his rounds in the park, meets* Visitors, *bows politely, and exchanges a few words with some of them.*

The Inspector [*advancing to* PROFESSOR RUBEK's *table and politely taking off his hat*]. I have the honor to wish you good morning, Mrs. Rubek. Good morning, Professor Rubek.

Professor Rubek. Good morning, good morning, Inspector.

The Inspector [*addressing himself to* MRS. RUBEK]. May I venture to ask if you have slept well?

Maia. Yes, thank you; excellently—for my part. I always sleep like a stone.

The Inspector. I am delighted to hear it. The first night in a strange place is often rather trying. And the Professor——?

Professor Rubek. Oh, my night's rest is never much to boast of—especially of late.

The Inspector [*with a show of sympathy*]. Oh—that is a pity. But after a few weeks' stay at the Baths—you will quite get over that.

Professor Rubek [*looking up at him*]. Tell me, Inspector —are any of your patients in the habit of taking baths during the night?

The Inspector [*astonished*]. During the night? No, I have never heard of such a thing.

Professor Rubek. Have you not?

The Inspector. No, I don't know of anyone so ill as to require such treatment.

Professor Rubek. Well, at any rate there is someone who is in the habit of walking about the park by night?

The Inspector [*smiling and shaking his head*]. No, Professor—that would be aganist the rules.

Maia [*impatiently*]. Good Heavens, Rubek, I told you so this morning—you must have dreamed it.

Professor Rubek [*dryly*]. Indeed? Must I? Thank you! [*Turning to* THE INSPECTOR.] The fact is, I got up last night—I couldn't sleep—and I wanted to see what sort of night it was——

The Inspector [*attentively*]. To be sure—and then——?

Professor Rubek. I looked out at the window—and caught sight of a white figure in there among the trees.

Maia [*smiling to* THE INSPECTOR]. And the Professor declares that the figure was dressed in a bathing costume——

Professor Rubek. —Or something like it, I said. Couldn't

distinguish very clearly. But I am sure it was something white.

The Inspector. Most remarkable. Was it a gentleman or a lady?

Professor Rubek. I could almost have sworn it was a lady. But then after it came another figure. And that one was quite dark—like a shadow——

The Inspector [*starting*]. A dark one? Quite black, perhaps?

Professor Rubek. Yes, I should almost have said so.

The Inspector [*a light breaking in upon him*]. And behind the white figure? Following close upon her——?

Professor Rubek. Yes—at a little distance——

The Inspector. Aha! Then I think I can explain the mystery, Professor.

Professor Rubek. Well, what was it then?

Maia [*simultaneously*]. Was the Professor really not dreaming?

The Inspector [*suddenly whispering, as he directs their attention toward the background on the right*]. Hush, if you please! Look there—— Don't speak loud for a moment.

A slender lady, dressed in fine, cream-white cashmere, and followed by a Sister of Mercy *in black, with a silver cross hanging by a chain on her breast, comes forward from behind the hotel and crosses the park toward the pavilion in front on the left. Her face is pale, and its lines seem to have stiffened; the eyelids are drooped and the eyes appear as though they saw nothing. Her dress comes down to her feet and clings to the body in perpendicular folds. Over her head, neck, breast, shoulders and arms she wears a large shawl of white crape. She keeps her arms crossed upon her breast. She carries her body immovably, and her steps are stiff and measured. The* Sister's *bearing is also measured, and she has the air of a servant. She keeps her brown piercing eyes incessantly fixed upon the lady.* Waiters, *with napkins on their arms, come forward in the hotel doorway, and cast curious glances at the strangers, who take no notice of anything, and, without looking round, enter the pavilion.*

Professor Rubek [*has risen slowly and involuntarily, and stands staring at the closed door of the pavilion*]. Who was that lady?

The Inspector. She is a stranger who has rented the little pavilion there.

Professor Rubek. A foreigner?

The Inspector. Presumably. At any rate they both came from abroad—about a week ago. They have never been here before.

Professor Rubek [*decidedly; looking at him*]. It was she I saw in the park last night.

The Inspector. No doubt it must have been. I thought so from the first.

Professor Rubek. What is this lady's name, Inspector?

The Inspector. She has registered herself as "Madame de Satow, with companion." We know nothing more.

Professor Rubek [*reflecting*]. Satow? Satow——?

Maia [*laughing mockingly*]. Do you know anyone of that name, Rubek? Eh?

Professor Rubek [*shaking his head*]. No, no one. Satow? It sounds Russian—or at all events Slavonic. [*To* THE INSPECTOR.] What language does she speak?

The Inspector. When the two ladies talk to each other, it is in a language I cannot make out at all. But at other times she speaks Norwegian like a native.

Professor Rubek [*exclaims with a start*]. Norwegian? You are sure you are not mistaken?

The Inspector. No, how could I be mistaken in that?

Professor Rubek [*looks at him with eager interest*]. You have heard her yourself?

The Inspector. Yes. I myself have spoken to her—several times.—Only a few words, however; she is far from communicative. But——

Professor Rubek. But Norwegian it was?

The Inspector. Thoroughly good Norwegian—perhaps with a little north country accent.

Professor Rubek [*gazing straight before him in amazement, whispers*]. That too!

Maia [*a little hurt and jarred*]. Perhaps this lady has been one of your models, Rubek? Search your memory.

Professor Rubek [*looks cuttingly at her*]. My models!

Maia [*with a provoking smile*]. In your younger days, I mean. You are said to have had such innumerable models —long ago, of course.

Professor Rubek [*in the same tone*]. Oh, no, little Frau Maia. I have in reality had only one single model. One and one only—for everything I have done.

The Inspector [*who has turned away and stands look-ing out to the left*]. If you'll excuse me, I think I will take my leave. I see someone coming whom it is not particularly agreeable to meet. Especially in the presence of ladies.

Professor Rubek [*looking in the same direction*]. That sportsman there? Who is it?

The Inspector. It is a certain Mr. Ulfheim, from——

Professor Rubek. Oh, Mr. Ulfheim——

The Inspector. —The bear killer, as they call him——

Professor Rubek. I know him.

The Inspector. Who does not know him?

Professor Rubek. Very slightly, however. Is he on your list of patients—at last?

The Inspector. No, strangely enough—not as yet. He comes here only once a year—on his way up to his hunting grounds.—Excuse me for the moment——[*Makes a movement to go into the hotel.*]

Ulfheim's Voice [*heard outside*]. Stop a moment, man! Devil take it all, can't you stop? Why do you always scuttle away from me?

The Inspector [*stops*]. I am not scuttling at all, Mr. Ulfheim.

ULFHEIM *enters from the left followed by a servant with a couple of sporting dogs in leash.* ULFHEIM *is in shooting costume, with high boots and a felt hat with a feather in it. He is a long, lank, sinewy personage, with matted hair and beard, and a loud voice. His appearance gives no pre-cise clue to his age, but he is no longer young.*

Ulfheim [*pounces upon* THE INSPECTOR]. Is this a way to receive strangers, hey? You scamper away with your tail between your legs—as if you had the devil at your heels.

The Inspector [*calmly, without answering him*]. Has Mr. Ulfheim arrived by the steamer?

Ulfheim [*growls*]. Haven't had the honor of seeing any steamer. [*With his arms akimbo.*] Don't you know that *I* sail my own cutter? [*To the* SERVANT.] Look well after your fellow creatures, Lars. But take care you keep them ravenous, all the same. Fresh meat bones—but not too much meat on them, do you hear? And be sure it's reeking raw, and bloody. And get something in your own belly while you're about it. [*Aiming a kick at him.*] Now then, go to hell with you!

The SERVANT *goes out with the dogs, behind the corner of the hotel.*

The Inspector. Would not Mr. Ulfheim like to go into the dining room in the meantime?

Ulfheim. In among all the half-dead flies and people? No, thank you a thousand times, Mr. Inspector.

The Inspector. Well, well, as you please.

Ulfheim. But get the housekeeper to prepare a hamper for me as usual. There must be plenty of provender in it —and lots of brandy——! You can tell her that I or Lars will come and play Old Harry with her if she doesn't——

The Inspector [*interrupting*]. We know your ways of old. [*Turning.*] Can I give the waiter any orders, Professor? Can I send Mrs. Rubek anything?

Professor Rubek. No, thank you; nothing for me.

Maia. Nor for me.

THE INSPECTOR *goes into the hotel.*

Ulfheim [*stares at them a moment; then lifts his hat*]. Why, blast me if here isn't a country tyke that has strayed into regular tiptop society.

Professor Rubek [*looking up*]. What do you mean by that, Mr. Ulfheim?

Ulfheim [*more quietly and politely*]. I believe I have the honor of addressing no less a person than the great Sculptor Rubek.

Professor Rubek [*nods*]. I remember meeting you once or twice—the autumn when I was last at home.

Ulfheim. That's many years ago now, though. And then you weren't so illustrious as I hear you've since become. At that time even a dirty bear hunter might venture to come near you.

Professor Rubek [*smiling*]. I don't bite even now.

Maia [*looks with interest at* ULFHEIM]. Are you really and truly a bear hunter?

Ulfheim [*seating himself at the next table, nearer the hotel*]. A bear hunter when I have the chance, madam. But I make the best of any sort of game that comes in my way —eagles, and wolves, and women, and elks, and reindeer —if only it's fresh and juicy and has plenty of blood in it. [*Drinks from his pocket flask.*]

Maia [*regarding him fixedly*]. But you like bear hunting best?

Ulfheim. I like it best, yes. For then one can have the knife handy at a pinch. [*With a slight smile.*] We both work in a hard material, madam—both your husband and I. He struggles with his marble blocks, I daresay; and I struggle with tense and quivering bear sinews. And we both of us win the fight in the end—subdue and master our material. We never rest till we've got the upper hand of it, though it fight never so hard.

Professor Rubek [*deep in thought*]. There's a great deal of truth in what you say.

Ulfheim. Yes, for I take it the stone has something to fight for too. It is dead, and determined by no manner of means to let itself be hammered into life. Just like the bear when you come and prod him up in his lair.

Maia. Are you going up into the forests now to hunt?

Ulfheim. I am going right up into the high mountains. —I suppose you have never been in the high mountains, madam?

Maia. No, never.

Ulfheim. Confound it all then, you must be sure and come up there this very summer! I'll take you with me— both you and the Professor, with pleasure.

Maia. Thanks. But Rubek is thinking of taking a sea trip this summer.

Professor Rubek. Round the coast—through the island channels.

Ulfheim. Ugh—what the devil would you do in those damnable sickly gutters—floundering about in the brackish ditchwater? Dishwater I should rather call it.

Maia. There, you hear, Rubek!

Ulfheim. No, much better come up with me to the mountains—away, clean away, from the trail and taint of men. You can't think what that means for me. But such a little lady——[*He stops.*]

The SISTER OF MERCY *comes out of the pavilion and goes into the hotel.*

[*Following her with his eyes.*] Just look at her, do! That night crow there!—Who is it that's to be buried?

Professor Rubek. I have not heard of anyone——

Ulfheim. Well, there's someone on the point of giving up the ghost, then—in one corner or another.—People that are sickly and rickety should have the goodness to see about getting themselves buried—the sooner the better.

Maia. Have you ever been ill yourself, Mr. Ulfheim?

Ulfheim. Never. If I had, I shouldn't be here.—But my nearest friends—they have been ill, poor things.

Maia. And what did you do for your nearest friends?

Ulfheim. Shot them, of course.

Professor Rubek [*looking at him*]. Shot them?

Maia [*moving her chair back*]. Shot them dead?

Ulfheim [*nods*]. I never miss, madam.

Maia. But how can you possibly shoot people!

Ulfheim. I am not speaking of people——

Maia. You said your nearest friends——

Ulfheim. Well, who should they be but my dogs?

Maia. Are your dogs your nearest friends?

Ulfheim. I have none nearer. My honest, trusty, absolutely loyal comrades—— When one of them turns sick and miserable—bang!—and there's my friend sent packing—to the other world.

The SISTER OF MERCY *comes out of the hotel with a tray on which is bread and milk. She places it on the table outside the pavilion, which she enters.*

[*Laughs scornfully.*] That stuff there—is that what you call food for human beings! Milk and water and soft, clammy bread. Ah, you should see my comrades feeding. Should you like to see it?

Maia [*smiling across to the* PROFESSOR *and rising*]. Yes, very much.

Ulfheim [*also rising*]. Spoken like a woman of spirit, madam! Come with me, then! They swallow whole great thumping meatbones—gulp them up and then gulp them down again. Oh, it's a regular treat to see them. Come along and I'll show you—and while we're about it, we can talk over this trip to the mountains——

He goes out by the corner of the hotel, MAIA *following him.*

Almost at the same moment the STRANGE LADY *comes out of the pavilion and seats herself at the table.*

THE LADY *raises her glass of milk and is about to drink, but stops and looks across at* RUBEK *with vacant, expressionless eyes.*

Professor Rubek [*remains sitting at his table and gazes fixedly and earnestly at her. At last he rises, goes some steps toward her, stops, and says in a low voice*]. I know you quite well, Irene.

The Lady [*in a toneless voice, setting down her glass*]. You can guess who I am, Arnold?

Professor Rubek [*without answering*]. And you recognize me, too, I see.

The Lady. With you it is quite another matter.

Professor Rubek. With me?—How so?

The Lady. Oh, you are still alive.

Professor Rubek [*not understanding*]. Alive——?

The Lady [*after a short pause*]. Who was the other? The woman you had with you—there at the table?

Professor Rubek [*a little reluctantly*]. She? That was my —my wife.

The Lady [*nods slowly*]. Indeed. That is well, Arnold. Someone, then, who does not concern me——

Professor Rubek [*nods*]. No, of course not——

The Lady. —One whom you have taken to you after my lifetime.

Professor Rubek [*suddenly looking hard at her*]. After your——? What do you mean by that, Irene?

Irene [*without answering*]. And the child? I hear the child is prospering too. Our child survives me—and has come to honor and glory.

Professor Rubek [*smiles as at a far-off recollection*]. Our child? Yes, we called it so—then.

Irene. In my lifetime, yes.

Professor Rubek [*trying to take a lighter tone*]. Yes, Irene.—I can assure you "our child" has become famous all the wide world over. I suppose you have read about it.

Irene [*nods*]. And has made its father famous too.—That was your dream.

Professor Rubek [*more softly, with emotion*]. It is to you I owe everything, everything, Irene—and I thank you.

Irene [*lost in thought for a moment*]. If I had then done what I had a right to do, Arnold——

Professor Rubek. Well? What then?

Irene. I should have killed that child.

Professor Rubek. Killed it, you say?

Irene [*whispering*]. Killed it—before I went away from you. Crushed it—crushed it to dust.

Professor Rubek [*shakes his head reproachfully*]. You would never have been able to, Irene. You had not the heart to do it.

Irene. No, in those days I had not that sort of heart.

Professor Rubek. But since then? Afterwards?

Irene. Since then I have killed it innumerable times. By daylight and in the dark. Killed it in hatred—and in revenge—and in anguish.

Professor Rubek [*goes close up to the table and asks softly*]. Irene—tell me now at last—after all these years—why did you go away from me? You disappeared so utterly —left not a trace behind——

Irene [*shaking her head slowly*]. Oh, Arnold—why should I tell you that now—from the world beyond the grave.

Professor Rubek. Was there someone else whom you had come to love?

Irene. There was one who had no longer any use for my love—any use for my life.

Professor Rubek [*changing the subject*]. H'm—don't let us talk any more of the past——

Irene. No, no—by all means let us not talk of what is beyond the grave—what is now beyond the grave for me.

Professor Rubek. Where have you been, Irene? All my inquiries were fruitless—you seemed to have vanished away.

Irene. I went into the darkness—when the child stood transfigured in the light.

Professor Rubek. Have you traveled much about the world?

Irene. Yes. Traveled in many lands.

Professor Rubek [*looks compassionately at her*]. And what have you found to do, Irene?

Irene [*turning her eyes upon him*]. Wait a moment; let me see—— Yes, now I have it. I have posed on the turntable in variety shows. Posed as a naked statue in living pictures. Raked in heaps of money. That was more than I could do with you; for you had none.—And then I turned the heads of all sorts of men. That, too, was more than I could do with you, Arnold. You kept yourself better in hand.

Professor Rubek [*hastening to pass the subject by*]. And then you have married, too?

Irene. Yes; I married one of them.

Professor Rubek. Who is your husband?

Irene. He was a South American. A distinguished diplomatist. [*Looks straight in front of her with a stony smile.*]

Him I managed to drive quite out of his mind; mad—incurably mad; inexorably mad.—It was great sport, I can tell you—while it was in the doing. I could have laughed within me all the time—if I had anything within me.

Professor Rubek. And where is he now?

Irene. Oh, in a churchyard somewhere or other. With a fine handsome monument over him. And with a bullet rattling in his skull.

Professor Rubek. Did he kill himself?

Irene. Yes, he was good enough to take that off my hands.

Professor Rubek. Do you not lament his loss, Irene?

Irene [*not understanding*]. Lament? What loss?

Professor Rubek. Why, the loss of Herr von Satow, of course.

Irene. His name was not Satow.

Professor Rubek. Was it not?

Irene. My second husband is called Satow. He is a Russian——

Professor Rubek. And where is he?

Irene. Far away in the Ural Mountains. Among all his gold mines.

Professor Rubek. So he lives there?

Irene [*shrugs her shoulders*]. Lives? Lives? In reality I have killed him——

Professor Rubek [*starts*]. Killed——!

Irene. Killed him with a fine sharp dagger which I always have with me in bed——

Professor Rubek [*vehemently*]. I don't believe you, Irene!

Irene [*with a gentle smile*]. Indeed you may believe it, Arnold.

Professor Rubek [*looks compassionately at her*]. Have you never had a child?

Irene. Yes, I have had many children.

Professor Rubek. And where are your children now?

Irene. I killed them.

Professor Rubek [*severely*]. Now you are telling me lies again!

Irene. I have killed them, I tell you—murdered them pitilessly. As soon as ever they came into the world. Oh, long, long before. One after the other.

Professor Rubek [*sadly and earnestly*]. There is something hidden behind everything you say.

Irene. How can I help that? Every word I say is whispered into my ear.

Professor Rubek. I believe I am the only one that can divine your meaning.

Irene. Surely you ought to be the only one.

Professor Rubek [*rests his hands on the table and looks intently at her*]. Some of the strings of your nature have broken.

Irene [*gently*]. Does not that always happen when a young warm-blooded woman dies?

Professor Rubek. Oh, Irene, have done with these wild imaginings——! You are living! Living—living!

Irene [*rises slowly from her chair and says, quivering*]. I was dead for many years. They came and bound me—laced my arms together behind my back—— Then they lowered me into a grave vault, with iron bars before the loophole. And with padded walls—so that no one on the earth above could hear the grave shrieks—— But now I am beginning, in a way, to rise from the dead. [*She seats herself again.*]

Professor Rubek [*after a pause*]. In all this, do you hold me guilty?

Irene. Yes.

Professor Rubek. Guilty of that—your death, as you call it.

Irene. Guilty of the fact that I had to die. [*Changing her tone to one of indifference.*] Why don't you sit down, Arnold?

Professor Rubek. May I?

Irene. Yes.—You need not be afraid of being frozen. I don't think I am quite turned to ice yet.

Professor Rubek [*moves a chair and seats himself at her table*]. There, Irene. Now we two are sitting together as in the old days.

Irene. A little way apart from each other—also as in the old days.

Professor Rubek [*moving nearer*]. It had to be so, then.

Irene. Had it?

Professor Rubek [*decisively*]. There had to be a distance between us——

Irene. Was it absolutely necessary, Arnold?

Professor Rubek [*continuing*]. Do you remember what you answered when I asked if you would go with me out into the wide world?

Irene. I held up three fingers in the air and swore that I would go with you to the world's end and to the end of life. And that I would serve you in all things——

Professor Rubek. As the model for my art——

Irene. —In frank, utter nakedness——

Professor Rubek [*with emotion*]. And you did serve me, Irene—so bravely—so gladly and ungrudgingly.

Irene. Yes, with all the pulsing blood of my youth, I served you!

Professor Rubek [*nodding, with a look of gratitude*]. That you have every right to say.

Irene. I fell down at your feet and served you, Arnold! [*Holding her clenched hand toward him.*] But you, you, —you——!

Professor Rubek [*defensively*]. I never did you any wrong! Never, Irene!

Irene. Yes, you did! You did wrong to my innermost, inborn nature——

Professor Rubek [*starting back*]. I——!

Irene. Yes, you! I exposed myself wholly and unreservedly to your gaze—— [*More softly.*] And never once did you touch me.

Professor Rubek. Irene, did you not understand that many a time I was almost beside myself under the spell of all your loveliness?

Irene [*continuing undisturbed*]. And yet—if you had touched me, I think I should have killed you on the spot. For I had a sharp needle always upon me—hidden in my hair—— [*Strokes her forehead meditatively.*] But after all—after all—that you could——

Professor Rubek [*looks impressively at her*]. I was an artist, Irene.

Irene [*darkly*]. That is just it. That is just it.

Professor Rubek. An artist first of all. And I was sick with the desire to achieve the great work of my life. [*Losing himself in recollection.*] It was to be called "The Resurrection Day"—figured in the likeness of a young woman, awakening from the sleep of death——

Irene. Our child, yes——

Professor Rubek [*continuing*]. It was to be the awakening of the noblest, purest, most ideal woman the world ever saw. Then I found you. You were what I required in every respect. And you consented so willingly—so gladly. You renounced home and kindred—and went with me.

Irene. To go with you meant for me the resurrection of my childhood.

Professor Rubek. That was just why I found in you all that I required—in you and in no one else. I came to look on you as a thing hallowed, not to be touched save in adoring thoughts. In those days I was still young, Irene. And the superstition took hold of me that if I touched you, if I desired you with my senses, my soul would be profaned, so that I should be unable to accomplish what I was striving for.—And I still think there was some truth in that.

Irene [*nods with a touch of scorn*]. The work of art first then the human being.

Professor Rubek. You must judge me as you will; but at that time I was utterly dominated by my great task—and exultantly happy in it.

Irene. And you achieved your great task, Arnold.

Professor Rubek. Thanks and praise be to you, I achieved my great task. I wanted to embody the pure woman as I saw her awakening on the Resurrection Day. Not marveling at anything new and unknown and undivined; but filled with a sacred joy at finding herself unchanged—she, the woman of earth—in the higher, freer, happier region—after the long, dreamless sleep of death. [*More softly.*] Thus did I fashion her.—I fashioned her in your image, Irene.

Irene [*laying her hands flat upon the table and leaning against the back of her chair*]. And then you were done with me——

Professor Rubek [*reproachfully*]. Irene!

Irene. You had no longer any use for me——

Professor Rubek. How can you say that!

Irene. —And began to look about you for other ideals——

Professor Rubek. I found none, none after you.

Irene. And no other models, Arnold?

Professor Rubek. You were no model to me. You were the fountainhead of my achievement.

Irene [*is silent for a short time*]. What poems have you made since? In marble I mean. Since the day I left you.

Professor Rubek. I have made no poems since that day —only frittered away my life in modeling.

Irene. And that woman, whom you are now living with——?

Professor Rubek [*interrupting vehemently*]. Do not speak of her now! It makes me tingle with shame.

Irene. Where are you thinking of going with her?

Professor Rubek [*slack and weary*]. Oh, on a tedious coasting voyage to the North, I suppose.

Irene [*looks at him, smiles almost imperceptibly, and whispers*]. You should rather go high up into the mountains. As high as ever you can. Higher, higher,—always higher, Arnold.

Professor Rubek [*with eager expectation*]. Are you going up there?

Irene. Have you the courage to meet me once again?

Professor Rubek [*struggling with himself, uncertainly*]. If we could—oh, if only we could——!

Irene. Why can we not do what we will? [*Looks at him and whispers beseechingly with folded hands.*] Come, come, Arnold! Oh, come up to me——!

MAIA *enters, glowing with pleasure, from behind the hotel, and goes quickly up to the table where they were previously sitting.*

Maia [*still at the corner of the hotel, without looking around*]. Oh, you may say what you please, Rubek, but— [*Stops, as she catches sight of* IRENE.]—— Oh, I beg your pardon—I see you have made an acquaintance.

Professor Rubek [*curtly*]. Renewed an acquaintance. [*Rises.*] What was it you wanted with me?

Maia. I only wanted to say this: you may do whatever you please, but *I* am not going with you on that disgusting steamboat.

Professor Rubek. Why not?

Maia. Because I want to go up on the mountains and into the forests—that's what I want. [*Coaxingly.*] Oh, you must let me do it, Rubek.—I shall be so good, so good afterwards!

Professor Rubek. Who is it that has put these ideas into your head?

Maia. Why he—that horrid bear killer. Oh you cannot conceive all the marvelous things he has to tell about the mountains. And about life up there! They're ugly, horrid, repulsive, most of the yarns he spins—for I almost believe he's lying—but wonderfully alluring all the same. Oh, won't you let me go with him? Only to see if what he says is true, you understand. May I, Rubek?

Professor Rubek. Yes, I have not the slightest objection. Off you go to the mountains—as far and as long as you please. I shall perhaps be going the same way myself.

Maia [*quickly*]. No, no, no, you needn't do that! Not on my account!

Professor Rubek. I want to go to the mountains. I have made up my mind to go.

Maia. Oh, thanks, thanks! May I tell the bear killer at once?

Professor Rubek. Tell the bear killer whatever you please.

Maia. Oh, thanks, thanks, thanks! [*Is about to take his hand; he repels the movement.*] Oh, how dear and good you are today, Rubek! [*She runs into the hotel.*]

At the same time the door of the pavilion is softly and noiselessly set ajar. The SISTER OF MERCY *stands in the opening, intently on the watch. No one sees her.*

Professor Rubek [*decidedly, turning to* IRENE]. Shall we meet up there then?

Irene [*rising slowly*]. Yes, we shall certainly meet.—I have sought for you so long.

Professor Rubek. When did you begin to seek for me, Irene?

Irene [*with a touch of jesting bitterness*]. From the moment I realized that I had given away to you something rather indispensable, Arnold. Something one ought never to part with.

Professor Rubek [*bowing his head*]. Yes, that is bitterly true. You gave me three or four years of your youth.

Irene. More, more than that I gave you—spendthrift as I then was.

Professor Rubek. Yes, you were prodigal, Irene. You gave me all your naked loveliness——

Irene. —To gaze upon——

Professor Rubek. —And to glorify——

Irene. Yes, for your own glorification.—And the child's.

Professor Rubek. And yours too, Irene.

Irene. But you have forgotten the most precious gift.

Professor Rubek. The most precious——? What gift was that?

Irene. I gave you my young, living soul. And that gift left me empty within—soulless. [*Looking at him with a fixed stare.*] It was that I died of, Arnold.

The SISTER OF MERCY *opens the door wide and makes room for her. She goes into the pavilion.*

Professor Rubek [stands and looks after her; then whispers]. Irene!

ACT SECOND

Near a mountain health resort. The landscape stretches, in the form of an immense treeless upland, toward a long mountain lake. Beyond the lake rises a range of peaks with blue-white snow in the clefts. In the foreground on the left a purling brook falls in severed streamlets down a steep wall of rock, and thence flows smoothly over the upland until it disappears to the right. Dwarf trees, plants, and stones along the course of the brook. In the foreground on the right a hillock, with a stone bench on the top of it.
It is a summer afternoon, toward sunset.

At some distance over the upland, on the other side of the brook, a troop of children is singing, dancing, and playing. Some are dressed in peasant costume, others in town-made clothes. Their happy laughter is heard, softened by distance, during the following.

PROFESSOR RUBEK *is sitting on the bench, with a plaid over his shoulders, and looking down at the children's play.*

Presently MAIA *comes forward from among some bushes on the upland to the left, well back, and scans the prospect with her hand shading her eyes. She wears a flat tourist cap, a short skirt, kilted up, reaching only midway between ankle and knee, and high, stout lace-boots. She has in her hand a long alpenstock.*

MAIA [*at last catches sight of* RUBEK *and calls*]. Hallo! [*She advances over the upland, jumps over the brook, with the aid of her alpenstock, and climbs up the hillock. Panting.*] Oh, how I have been rushing around looking for you, Rubek.

Professor Rubek [nods indifferently and asks]. Have you just come from the hotel?

Maia. Yes, that was the last place I tried—that flytrap.

Professor Rubek [*looking at her for a moment*]. I noticed that you were not at the dinner table.

Maia. No, we had our dinner in the open air, we two.

Professor Rubek. "We two"? What two?

Maia. Why, I and that horrid bear killer, of course.

Professor Rubek. Oh, he.

Maia. Yes. And first thing tomorrow morning we are going off again.

Professor Rubek. After bears?

Maia. Yes. Off to kill a brown-boy.

Professor Rubek. Have you found the tracks of any?

Maia [*with superiority*]. You don't suppose that bears are to be found in the naked mountains, do you?

Professor Rubek. Where, then?

Maia. Far beneath. On the lower slopes; in the thickest parts of the forest. Places your ordinary townfolk could never get through——

Professor Rubek. And you two are going down there tomorrow?

Maia [*throwing herself down among the heather*]. Yes, so we have arranged.—Or perhaps we may start this evening.—If you have no objection, that's to say?

Professor Rubek. I? Far be it from me to——

Maia [*quickly*]. Of course, Lars goes with us—with the dogs.

Professor Rubek. I feel no curiosity as to the movements of Mr. Lars and his dogs. [*Changing the subject.*] Would you not rather sit properly on the seat?

Maia [*drowsily*]. No, thank you. I'm lying so delightfully in the soft heather.

Professor Rubek. I can see that you are tired.

Maia [*yawning*]. I almost think I'm beginning to feel tired.

Professor Rubek. You don't notice it till afterwards— when the excitement is over——

Maia [*in a drowsy tone*]. Just so. I will lie and close my eyes.

A short pause.

[*with sudden impatience*]. Ugh, Rubek—how can you endure to sit there listening to these children's screams! And to watch all the capers they are cutting, too!

Professor Rubek. There is something harmonious—almost like music—in their movements, now and then; amid all the clumsiness. And it amuses me to sit and watch for these isolated moments—when they come.

Maia [*with a somewhat scornful laugh*]. Yes, you are always, always an artist.

Professor Rubek. And I propose to remain one.

Maia [*lying on her side, so that her back is turned to him*]. There's not a bit of the artist about him.

Professor Rubek [*with attention*]. Who is it that's not an artist?

Maia [*again in a sleepy tone*]. Why, he—the other one, of course.

Professor Rubek. The bear hunter, you mean?

Maia. Yes. There's not a bit of the artist about him—not the least little bit.

Professor Rubek [*smiling*]. No, I believe there's no doubt about that.

Maia [*vehemently, without moving*]. And so ugly as he is! [*Plucks up a tuft of heather and throws it away.*] So ugly, so ugly! Isch!

Professor Rubek. Is that why you are so ready to set off with him—out into the wilds?

Maia [*curtly*]. I don't know. [*Turning toward him.*] You are ugly, too, Rubek.

Professor Rubek. Have you only discovered it?

Maia. No, I have seen it for long.

Professor Rubek [*shrugging his shoulders*]. One doesn't grow younger. One doesn't grow younger, Frau Maia.

Maia. It's not that sort of ugliness that I mean at all. But there has come to be such an expression of fatigue, of utter weariness, in your eyes—when you deign, once in a while, to cast a glance at me.

Professor Rubek. Have you noticed that?

Maia [*nods*]. Little by little this evil look has come into your eyes. It seems almost as though you were nursing some dark plot against me.

Professor Rubek. Indeed? [*In a friendly but earnest tone.*] Come here and sit beside me, Maia; and let us talk a little.

Maia [*half rising*]. Then will you let me sit upon your knee? As I used to in the early days?

Professor Rubek. No, you mustn't—people can see us from the hotel. [*Moves a little.*] But you can sit here on the bench—at my side.

Maia. No, thank you; in that case I'd rather lie here,

where I am. I can hear you quite well here. [*Looks inquiringly at him.*] Well, what is it you want to say to me?

Professor Rubek [*begins slowly*]. What do you think was my real reason for agreeing to make this tour?

Maia. Well—I remember you declared, among other things, that it was going to do me such a tremendous lot of good. But—but——

Professor Rubek. But——?

Maia. But now I don't believe the least little bit that that was the reason——

Professor Rubek. Then what is your theory about it now?

Maia. I think now that it was on account of that pale lady.

Professor Rubek. Madame von Satow——!

Maia. Yes, she who is always hanging at our heels. Yesterday evening she made her appearance up here too.

Professor Rubek. But what in all the world——!

Maia. Oh, I know you knew her very well indeed—long before you knew me.

Professor Rubek. And had forgotten her, too—long before I knew you.

Maia [*sitting upright*]. Can you forget so easily, Rubek?

Professor Rubek [*curtly*]. Yes, very easily indeed. [*Adds harshly.*] When I want to forget.

Maia. Even a woman who has been a model to you?

Professor Rubek. When I have no more use for her——

Maia. One who has stood to you undressed?

Professor Rubek. That means nothing—nothing for us artists. [*With a change of tone.*] And then—may I venture to ask—how was *I* to guess that she was in this country?

Maia. Oh, you might have seen her name in a Visitors' List—in one of the newspapers.

Professor Rubek. But I had no idea of the name she now goes by. I had never heard of any Herr von Satow.

Maia [*affecting weariness*]. Oh, well then, I suppose it must have been for some other reason that you were so set upon this journey.

Professor Rubek [*seriously*]. Yes, Maia—it was for another reason. A quite different reason. And that is what we must sooner or later have a clear explanation about.

Maia [*in a fit of suppressed laughter*]. Heavens, how solemn you look!

Professor Rubek [*suspiciously scrutinizing her*]. Yes, perhaps a little more solemn than necessary.

Maia. How so——?

Professor Rubek. And that is a very good thing for us both.

Maia. You begin to make me feel curious, Rubek.

Professor Rubek. Only curious? Not a little bit uneasy.

Maia [*shaking her head*]. Not in the least.

Professor Rubek. Good. Then listen.—You said that day down at the Baths that it seemed to you I had become very nervous of late——

Maia. Yes, and you really have.

Professor Rubek. And what do you think can be the reason of that?

Maia. How can I tell——? [*Quickly.*] Perhaps you have grown weary of this constant companionship with me.

Professor Rubek. Constant——? Why not say "everlasting"?

Maia. Daily companionship, then. Here have we two solitary people lived down there for four or five mortal years, and scarcely been an hour away from each other.—We two all by ourselves.

Professor Rubek [*with interest*]. Well? And then——?

Maia [*a little oppressed*]. You are not a particularly sociable man, Rubek. You like to keep yourself to yourself and think your own thoughts. And of course I can't talk properly to you about your affairs. I know nothing about art and that sort of thing—— [*With an impatient gesture.*] And care very little either, for that matter!

Professor Rubek. Well, well; and that's why we generally sit by the fireside, and chat about your affairs.

Maia. Oh, good gracious—I have no affairs to chat about.

Professor Rubek. Well, they are trifles, perhaps; but at any rate the time passes for us in that way as well as another, Maia.

Maia. Yes, you are right. Time passes. It is passing away from you, Rubek.—And I suppose it is really that that makes you so uneasy——

Professor Rubek [*nods vehemently*]. And so restless! [*Writhing in his seat.*] No, I shall soon not be able to endure this pitiful life any longer.

Maia [*rises and stands for a moment looking at him*]. If you want to get rid of me, you have only to say so.

Professor Rubek. Why will you use such phrases? Get rid of you?

Maia. Yes, if you want to have done with me, please say so right out. And I will go that instant.

Professor Rubek [*with an almost imperceptible smile*]. Do you intend that as a threat, Maia?

Maia. There can be no threat for you in what I said.

Professor Rubek [*rising*]. No, I confess you are right there. [*Adds after a pause.*] You and I cannot possibly go on living together like this——

Maia. Well? And then——?

Professor Rubek. There is no "then" about it. [*With emphasis on his words.*] Because we two cannot go on living together alone—it does not necessarily follow that we must part.

Maia [*smiles scornfully*]. Only draw away from each other a little, you mean?

Professor Rubek [*shakes his head*]. Even that is not necessary.

Maia. Well then? Come out with what you want to do with me.

Professor Rubek [*with some hesitation*]. What I now feel so keenly—and so painfully—that I require, is to have someone about me who really and truly stands close to me——

Maia [*interrupts him anxiously*]. Don't *I* do that, Rubek?

Professor Rubek [*waving her aside*]. Not in that sense. What I need is the companionship of another person who can, as it were, complete me—supply what is wanting in me—be one with me in all my striving.

Maia [*slowly*]. It's true that things like that are a great deal too hard for me.

Professor Rubek. Oh, no, they are not at all in your line, Maia.

Maia [*with an outburst*]. And heaven knows I don't want them to be, either!

Professor Rubek. I know that very well.—And it was with no idea of finding any such help in my lifework that I married you.

Maia [*observing him closely*]. I can see in your face that you are thinking of someone else.

Professor Rubek. Indeed? I have never noticed before that you were a thought reader. But you can see that, can you?

Maia. Yes, I can. Oh, I know you so well, so well, Rubek.

Professor Rubek. Then perhaps you can also see who it is I am thinking of?

Maia. Yes, indeed I can.

Professor Rubek. Well? Have the goodness to——?

Maia. You are thinking of that—that model you once used for—— [*Suddenly letting slip the train of thought.*] Do you know, the people down at the hotel think she's mad.

Professor Rubek. Indeed? And pray what do the people down at the hotel think of you and the bear killer?

Maia. That has nothing to do with the matter. [*Continuing the former train of thought.*] But it was this pale lady you were thinking of.

Professor Rubek [*calmly*]. Precisely, of her.—When I had no more use for her—and when, besides, she went away from me—vanished without a word——

Maia. Then you accepted me as a sort of makeshift, I suppose?

Professor Rubek [*more unfeelingly*]. Something of the sort, to tell the truth, little Maia. For a year or a year and a half I had lived there lonely and brooding, and had put the last touch—the very last touch, to my work. "The Resurrection Day" went out over the world and brought me fame—and everything else that heart could desire. [*With greater warmth.*] But I no longer loved my own work. Men's laurels and incense nauseated me, till I could have rushed away in despair and hidden myself in the depths of the woods. [*Looking at her.*] You, who are a thought reader—can you guess what then occurred to me?

Maia [*lightly*]. Yes, it occurred to you to make portrait busts of gentlemen and ladies.

Professor Rubek [*nods*]. To order, yes. With animals' faces behind the masks. Those I threw in gratis—into the bargain, you understand. [*Smiling.*] But that was not precisely what I had in my mind.

Maia. What, then?

Professor Rubek [*again serious*]. It was this, that all the talk about the artist's vocation and the artist's mission, and so forth, began to strike me as being very empty, and hollow, and meaningless at bottom.

Maia. Then what would you put in its place?

Professor Rubek. Life, Maia.

Maia. Life?

Professor Rubek. Yes, is not life in sunshine and in beauty a hundred times better worth while than to hang about to the end of your days in a raw, damp hole, and wear yourself out in a perpetual struggle with lumps of clay and blocks of stone?

Maia [*with a little sigh*]. Yes, I have always thought so, certainly.

Professor Rubek. And then I had become rich enough to live in luxury and in indolent, quivering sunshine. I was able to build myself the villa on the Lake of Taunitz, and the palazzo in the capital,—and all the rest of it.

Maia [*taking up his tone*]. And last but not least, you could afford to treat yourself to me, too. And you gave me leave to share in all your treasures.

Professor Rubek [*jesting, so as to turn the conversation*]. Did I not promise to take you up with me to a high mountain and show you all the glory of the world?

Maia [*with a gentle expression*]. You have perhaps taken me up with you to a high enough mountain, Rubek —but you have not shown me all the glory of the world.

Professor Rubek [*with a laugh of irritation*]. How insatiable you are, Maia! Absolutely insatiable! [*With a vehement outburst.*] But do you know what is the most hopeless thing of all, Maia? Can you guess that?

Maia [*with quiet defiance*]. Yes, I suppose it is that you have gone and tied yourself to me—for life.

Professor Rubek. I would not have expressed myself so heartlessly.

Maia. But you would have meant it just as heartlessly.

Professor Rubek. You have no clear idea of the inner workings of an artist's nature.

Maia [*smiling and shaking her head*]. Good heavens, I haven't even a clear idea of the inner workings of my own nature.

Professor Rubek [*continuing undisturbed*]. I live at such high speed, Maia. We live so, we artists. I, for my part, have lived through a whole lifetime in the few years we two have known each other. I have come to realize that

I am not at all adapted for seeking happiness in indolent enjoyment. Life does not shape itself that way for me and those like me. I must go on working—producing one work after another—right up to my dying day. [*Forcing himself to continue.*] That is why I cannot get on with you any longer, Maia—not with you alone.

Maia [*quietly*]. Does that mean, in plain language, that you have grown tired of me?

Professor Rubek [*bursts forth*]. Yes, that is what it means! I have grown tired—intolerably tired and fretted and unstrung—in this life with you! Now you know it. [*Controlling himself.*] These are hard, ugly words I am using. I know that very well. And you are not at all to blame in this matter;—that I willingly admit. It is simply and solely I myself, who have once more undergone a revolution—[*Half to himself.*]—an awakening to my real life.

Maia [*involuntarily folding her hands*]. Why in all the world should we not part then?

Professor Rubek [*looks at her in astonishment*]. Should you be willing to?

Maia [*shrugging her shoulders*]. Oh, yes—if there's nothing else for it, then——

Professor Rubek [*eagerly*]. But there is something else for it. There is an alternative——

Maia [*holding up her forefinger*]. Now you are thinking of the pale lady again!

Professor Rubek. Yes, to tell the truth, I cannot help constantly thinking of her. Ever since I met her again. [*A step nearer her.*] For now I will tell you a secret, Maia.

Maia. Well?

Professor Rubek [*touching his own breast*]. In here, you see—in here I have a little Bramah-locked casket. And in that casket all my sculptor's visions are stored up. But when she disappeared and left no trace, the lock of the casket snapped to. And she had the key—and she took it away with her.—You, little Maia, you had no key; so all that the casket contains must lie unused. And the years pass! And I have no means of getting at the treasure.

Maia [*trying to repress a subtle smile*]. Then get her to open the casket for you again——

Professor Rubek [*not understanding*]. Maia——?

Maia. —for here she is, you see. And no doubt it's on account of this casket that she has come.

Professor Rubek. I have not said a single word to her on this subject!

Maia [*looks innocently at him*]. My dear Rubek—is it worth-while to make all this fuss and commotion about so simple a matter?

Professor Rubek. Do you think this matter is so absolutely simple?

Maia. Yes, certainly I think so. Do you attach yourself to whoever you most require. [*Nods to him.*] I shall always manage to find a place for myself.

Professor Rubek. Where do you mean?

Maia [*unconcerned, evasively*]. Well—I need only take myself off to the villa, if it should be necessary. But it won't be; for in town—in all that great house of ours—there must surely, with a little good will, be room enough for three.

Professor Rubek [*uncertainly*]. And do you think that would work in the long run?

Maia [*in a light tone*]. Very well, then—if it won't work, it won't. It is no good talking about it.

Professor Rubek. And what shall we do then, Maia—if it does not work?

Maia [*untroubled*]. Then we two will simply get out of each other's way—part entirely. I shall always find something new for myself, somewhere in the world. Something free! Free! Free!—No need to be anxious about that, Professor Rubek! [*Suddenly points off to the right.*] Look there! There we have her.

Professor Rubek [*turning*]. Where?

Maia. Out on the plain. Striding—like a marble statue. She is coming this way.

Professor Rubek [*stands gazing with his hand over his eyes*]. Does not she look like the Resurrection incarnate? [*To himself.*] And her I could displace—and move into the shade! Remodel her—— Fool that I was!

Maia. What do you mean by that?

Professor Rubek [*putting the question aside*]. Nothing. Nothing that you would understand.

IRENE *advances from the right over the upland. The children at their play have already caught sight of her and run to meet her. She is now surrounded by them; some appear confident and at ease, others uneasy and timid. She talks low to them and indicates that they are to*

*go down to the hotel; she herself will rest a little beside the
brook. The children run down over the slope to the left,
halfway to the back.* IRENE *goes up to the wall of rock,
and lets the rillets of the cascade flow over her hands,
cooling them.*

Maia [*in a low voice*]. Go down and speak to her alone,
Rubek.

Professor Rubek. And where will you go in the meantime?

Maia [*looking significantly at him*]. Henceforth I shall
go my own ways. [*She descends from the hillock and leaps
over the brook, by aid of her alpenstock. She stops beside
IRENE.*] Professor Rubek is up there, waiting for you,
madam.

Irene. What does he want?

Maia. He wants you to help him to open a casket that
has snapped to.

Irene. Can I help him in that?

Maia. He says you are the only person that can.

Irene. Then I must try.

Maia. Yes, you really must, madam. [*She goes down by
the path to the hotel.*]

In a little while PROFESSOR RUBEK *comes down to* IRENE,
but stops with the brook between them.

Irene [*after a short pause*]. She—the other one—said
that you had been waiting for me.

Professor Rubek. I have waited for you year after year
—without myself knowing it.

Irene. I could not come to you, Arnold. I was lying down
there, sleeping the long, deep, dreamful sleep.

Professor Rubek. But now you have awakened, Irene!

Irene [*shakes her head*]. I have the heavy, deep sleep
still in my eyes.

Professor Rubek. You shall see that day will dawn and
lighten for us both.

Irene. Do not believe that.

Professor Rubek [*urgently*]. I do believe it! And I know
it! Now that I have found you again——

Irene. Risen from the grave.

Professor Rubek. Transfigured!

Irene. Only risen, Arnold. Not transfigured.

*He crosses over to her by means of steppingstones below
the cascade.*

Professor Rubek. Where have you been all day, Irene?

Irene [*pointing*]. Far, far over there, on the great dead
waste——

Professor Rubek [*turning the conversation*]. You have
not your—your friend with you today, I see.

Irene [*smiling*]. My friend is keeping a close watch on
me, none the less.

Professor Rubek. Can she?

Irene [*glancing furtively around*]. You may be sure she
can—wherever I may go. She never loses sight of me——
[*Whispering.*] Until, one fine sunny morning, I shall kill
her.

Professor Rubek. Would you do that?

Irene. With the utmost delight—if only I could manage
it.

Professor Rubek. Why do you want to?

Irene. Because she deals in witchcraft. [*Mysteriously.*]
Only think, Arnold—she has changed herself into my
shadow.

Professor Rubek [*trying to calm her*]. Well, well, well—
a shadow we must all have.

Irene. I am my own shadow. [*With an outburst.*] Do
you not understand that!

Professor Rubek [*sadly*]. Yes, yes, Irene, I understand it.

*He seats himself on a stone beside the brook. She stands
behind him, leaning against the wall of rock.*

Irene [*after a pause*]. Why do you sit there turning
your eyes away from me?

Professor Rubek [*softly, shaking his head*]. I dare not—
I dare not look at you.

Irene. Why dare you not look at me any more?

Professor Rubek. You have a shadow that tortures me.
And *I* have the crushing weight of my conscience.

Irene [*with a glad cry of deliverance*]. At last!

Professor Rubek [*springs up*]. Irene—what is it!

Irene [*motioning him off*]. Keep still, still, still! [*Draws
a deep breath and says, as though relieved of a burden.*]
There! Now they let me go. For this time.—Now we can
sit down and talk as we used to—when I was alive.

Professor Rubek. Oh, if only we could talk as we used to.

Irene. Sit there, where you were sitting. I will sit here beside you.

He sits down again. She seats herself on another stone, close to him.

Irene [*after a short interval of silence*]. Now I have come back to you from the uttermost regions, Arnold.

Professor Rubek. Aye, truly, from an endless journey.

Irene. Come home to my lord and master——

Professor Rubek. To our home;—to our own home, Irene.

Irene. Have you looked for my coming every single day?

Professor Rubek. How dared I look for you?

Irene [*with a sidelong glance*]. No, I suppose you dared not. For you understood nothing.

Professor Rubek. Was it really not for the sake of someone else that you all of a sudden disappeared from me in that way?

Irene. Might it not quite well be for your sake, Arnold?

Professor Rubek [*looks doubtfully at her*]. I don't understand you——?

Irene. When I had served you with my soul and with my body—when the statue stood there finished—our child as you called it—then I laid at your feet the most precious sacrifice of all—by effacing myself for all time.

Professor Rubek [*bows his head*]. And laying my life waste.

Irene [*suddenly firing up*]. It was just that I wanted! Never, never should you create anything again—after you had created that only child of ours.

Professor Rubek. Was it jealousy that moved you, then?

Irene [*coldly*]. I think it was rather hatred.

Professor Rubek. Hatred? Hatred for me?

Irene [*again vehemently*]. Yes, for you—for the artist who had so lightly and carelessly taken a warm-blooded body, a young human life, and worn the soul out of it—because you needed it for a work of art.

Professor Rubek. And you can say that—you who threw yourself into my work with such saintlike passion and such ardent joy?—that work for which we two met together every morning, as for an act of worship.

Irene [*coldly, as before*]. I will tell you one thing, Arnold.

Professor Rubek. Well?

Irene. I never loved your art, before I met you.—Nor after either.

Professor Rubek. But the artist, Irene?

Irene. The artist I hate.

Professor Rubek. The artist in me too?

Irene. In you most of all. When I unclothed myself and stood for you, then I hated you, Arnold——

Professor Rubek [*warmly*]. That you did not, Irene! That is not true!

Irene. I hated you, because you could stand there so unmoved——

Professor Rubek [*laughs*]. Unmoved? Do you think so?

Irene. —at any rate so intolerably self-controlled. And because you were an artist and an artist only—not a man! [*Changing to a tone fully of warmth and feeling.*] But that statue in the wet, living clay, that I loved—as it rose up, a vital human creature, out of those raw, shapeless masses —for that was our creation, our child. Mine and yours.

Professor Rubek [*sadly*]. It was so in spirit and in truth.

Irene. Let me tell you, Arnold—it is for the sake of this child of ours that I have undertaken this long pilgrimage.

Professor Rubek [*suddenly alert*]. For the statue's——?

Irene. Call it what you will. I call it our child.

Professor Rubek. And now you want to see it? Finished? In marble, which you always thought so cold? [*Eagerly.*] You do not know, perhaps, that it is installed in a great museum somewhere—far out in the world?

Irene. I have heard a sort of legend about it.

Professor Rubek. And museums were always a horror to you. You called them grave vaults——

Irene. I will make a pilgrimage to the place where my soul and my child's soul lie buried.

Professor Rubek [*uneasy and alarmed*]. You must never see that statue again! Do you hear, Irene! I implore you——! Never, never see it again!

Irene. Perhaps you think it would mean death to me a second time?

Professor Rubek [*clenching his hands together*]. Oh, I don't know what I think. But how could I ever imagine that you would fix your mind so immovably on that statue? You, who went away from me—before it was completed.

Irene. It was completed. That was why I could go away from you—and leave you alone.

Professor Rubek [*sits with his elbows upon his knees, rocking his head from side to side, with his hands before his eyes*]. It was not what it afterwards became.

Irene [*quietly, but quick as lightning, half-unsheathes a narrow-bladed sharp knife which she carries in her breast, and asks in a hoarse whisper*]. Arnold—have you done any evil to our child?

Professor Rubek [*evasively*]. Any evil?—How can I be sure what you would call it?

Irene [*breathless*]. Tell me at once: what have you done to the child?

Professor Rubek. I will tell you, if you will sit and listen quietly to what I say.

Irene [*hides the knife*]. I will listen as quietly as a mother can when she——

Professor Rubek [*interrupting*]. And you must not look at me while I am telling you.

Irene [*moves to a stone behind his back*]. I will sit here, behind you. Now tell me.

Professor Rubek [*takes his hands from before his eyes and gazes straight in front of him*]. When I had found you, I knew at once how I should make use of you for my lifework.

Irene. "The Resurrection Day" you called your life-work.—I call it "our child."

Professor Rubek. I was young then—with no knowledge of life. The Resurrection, I thought, would be most beauti-fully and exquisitely figured as a young unsullied woman —with none of our earth-life's experiences—awakening to light and glory without having to put away from her anything ugly and impure.

Irene [*quickly*]. Yes—and so I stand there now, in our work?

Professor Rubek [*hesitating*]. Not absolutely and en-tirely so, Irene.

Irene [*in rising excitement*]. Not absolutely——? Do I not stand as I always stood for you?

Professor Rubek [*without answering*]. I learned worldly wisdom in the years that followed, Irene. "The Resurrec-tion Day" became in my mind's eye something more and something—something more complex. The little round plinth on which your figure stood erect and solitary—it no longer afforded room for all the imagery I now wanted to add——

Irene [*gropes for her knife, but desists*]. What imagery did you add then? Tell me!

Professor Rubek. I imaged that which I saw with my eyes around me in the world. I had to include it—I could not help it, Irene. I expanded the plinth—made it wide and spacious. And on it I placed a segment of the curving, bursting earth. And up from the fissures of the soil there now swarm men and women with dimly suggested animal faces. Women and men—as I knew them in real life.

Irene [*in breathless suspense*]. But in the middle of the rout there stands the young woman radiant with the joy of light? Do I not stand so, Arnold?

Professor Rubek [*evasively*]. Not quite in the middle. I had unfortunately to move that figure a little back. For the sake of the general effect, you understand. Otherwise it would have dominated the whole too much.

Irene. But the joy in the light still transfigures my face?

Professor Rubek. Yes, it does, Irene—in a way. A little subdued perhaps—as my altered idea required.

Irene [*rising noiselessly*]. That design expresses the life you now see, Arnold.

Professor Rubek. Yes, I suppose it does.

Irene. And in that design you have shifted me back, a little toned down—to serve as a background figure—in a group. [*She draws the knife.*]

Professor Rubek. Not a background figure. Let us say, at most, a figure not quite in the foreground—or something of that sort.

Irene [*whispers hoarsely*]. There you uttered your own doom. [*On the point of striking.*]

Professor Rubek [*turns and looks up at her*]. Doom?

Irene [*hastily hides the knife, and says as though choked with agony*]. My whole soul—you and I—we, we we and our child were in that solitary figure.

Professor Rubek [*eagerly, taking off his hat and drying the drops of sweat upon his brow*]. Yes, but let me tell you, too, how I have placed myself in the group. In front, beside a fountain—as it were here—sits a man weighed down with guilt, who cannot quite free himself from the earth-crust. I call him remorse for a forfeited life. He sits there and dips his fingers in the purling stream—to wash them clean—and he is gnawed and tortured by the thought that never, never will he succeed. Never in all eternity will he attain to freedom and the new life. He will remain forever prisoned in his hell.

Irene [*hardly and coldly*]. Poet!

Professor Rubek. Why poet?

Irene. Because you are nerveless and sluggish and full of forgiveness for all the sins of your life, in thought and in act. You have killed my soul—so you model yourself in remorse, and self-accusation, and penance—[*Smiling.*] —and with that you think your account is cleared.

Professor Rubek [*defiantly*]. I am an artist, Irene. And I take no shame to myself for the frailties that perhaps cling to me. For I was born to be an artist, you see. And, do what I may, I shall never be anything else.

Irene [*looks at him with a lurking evil smile, and says gently and softly*]. You are a poet, Arnold. [*Softly strokes his hair.*] You dear, great, middle-aged child,—is it possible that you cannot see that!

Professor Rubek [*annoyed*]. Why do you keep on calling me a poet?

Irene [*with malign eyes*]. Because there is something apologetic in the word, my friend. Something that suggests forgiveness of sins—and spreads a cloak over all frailty. [*With a sudden change of tone.*] But *I* was a human being —then! And I, too, had a life to live,—and a human destiny to fulfill. And all that, look you, I let slip—gave it all up in order to make myself your bondwoman.—Oh, it was self-murder—a deadly sin against myself! [*Half whispering.*] And that sin I can never expiate!

She seats herself near him beside the brook, keeps close, though unnoticed, watch upon him, and, as though in absence of mind, plucks some flowers from the shrubs around them.

[*With apparent self-control.*] I should have borne children into the world—many children—real children—not such children as are hidden away in grave vaults. That was my vocation. I ought never to have served you—poet.

Professor Rubek [*lost in recollection*]. Yet those were beautiful days, Irene. Marvelously beautiful days—as I now look back upon them——

Irene [*looking at him with a soft expression*]. Can you

remember a little word that you said—when you had finished—finished with me and with our child? [*Nods to him.*] Can you remember that little word, Arnold?

Professor Rubek [*looks inquiringly at her*]. Did I say a little word then, which you still remember?

Irene. Yes, you did. Can you not recall it?

Professor Rubek [*shaking his head*]. No, I can't say that I do. Not at the present moment, at any rate.

Irene. You took both my hands and pressed them warmly. And I stood there in breathless expectation. And then you said: "So now, Irene, I thank you from my heart. This," you said, "has been a priceless episode for me."

Professor Rubek [*looks doubtfully at her*]. Did I say "episode"? It is not a word I am in the habit of using.

Irene. You said "episode."

Professor Rubek [*with assumed cheerfulness*]. Well, well —after all, it was in reality an episode.

Irene [*curtly*]. At that word I left you.

Professor Rubek. You take everything so painfully to heart, Irene.

Irene [*drawing her hand over her forehead*]. Perhaps you are right. Let us shake off all the hard things that go to the heart. [*Plucks off the leaves of a mountain rose and strews them on the brook.*] Look there, Arnold. There are our birds swimming.

Professor Rubek. What birds are they?

Irene. Can you not see? Of course they are flamingos. Are they not rose red?

Professor Rubek. Flamingos do not swim. They only wade.

Irene. Then they are not flamingos. They are sea gulls.

Professor Rubek. They may be sea gulls with red bills, yes. [*Plucks broad green leaves and throws them into the brook.*] Now I send out my ships after them.

Irene. But there must be no harpoon men on board.

Professor Rubek. No, there shall be no harpoon men. [*Smiles to her.*] Can you remember the summer when we used to sit like this outside the little peasant hut on the Lake of Taunitz?

Irene [*nods*]. On Saturday evenings, yes,—when we had finished our week's work——

Professor Rubek. —And taken the train out to the lake—to stay there over Sunday——

Irene [*with an evil gleam of hatred in her eyes*]. It was an episode, Arnold.

Professor Rubek [*as if not hearing*]. Then, too, you used to set birds swimming in the brook. They were water lilies which you——

Irene. They were white swans.

Professor Rubek. I meant swans, yes. And I remember that I fastened a great furry leaf to one of the swans. It looked like a burdock leaf——

Irene. And then it turned into Lohengrin's boat—with the swan yoked to it.

Professor Rubek. How fond you were of that game, Irene.

Irene. We played it over and over again.

Professor Rubek. Every single Saturday, I believe,—all the summer through.

Irene. You said I was the swan that drew your boat.

Professor Rubek. Did I say so? Yes, I daresay I did. [*Absorbed in the game.*] Just see how the sea gulls are swimming down the stream!

Irene [*laughing*]. And all your ships have run ashore.

Professor Rubek [*throwing more leaves into the brook*]. I have ships enough in reserve. [*Follows the leaves with his eyes, throws more into the brook, and says after a pause.*] Irene,—I have bought the little peasant hut beside the Lake of Taunitz.

Irene. Have you bought it? You often said you would, if you could afford it.

Professor Rubek. The day came when I could afford it easily enough; and so I bought it.

Irene [*with a sidelong look at him*]. Then do you live out there now—in our old house?

Professor Rubek. No, I have had it pulled down long ago. And I have built myself a great, handsome, comfortable villa on the site—with a park around it. It is there that we—[*Stops and corrects himself.*]—there that I usually live during the summer.

Irene [*mastering herself*]. So you and—and the other one live out there now?

Professor Rubek [*with a touch of defiance*]. Yes. When my wife and I are not traveling—as we are this year.

Irene [*looking far before her*]. Life was beautiful, beautiful by the Lake of Taunitz.

Professor Rubek [*as though looking back into himself*]. And yet, Irene——

Irene [*completing his thought*]. —Yet we two let slip all that life and its beauty.

Professor Rubek [*softly, urgently*]. Does repentance come too late, now?

Irene [*does not answer, but sits silent for a moment; then she points over the upland*]. Look there, Arnold,—now the sun is going down behind the peaks. See what a red glow the level rays cast over all the heathery knolls out yonder.

Professor Rubek [*looks where she is pointing*]. It is long since I have seen a sunset in the mountains.

Irene. Or a sunrise?

Professor Rubek. A sunrise I don't think I have ever seen.

Irene [*smiles as though lost in recollection*]. *I* once saw a marvelously lovely sunrise.

Professor Rubek. Did you? Where was that?

Irene. High, high up on a dizzy mountaintop.—You beguiled me up there by promising that I should see all the glory of the world if only I—— [*She stops suddenly.*]

Professor Rubek. If only you——? Well?

Irene. I did as you told me—went with you up to the heights. And there I fell upon my knees, and worshiped you, and served you. [*Is silent for a moment; then says softly.*] Then I saw the sunrise.

Professor Rubek [*turning the conversation*]. Should you not like to come and live with us in the villa down there?

Irene [*looks at him with a scornful smile*]. With you—and the other woman?

Professor Rubek [*urgently*]. With me—as in our days of creation. You could open all that is locked up in me. Can you not find it in your heart, Irene?

Irene [*shaking her head*]. I have no longer the key to you, Arnold.

Professor Rubek. You have the key! You and you alone possess it! [*Beseechingly.*] Help me—that I may be able to live my life over again!

Irene [*immovable as before*]. Empty dreams! Idle—dead dreams. For the life you and I led there is no resurrection.

Professor Rubek [*curtly, breaking off*]. Then let us go on playing.

Irene. Yes, playing, playing—only playing!

They sit and strew leaves and petals over the brook, where
they float and sail away.

Up the slope to the left at the back come ULFHEIM *and*
MAIA *in hunting costume. After them comes the* SERVANT
with the leash of dogs, with which he goes out to the right.

Professor Rubek [*catching sight of them*]. Ah! there is
little Maia, going out with the bear hunter.

Irene. Your lady, yes.

Professor Rubek. Or the other's.

Maia [*looks around as she is crossing the upland, sees
the two sitting by the brook, and calls out*]. Good night,
Professor! Dream of me. Now I am going off on my ad-
ventures!

Professor Rubek [*calls back to her*]. What sort of an
adventure is this to be?

Maia [*approaching*]. I am going to let life take the
place of all the rest.

Professor Rubek [*mockingly*]. Aha! so you too are going
to do that, little Maia?

Maia. Yes. And I've made a verse about it, and this is
how it goes: [*Sings triumphantly*]

I am free! I am free! I am free!
No more life in the prison for me!
I am free as a bird! I am free!

For I believe I have awakened now—at last.

Professor Rubek. It almost seems so.

Maia [*drawing a deep breath*]. Oh—how divinely light
one feels on waking!

Professor Rubek. Good night, Frau Maia—and good
luck to——

Ulfheim [*calls out, interposing*]. Hush, hush!—for the
devil's sake let's have none of your wizard wishes. Don't
you see that we are going out to shoot——

Professor Rubek. What will you bring me home from
the hunting, Maia?

Maia. You shall have a bird of prey to model. I shall
wing one for you.

Professor Rubek [*laughs mockingly and bitterly*]. Yes,
to wing things—without knowing what you are doing—
that has long been quite in your way.

Maia [*tossing her head*]. Oh, just let me take care of
myself for the future, and I wish you then——! [*Nods and*

laughs roguishly.] Good-by—and a good, peaceful summer night on the upland!

Professor Rubek [*jestingly*]. Thanks! and all the ill-luck in the world over you and your hunting!

Ulfheim [*roaring with laughter*]. There now, that is a wish worth having!

Maia [*laughing*]. Thanks, thanks, thanks, Professor!

They have both crossed the visible portion of the upland, and go out through the bushes to the right.

Professor Rubek [*after a short pause*]. A summer night on the upland! Yes, that would have been life!

Irene [*suddenly, with a wild expression in her eyes*]. Will you spend a summer night on the upland—with me?

Professor Rubek [*stretching his arms wide*]. Yes, yes—come!

Irene. My adored lord and master!

Professor Rubek. Oh, Irene!

Irene [*hoarsely, smiling and groping in her breast*]. It will be only an episode—— [*Quickly, whispering.*] Hush! —do not look round, Arnold!

Professor Rubek [*also in a low voice*]. What is it?

Irene. A face that is staring at me.

Professor Rubek [*turns involuntarily*]. Where? [*With a start.*] Ah——!

The SISTER OF MERCY's *head is partly visible among the bushes beside the descent to the left. Her eyes are immovably fixed on* IRENE.

Irene [*rises and says softly*]. We must part then. No, you must remain sitting. Do you hear? You must not go with me. [*Bends over him and whispers.*] Till we meet again— tonight—on the upland.

Professor Rubek. And you will come, Irene?

Irene. Yes, surely I will come. Wait for me here.

Professor Rubek [*repeats dreamily*]. Summer night on the upland. With you. With you. [*His eyes meet hers.*] Oh, Irene—that might have been our life.—And that we have forfeited—we two.

Irene. We see the irretrievable only when—— [*Breaks off.*]

Professor Rubek [*looks inquiringly at her*]. When——?

Irene. When we dead awaken.

Professor Rubek [*shakes his head mournfully*]. What do
we really see then?

Irene. We see that we have never lived. [*She goes
toward the slope and descends.*]

The SISTER OF MERCY *makes way for her and follows her.*
PROFESSOR RUBEK *remains sitting motionless beside the
brook.*

Maia [*is heard singing triumphantly among the hills*].

> I am free! I am free! I am free!
> No more life in the prison for me!
> I am free as a bird! I am free!

ACT THIRD

*A wild riven mountainside, with sheer precipices at the
back. Snow-clad peaks rise to the right, and lose themselves in drifting mists. To the left, on a stone-scree, stands
an old, half-ruined hut. It is early morning. Dawn is
breaking. The sun has not yet risen.*

MAIA *comes, flushed and irritated, down over the stone-
scree on the left.* ULFHEIM *follows, half angry, half laughing, holding her fast by the sleeve.*

MAIA [*trying to tear herself loose*]. Let me go! Let me
go, I say!

Ulfheim. Come, come! are you going to bite now? You're
as snappish as a wolf.

Maia [*striking him over the hand*]. Let me go, I tell you!
And be quiet!

Ulfheim. No, confound me if I will!

Maia. Then I will not go another step with you. Do you
hear?—not a single step!

Ulfheim. Ho, ho! How can you get away from me, here,
on the wild mountainside?

Maia. I will jump over the precipice yonder, if need
be——

Ulfheim. And mangle and mash yourself up into dogs'
meat! A juicy morsel! [*Lets go his hold.*] As you please.
Jump over the precipice if you want to. It's a dizzy drop.

There's only one narrow footpath down it, and that's almost impassable.

Maia [*dusts her skirt with her hand, and looks at him with angry eyes*]. Well, you are a nice one to go hunting with!

Ulfheim. Say, rather, sporting.

Maia. Oh! So you call this sport, do you?

Ulfheim. Yes, I venture to take that liberty. It is the sort of sport I like best of all.

Maia [*tossing her head*]. Well—I must say! [*After a pause; looks searchingly at him.*] Why did you let the dogs loose up there?

Ulfheim [*blinking his eyes and smiling*]. So that they too might do a little hunting on their own account, don't you see?

Maia. There's not a word of truth in that! It wasn't for the dogs' sake that you let them go.

Ulfheim [*still smiling*]. Well, why did I let them go then? Let us hear.

Maia. You let them go because you wanted to get rid of Lars. He was to run after them and bring them in again, you said. And in the meantime——. Oh, it was a pretty way to behave!

Ulfheim. In the meantime?

Maia [*curtly breaking off*]. No matter!

Ulfheim [*in a confidential tone*]. Lars won't find them. You may safely swear to that. He won't come with them before the time's up.

Maia [*looking angrily at him*]. No, I daresay not.

Ulfheim [*catching at her arm*]. For Lars—he knows my—my methods of sport, you see.

Maia [*eludes him, and measures him with a glance*]. Do you know what you look like, Mr. Ulfheim?

Ulfheim. I should think I'm probably most like myself.

Maia. Yes, there you're exactly right. For you're the living image of a faun.

Ulfheim. A faun?

Maia. Yes, precisely; a faun.

Ulfheim. A faun! Isn't that a sort of monster? Or a kind of wood demon, as you might call it?

Maia. Yes, just the sort of creature you are. A thing with a goat's beard and goat legs. Yes, and the faun has horns too!

Ulfheim. So, so!—has he horns too?

Maia. A pair of ugly horns, just like yours, yes.

Ulfheim. Can you see the poor little horns *I* have?

Maia. Yes, I seem to see them quite plainly.

Ulfheim [*taking the dogs' leash out of his pocket*]. Then I had better see about tying you.

Maia. Have you gone quite mad? Would you tie me?

Ulfheim. If I am a demon, let me be a demon! So that's the way of it! You can see the horns, can you?

Maia [*soothingly*]. There, there, there! Now try to behave nicely, Mr. Ulfheim. [*Breaking off.*] But what has become of that hunting castle of yours, that you boasted so much of? You said it lay somewhere hereabouts.

Ulfheim [*points with a flourish to the hut*]. There you have it, before your very eyes.

Maia [*looks at him*]. That old pigsty!

Ulfheim [*laughing in his beard*]. It has harbored more than one king's daughter, I can tell you.

Maia. Was it there that that horrid man you told me about came to the king's daughter in the form of a bear?

Ulfheim. Yes, my fair companion of the chase—this is the scene. [*With a gesture of invitation.*] If you would deign to enter——

Maia. Isch! If ever I set foot in it——! Isch!

Ulfheim. Oh, two people can doze away a summer night in there comfortably enough. Or a whole summer, if it comes to that!

Maia. Thanks! One would need to have a pretty strong taste for that kind of thing. [*Impatiently.*] But now I am tired both of you and the hunting expedition. Now I am going down to the hotel—before people awaken down there.

Ulfheim. How do you propose to get down from here?

Maia. That's your affair. There must be a way down somewhere or other, I suppose.

Ulfheim [*pointing toward the back*]. Oh, certainly! There is a sort of way—right down the face of the precipice yonder——

Maia. There, you see. With a little good will——

Ulfheim. —But just you try if you dare go that way.

Maia [*doubtfully*]. Do you think I can't?

Ulfheim. Never in this world—if you don't let me help you.

Maia [*uneasily*]. Why, then come and help me! What else are you here for?

Ulfheim. Would you rather I should take you on my back——?

Maia. Nonsense!

Ulfheim. —Or carry you in my arms?

Maia. Now do stop talking that rubbish!

Ulfheim [*with suppressed exasperation*]. I once took a young girl—lifted her up from the mire of the streets and carried her in my arms. Next my heart I carried her. So I would have borne her all through life—lest haply she should dash her foot against a stone. For her shoes were worn very thin when I found her——

Maia. And yet you took her up and carried her next your heart?

Ulfheim. Took her up out of the gutter and carried her as high and as carefully as I could. [*With a growling laugh.*] And do you know what I got for my reward?

Maia. No. What did you get?

Ulfheim [*looks at her, smiles and nods*]. I got the horns! The horns that you can see so plainly. Is not that a comical story, madam bear murderess?

Maia. Oh, yes, comical enough! But I know another story that is still more comical.

Ulfheim. How does that story go?

Maia. This is how it goes. There was once a stupid girl, who had both a father and a mother—but a rather poverty-stricken home. Then there came a high and mighty seigneur into the midst of all this poverty. And he took the girl in his arms—as you did—and traveled far, far away with her——

Ulfheim. Was she so anxious to be with him?

Maia. Yes, for she was stupid, you see.

Ulfheim. And he, no doubt, was a brilliant and beautiful personage?

Maia. Oh, no, he wasn't so superlatively beautiful either. But he pretended that he would take her with him to the top of the highest of mountains, where there were light and sunshine without end.

Ulfheim. So he was a mountaineer, was he, that man?

Maia. Yes, he was—in his way.

Ulfheim. And then he took the girl up with him——?

Maia [*with a toss of the head*]. Took her up with him finely, you may be sure! Oh, no! he beguiled her into a cold, clammy cage, where—as it seemed to her—there was neither sunlight nor fresh air, but only gilding and great petrified ghosts of people all round the walls.

Ulfheim. Devil take me, but it served her right!

Maia. Yes, but don't you think it's quite a comical story, all the same?

Ulfheim [*looks at her a moment*]. Now listen to me, my good companion of the chase——

Maia. Well, what is it now?

Ulfheim. Should not we two tack our poor shreds of life together?

Maia. Is his worship inclined to set up as a patching tailor?

Ulfheim. Yes, indeed he is. Might not we two try to draw the rags together here and there—so as to make some sort of a human life out of them?

Maia. And when the poor tatters were quite worn out—what then?

Ulfheim [*with a large gesture*]. Then there we shall stand, free and serene—as the man and woman we really are!

Maia [*laughing*]. You with your goat legs, yes!

Ulfheim. And you with your—— Well, let that pass.

Maia. Yes, come—let us pass—on.

Ulfheim. Stop! Whither away, comrade?

Maia. Down to the hotel, of course.

Ulfheim. And afterwards?

Maia. Then we'll take a polite leave of each other, with thanks for pleasant company.

Ulfheim. Can we part, we two? Do you think we can?

Maia. Yes, you didn't manage to tie me up, you know.

Ulfheim. I have a castle to offer you——

Maia [*pointing to the hut*]. A fellow to that one?

Ulfheim. It has not fallen to ruin yet.

Maia. And all the glory of the world, perhaps?

Ulfheim. A castle, I tell you——

Maia. Thanks! I have had enough of castles.

Ulfheim. —With splendid hunting grounds stretching for miles around it.

Maia. Are there works of art too in this castle?

Ulfheim [*slowly*]. Well, no—it's true there are no works of art; but——

Maia [*relieved*]. Ah! that's one good thing, at any rate!

Ulfheim. Will you go with me, then—as far and as long as I want you?

Maia. There is a tame bird of prey keeping watch upon me.

Ulfheim [*wildly*]. We'll put a bullet in his wing, Maia!

Maia [*looks at him a moment, and says resolutely*]. Come then, and carry me down into the depths.

Ulfheim [*puts his arm round her waist*]. It is high time! The mist is upon us!

Maia. Is the way down terribly dangerous?

Ulfheim. The mountain mist is more dangerous still.

She shakes him off, goes to the edge of the precipice and looks over, but starts quickly back.

Ulfheim [*goes toward her, laughing*]. What? Does it make you a little giddy?

Maia [*faintly*]. Yes, that too. But go and look over. Those two, coming up——

Ulfheim [*goes and bends over the edge of the precipice*]. It's only your bird of prey—and his strange lady.

Maia. Can't we get past them—without their seeing us?

Ulfheim. Impossible! The path is far too narrow. And there's no other way down.

Maia [*nerving herself*]. Well, well—let us face them here, then!

Ulfheim. Spoken like a true bear killer, comrade!

PROFESSOR RUBEK *and* IRENE *appear over the edge of the precipice at the back. He has his plaid over his shoulders; she has a fur cloak thrown loosely over her white dress, and a swansdown hood over her head.*

Professor Rubek [*still only half visible above the edge*]. What, Maia! So we two meet once again?

Maia [*with assumed coolness*]. At your service. Won't you come up?

PROFESSOR RUBEK *climbs right up and holds out his hand to* IRENE, *who also comes right to the top.*

Professor Rubek [*coldly to* MAIA]. So you, too, have been all night on the mountain,—as we have?

Maia. I have been hunting—yes. You gave me permission, you know.

Ulfheim [*pointing downward*]. Have you come up that path there?

Professor Rubek. As you saw.

Ulfheim. And the strange lady too?

Professor Rubek. Yes, of course. [*With a glance at* MAIA.] Henceforth the strange lady and I do not intend our ways to part.

Ulfheim. Don't you know, then, that it is a deadly dangerous way you have come?

Professor Rubek. We thought we would try it, nevertheless. For it did not seem particularly hard at first.

Ulfheim. No, at first nothing seems hard. But presently you may come to a tight place where you can neither get forward nor back. And then you stick fast, Professor! Mountain-fast, as we hunters call it.

Professor Rubek [*smiles and looks at him*]. Am I to take these as oracular utterances, Mr. Ulfheim?

Ulfheim. Lord preserve me from playing the oracle! [*Urgently, pointing up toward the heights.*] But don't you see that the storm is upon us? Don't you hear the blasts of wind?

Professor Rubek [*listening*]. They sound like the prelude to the Resurrection Day.

Ulfheim. They are storm blasts from the peaks, man! Just look how the clouds are rolling and sinking—soon they'll be all around us like a winding sheet!

Irene [*with a start and shiver*]. I know that sheet!

Maia [*drawing* ULFHEIM *away*]. Let us make haste and get down.

Ulfheim [*to* PROFESSOR RUBEK]. I cannot help more than one. Take refuge in the hut in the meantime—while the storm lasts. Then I shall send people up to fetch the two of you away.

Irene [*in terror*]. To fetch us away! No, no!

Ulfheim [*harshly*]. To take you by force if necessary—for it's a matter of life and death here. Now, you know it. [*To* MAIA.] Come, then—and don't fear to trust yourself in your comrade's hands.

Maia [*clinging to him*]. Oh, how I shall rejoice and sing, if I get down with a whole skin!

Ulfheim [*begins the descent and calls to the others*]. You'll wait, then, in the hut, till the men come with ropes, and fetch you away.

ULFHEIM, *with* MAIA *in his arms, clambers rapidly but warily down the precipice.*

Irene [*looks for some time at* PROFESSOR RUBEK *with terror-stricken eyes*]. Did you hear that, Arnold?—men are coming up to fetch me away! Many men will come up here——

Professor Rubek. Do not be alarmed, Irene!

Irene [*in growing terror*]. And she, the woman in black —she will come too. For she must have missed me long ago. And then she will seize me, Arnold! And put me in the strait-waistcoat. Oh, she has it with her, in her box. I have seen it with my own eyes——

Professor Rubek. Not a soul shall be suffered to touch you.

Irene [*with a wild smile*]. Oh, no—I myself have a resource against that.

Professor Rubek. What resource do you mean?

Irene [*drawing out the knife*]. This!

Professor Rubek [*tries to seize it*]. Have you a knife?

Irene. Always, always—both day and night—in bed as well!

Professor Rubek. Give me that knife, Irene!

Irene [*concealing it*]. You shall not have it. I may very likely find a use for it myself.

Professor Rubek. What use can you have for it, here?

Irene [*looks fixedly at him*]. It was intended for you, Arnold.

Professor Rubek. For me!

Irene. As we were sitting by the Lake of Taunitz last evening——

Professor Rubek. By the Lake of——

Irene. Outside the peasant's hut—and playing with swans and water lilies——

Professor Rubek. What then—what then?

Irene. And when I heard you say with such deathly, icy coldness—that I was nothing but an episode in your life——

Professor Rubek. It was you that said that, Irene, not I.

Irene [*continuing*]. —Then I had my knife out. I wanted to stab you in the back with it.

Professor Rubek [*darkly*]. And why did you hold your hand?

Irene. Because it flashed upon me with a sudden horror that you were dead already—long ago.

Professor Rubek. Dead?

Irene. Dead. Dead, you as well as I. We sat there by the

Lake of Taunitz, we two clay-cold bodies—and played with each other.

Professor Rubek. I do not call that being dead. But you do not understand me.

Irene. Then where is the burning desire for me that you fought and battled against when I stood freely forth before you as the woman arisen from the dead?

Professor Rubek. Our love is assuredly not dead, Irene.

Irene. The love that belongs to the life of earth—the beautiful, miraculous earth life—the inscrutable earth life —that is dead in both of us.

Professor Rubek [*passionately*]. And do you know that just that love—it is burning and seething in me as hotly as ever before?

Irene. And I? Have you forgotten who I now am?

Professor Rubek. Be who or what you please, for aught I care! For me, you are the woman I see in my dreams of you.

Irene. I have stood on the turntable—naked—and made a show of myself to many hundreds of men—after you.

Professor Rubek. It was I that drove you to the turntable—blind as I then was—I, who placed the dead clay image above the happiness of life—of love.

Irene [*looking down*]. Too late—too late!

Professor Rubek. Not by a hairsbreadth has all that has passed in the interval lowered you in my eyes.

Irene [*with head erect*]. Nor in my own!

Professor Rubek. Well, what then! Then we are free— and there is still time for us to live our life, Irene.

Irene [*looks sadly at him*]. The desire for life is dead in me, Arnold. Now I have arisen. And I look for you. And I find you.—And then I see that you and life lie dead—as I have lain.

Professor Rubek. Oh, how utterly you are astray! Both in us and around us life is fermenting and throbbing as fiercely as ever!

Irene [*smiling and shaking her head*]. The young woman of your Resurrection Day can see all life lying on its bier.

Professor Rubek [*throwing his arms violently around her*]. Then let two of the dead—us two—for once live life to its uttermost—before we go down to our graves again!

Irene [*with a shriek*]. Arnold!

Professor Rubek. But not here in the half darkness! Not here with this hideous dank shroud flapping around us——

Irene [*carried away by passion*]. No, no—up in the light, and in all the glittering glory! Up to the Peak of Promise!

Professor Rubek. There we will hold our marriage feast, Irene—oh, my beloved!

Irene [*proudly*]. The sun may freely look on us, Arnold.

Professor Rubek. All the powers of light may freely look on us—and all the powers of darkness, too. [*Seizes her hand.*] Will you then follow me, oh, my grace-given bride?

Irene [*as though transfigured*]. I follow you, freely and gladly, my lord and master!

Professor Rubek [*drawing her along with him*]. We must first pass through the mists, Irene, and then——

Irene. Yes, through all the mists, and then right up to the summit of the tower that shines in the sunrise.

The mist clouds close in over the scene—PROFESSOR RUBEK *and* IRENE, *hand in hand, climb up over the snow field to the right and soon disappear among the lower clouds. Keen storm gusts hurtle and whistle through the air. The* SISTER OF MERCY *appears upon the stone-scree to the left. She stops and looks around silently and searchingly.*

MAIA *can be heard singing triumphantly far in the depths below.*

Maia.

> I am free! I am free! I am free!
> No more life in the prison for me!
> I am free as a bird! I am free!

Suddenly a sound like thunder is heard from high up on the snow field, which glides and whirls downwards with headlong speed. PROFESSOR RUBEK *and* IRENE *can be dimly discerned as they are whirled along with the masses of snow and buried in them.*

The Sister of Mercy [*gives a shriek, stretches out her arms toward them and cries*]. Irene! [*Stands silent a moment, then makes the sign of the cross before her in the air, and says.*] Pax vobiscum!

MAIA'S *triumphant song sounds from still farther down below.*

DRAMABOOKS